Robbing Banks

Robbing Banks

An American History
1831-1999

L.R. KIRCHNER

Rockville Centre, NY

Published by
SARPEDON
An Imprint of Combined Publishing

For additional information contact Sarpedon Publishers,
49 Front Street, Rockville Centre, NY 11570.

For sales or rights inquiries contact Combined Publishing,
476 West Elm St., Conshohocken, PA 19428

ISBN 1-885119-64-X

Cataloging-in-publication data is available from
Library of Congress.

10 9 8 7 6 5 4 3 2 1

PRINTED IN THE UNITED STATES OF AMERICA

Contents

❦

Acknowledgments

Without question, the assistance of my wife, Janet, was paramount in the completion of this work. Her support and patience are greatly appreciated, for not only did she stand by this project, her inspiration was a source of strength despite any hardship that came along.

My sincere thanks go out to Richard Lawrence Miller, successful author and crackerjack editor. His contributions to *Robbing Banks* were invaluable. Besides, he has been sworn to secrecy to not divulge the sort of mistakes I am capable of committing. In addition, thanks to Sarpedon's Sam Southworth, who believed in the manuscript, Donn Teal, who copyedited it, and especially Daryl Horrocks, whose editorial and organizational expertise whipped the final book into shape. Thanks, too, for the understanding and benevolence of my old friends Brian Diddle, owner of Precision Printing, and Zeno Yates, of Business Benefits Systems, for their belief in the literary merits of this work. Bill Apel and John Bauer also assisted in this project and my appreciation is heartfelt.

There is no way this work could have been finished without the cooperation of law-enforcement personnel throughout the nation. The input from city, state, and federal (FBI, ATF, DEA, and U.S. Treasury) bank robbery specialists has been invaluable, as was the assistance of Kansas City's Regional Crime Lab. My thanks also go out to wire services and newspapers all over the United States for their contributions. Last, but not least, thanks to the convicted and paroled bank robbers who gave me, somewhat guardedly, insight into their world.

Of course, Gloria Glynn knows how important this project was: this one's for her!

Introduction

Even though bank robberies have been recognized over the years as a national epidemic, it may seem curious to some people that an author would even consider taking an up-close and personal look at such a nefarious profession. After all, today's robbers are, for the most part, crude amateurs possessing little of the romantic aura of yesteryear's brigands. Today, the fine art of illegally removing capital from a financial institution has often been reduced to the practice of crude thuggery or impulsive strong-arm holdups. This is not to say that old-style desperados were invariably suave or elegant; they were not. However, there was something about the old-time robber that captured the American public's attention and, frequently, admiration. The perception begs the question: "How were the old-timers different from today's petty thugs?"

The populace romanticizes the fanciful robber who rode a horse into the sleepy little town on a hot afternoon. Tying his mount in front of the bank, he strolled in, demanded the money and, without firing a shot, quietly rode away into the sunset. There were a few men who came close to fitting this description but, for the most part, they simply did not exist.

Then there were the more flamboyant legends who vaulted across the counter and, with bag in hand, demanded of the teller, "fill 'er up!" Jesse James and his brother Frank gained a considerable amount of news space with such exploits, and their careers helped form the mystique surrounding robbing banks. Countless imitators have envisioned themselves as reincarnations of these two idealized outlaws.

Nonetheless, despite all the breathless press accounts that accompanied their exploits, their was a sinister downside in the James boys' line of work: they sometimes killed people. Even so, they did capture the ambience of the quintessential outlaw robbers.

We will take an in-depth look at Frank and Jesse James, but only to set a common stage upon which all our other bank robbers will walk. In establishing a working profile of the men and women in this criminal profession we will find that somewhere in the dark recesses of a large selection of bank robbers' minds lurk the spirits of the James brothers. Like it or not, these two men have been admired for their achievements.

We will also look at many would-be famous robbers who failed miserably in this line of work. They fell far short in their quest to be consummate bank robbers and, ironically, thereby secured their own niches in history. Although many of these unfortunates never seemed to get it right when it came to their chosen walk of life, we shall find that their failures provide fully as much insight into the busines of bank robbing as the more spectacular—and far fewer—success stories.

Differentiating between the violent and nonviolent larcenist is also important. The distinction does not arise from whether the bank robber possessed a weapon, but from what he or she did with it. There are those desperados who in their villainy went that extra irrational step and murdered innocent people. In such instances the general perception of bank robbers changes. Suddenly the "Robin Hood" degenerates into just another killer. The public and the constabulary turn from grudgingly admiring the outlaw for his thrilling deeds of derring-do to wanting the thug arrested and hanged. An unwarranted transition from robbery to murder caused the downfall of many previously successful bank robbers.

The more notable thieves were excellent "salesmen." Some had the skill to convince employees of the institution being held up that handing over the money would be in their best interest. Bodily harm was of course the implied consequence of refusal, but the best bank robbers rarely had to make good on their threats. This "salesman" characteristic set some robbers apart from the run-of-the-mill armed bandit: they essentially persuaded a victim into giving up treasure. As their fame grew, it became known that these rogues would not be so likely to shoot you if you went along with them. Some charismatic holdup men of the 1930s, '40s and '50s fall into this category. Even today a few robbers still use good sales manners to contribute to their success, though the technique is far from as common as it used to be.

Bank robbery can be violent both emotionally and physically. Therefore we shall also examine the variety of bandit known as the "killer thief." There now seem to be more of these miscreants than in the old days of the industry. And the primary reason, ironically, is improved defenses against bank robbing: modern security devices and knowledgeable law enforcement personnel. In the old days there were no closed-circuit television systems, secret alarms, or exploding money packets; the bad guys were not chased by helicopters with infrared heat sensors. Cops didn't have computers and rapid land communications to foul up the hasty escape. Bank robbers today no longer have the luxury of spending valuable time charming the captive employees. It's a time thing, and time is no longer favorable to robbers or victims.

Today there is also another component in this new and vicious approach to bank robbery: drugs. Many bank robbers are now involved in the sale or consumption of illegal narcotics. The heist is made specifically to obtain money to purchase this expensive commodity, for dealing or using. Such robbers tend to shoot first if their demands are not met. Gone is the social polish of yesteryear's cool and calculating crook. The new breed of desperado is the snatch-and-grab kind, and is far more dangerous to lawmen and the public. These men and women have very little in common with the "legends" of the bank robbing profession. We will, however, look at some of the more infamous in this new category, even if their efforts have more to do with brutality than with robbing banks. This kind of robber is the most difficult kind of thief to anticipate; he is the one who prompts the outrage at today's rash of bank robberies. He can, and often does, kill.

Holding up financial institutions has a long and fascinating history. Some individuals, although thieves, had style; they commanded attention. They were good in their "profession" and we shall look at some of the more interesting characters in the assortment. This is in no way to condone what they did, but is rather a chance to see what the real experts were like, and perhaps to learn from their exploits. We have come to believe the bank robbers in today's world are, for the most part, only dimwitted shadows of their predecessors. The business has had a few real professionals, but it has also had many morons who weren't worth the label "bank robber." We will look at both, not in an admiring but in a factual way. The reader may then assess the merits, if any, of each of them.

And there is yet another kind of robber we need to understand: the burglar-robber who enters the establishment by stealth and takes the money without making human contact with his prey. These men are adept at getting around alarms and safeguards by picking, prying, drilling, or blasting. This requires a different set of skills than those possessed by the strong-arm holdup man, and this field has some real superstars. These men take more money per heist than the armed robber, but in many ways they also take more chances. We would not get a true picture of robbers if we excluded such "box men." No two burglar-bank robbers ever work the same way, and their successful jobs are marked by a distinct signature. Robbers who do not measure up in this occupation will also leave their name on their jobs, much to their chagrin: to be listed among the inmates of some corrections institution as a bumbling bank burglar is not a sign of status.

Although the success of a burglar-robber is of course measured by his anonymity, a scant number of such thieves have made a few huge scores and then come to the light of day by spending time behind bars. There they are considered legends of the trade. These men are not only respected by their peers but are occasionally admired by the police and banking institutions themselves. After all, elaborate security systems are likely to be a source of pride; respect, however grudging, is likely to be extended to the robber who can beat them.

We'll also discover the role of public relations in the careers of most of the rascals we examine. The James Gang may be considered the first celebrity bank robbers, but only because Eddie Green of Malden, Massachusetts, didn't have suitable P.R. Some of our desperadoes deserved all the press they accumulated; others did not. As a group, however, bank robbers love good press coverage. Some go out of their way to get it, and many have used it to their advantage.

It would be virtually impossible to list all the notable figures who have engaged in the bank robbing business. My intention is to give examples of some of the criminals and what methods they used. In the early days, there were few variations on the basic techniques. As security systems became more modern, and the police more sophisticated, approaches to robbing banks evolved with the times. What I have tried to do is show who some masters of this profession were across different eras, and how they, in turn, influenced the actions of the banking industry and law enforcement. The less successful villains along the way serve to emphasize how difficult robbing banks can be.

As we reach the modern age in the following pages, we encounter several cases that are still pending as well as some robbers who are still serving time in prison; therefore, for legal and other practical reasons several of the robbers' names have been changed. The stories remain factual, and I trust that the aliases I have assigned will not detract from the reader's interest.

We are now ready to stroll through our gallery of rogues, looking at the good, the bad, and the best!

Chapter 1

Horses and Colts

"Society prepares the crime; the criminal commits it."
—V. Alfieri

Shortly after the Pilgrims planted their feet on Plymouth Rock, there was a problem with thieves. Crime crept like a plague from the boats of the Pilgrims, bringing to the new land all of the old conditions—both good and bad—that had defined Europe throughout the centuries. Robbing banks, however, had never been an established practice in the Old World. Instead, it can be chalked up as one of the great innovations in civilization brought to fruition in the new frontier nation—the United States.

Until the 1800s, most people did business in metal money: gold and silver. The practice of using bars or ingots of precious metal, parallel with minted coins, had lasted for millennia. Coins of the realm in America were a holdover from Great Britain, France, Spain, and other colonial powers. Shortly before the ratification of the Constitution in the late 1770s, America began to mint its own coins. But on a state-by-state basis the use of paper money, or scrip, gradually developed into the legal tender of trade and commerce. Since gold and silver were heavy, the lighter form of money was advantageous, not least to those with ambitions to steal it in large quantities.

The first federally chartered American bank was The Bank of North America, established in 1782, though there had been banks in the Colonies before this first *official* bank. Bankers would be caretakers of large amounts of gold and silver, for a price, and either safeguard it or ship it for the owner. The fee charged by the banker amounted to a sort of reverse interest. The banker's profit would be his fees for guarding the funds of others. In this way the bank could make money on each and every client the business could attract. By the same token, the bank could then lend money to others to satisfy their business needs. Again a fee was charged for the lending of money and the bank profited further. By and large the bank became one of the hallmark businesses of the community. The banker got to live in the big house on the hill, often to the chagrin of other citizens.

Banks were, of course, established to take care of community business barons, high rollers of the day, who had an excess of funds from their occupations. These gentlemen needed someplace safe to keep their money and, likewise, a place to borrow more money to increase their wealth. This relationship between banks and the wealthy allowed many bank robbers over the years to pursue their ill-gotten gains with tacit blessings from the community, mostly because of the jealousy that customarily accompanies sentiments toward the rich.

In the early years, bank security was lackluster. In most cases safes were nothing more than strongboxes, made from hand-forged iron edges, hinges, rivets, and wood. They were not much to look at and not difficult to disassemble. In those nascent days of the profession, however, it simply didn't occur to most thieves to steal money from a fixed institution in the center of a town. It would take a number of enlightened pioneers to show the way.

Petty thievery has always been in style, but during the 1700s and early 1800s the real pros—and precursors of our current subject— were the highway robbers. Lurking in woods or other sparsely populated areas, highwaymen preyed on the communications network that connected businesses, the wealthy, and banks. Large shipments of gold and silver fell victim to these thieves of the byways who often brought wagons or pack animals along to carry their loot. In frontier America these crimes took the form of stagecoach hold-ups, later evolving into train robberies or armored-car heists. Although many bank robbers would come to alternate their raids on institutions with the older tradition of highway robbery, until 1831 most pillagers hadn't yet figured out that they would hit the jackpot if they simply hit the bank itself— acquiring the money at its source.

As the banking industry evolved, money handlers discovered how to build sturdy, permanently affixed strongboxes into their places of business. This construction was in the form of forged-iron plates held together with rivets and bolted to the floor. As for the transfer of funds, stagecoach lines added the shotgun guard, making the occasional armed highway robbery just a little more challenging to the men on horseback or afoot. An atmosphere of safety developed within the banking profession as a result.

Banks sprang up throughout the country and for the most part were considered valuable assets to a community—although the bankers perpetually remained objects of as much envy as respect. The rates, fees, or interest the banker charged to watch over someone else's money could vary widely from area to area and were not regulated. The banker, living in the house that was always somehow bigger and more lavishly furnished than his neighbors', had his critics.

The first recorded bank robbery was actually a burglary committed in New York City. An Englishman named Edward Smith removed $245,000 from a Wall Street bank in March of 1831. He used a type of duplicate key arrangement, still unknown, to gain access. Captured after a very short spending spree, he was sentenced to Sing Sing prison for five years. His efforts did not go unnoticed, however, and banks began looking into their then nonexistent security systems. The early safes were no longer good enough to keep the money of depositors secure. It would be a safe bet that Mr. Smith didn't have a lot of trouble pulling off the first robbery of an American bank, since the first noteworthy safe manufacturer was the Mosler Safe Co. in Britain; safes only began to be built in America after 1834.

With the opening of the American West a new form of frontier finance began to emerge, reminiscent of the days before scrip. Travelers, adventurers, traders, and early prospectors began using gold dust and nuggets as a medium of exchange. The discovery of gold and silver in the western territories was instrumental in the rapid expansion of these areas. Needless to say bankers moved where the wealth was. Small banks sprouted up in gold- and silver-mining towns, at least until the veins ran out. The transport of this form of money became one of the trickier aspects of doing business. And the highwaymen still followed the riches, plying their trade.

Between 1874 and 1882, a crusty old man known as Black Bart (Charles E. Bowles) made a name for himself robbing stagecoaches in

California. His method was to wave down a stagecoach on the road by brandishing a shotgun. He acquired the handle "Black Bart" from the long black coat and hat he always wore; his face was covered either with a bandanna or a feed sack. He was only one of the more colorful of the hundreds who were engaged in this practice; thankfully, at no time during the commission of his crimes did he shoot anybody. Bart was eventually captured by a Pinkerton agent, and served several years in prison for his crimes; the man then disappeared into Western legend forever.

The Pinkertons were a private police force, available for hire to banks, railroads, and, as during the Civil War, the U.S. government. Along with other firms that featured "commercial vigilantes," the Pinkertons were empowered to catch criminals and deliver them to the justice system. America's first official police department was formed in 1844 in New York City, and was copied shortly thereafter by Boston, Philadelphia, and every other municipality with enough tax income to pay for one.

By the mid-nineteenth century, banks had installed not only better equipment, but vaults in which to keep money safe. Doors to these vaults became ever more thick and elaborate in design. Nevertheless, a wave of robbers and burglars discovered that getting into early safes and vaults was not difficult. For the most part the bank building itself was still made of wood. Coming through the roof, up through the floor, or even through the wall, were the most common routes of access for the burglar.

Robbers' tools were simple woodworking instruments, with the addition of the occasional bit of black powder explosive. Over the years manufacturers added such things as combination, clockwork, and tumbler and pin locking devices to their inventions. Big brass doors on the vaults, however, were more for visual appeal to bank customers than for the bad guys. Many early safes and vaults even had the bank's name in huge engraved lettering on these doors, with lots of shiny brass knobs and wheels. It made depositors feel their bank was secure; never mind that the building itself was only wood.

In the field of bank robbing, burglars had a full three-decade head start on their gun-wielding counterparts. Until the Civil War, in fact, daylight armed robbery of a bank was generally unheard of. As the frontier inexorably moved west, Indians were the primary threat to public order and had the tendency to bind communities together in common cause. Towns and cities that subsequently became large enough to house a bank seldom were large enough to sustain a social underclass inclined toward crime. And in America, individuals intensely desirous of wealth could always keep moving west, where land was unlimited and prospectors kept discovering new veins of gold. In the east, more established cities had not yet taken the full brunt of the great immigration waves from the Old World that would result in large, though often temporary, ethnic ghettos. Ironically, the first big batch of non-Anglo-Saxon immigrants, the Irish, would find their calling in the New World as police.

The average American was also well aware of how robbers were dealt with in the mid-1800s. Though communities may have lacked the men in blue that we know today, they could instead rely on the entire citizenry of the town to uphold the law. After all, there were far more honest citizens than crooks. The good people of those towns had made it to the Promised Land through great hardship, and certainly weren't about to let some low-life street thug steal their money. Thieves ran the great risk of armed confrontation with a citizenry not averse to violence. If bullets from quickly drawn guns didn't deliver summary justice immediately, the captured thief—after tarring and feathering—would likely swing from the end of a hastily rigged noose. Some of these ill-advised scoundrels would then hang there, bullet holes or not, as a deterrent to other would-be thieves.

In Western communities, lynchings were the preeminent social event, especially if the robber was well known. A local holdup man, or a stranger who had received enough publicity, could and did draw a crowd. Vendors sold popcorn, flags, peanuts, and cold drinks, giving the event a carnival atmosphere. Many small towns didn't have a court system, so there were a lot of impromptu executions. For towns that did have a sitting judge these hangings could be advertised a week or two in advance in order to give people a chance to attend. Hangings were a big boost to the local economy and a good chance for neighbors to get together. Of course, more than a few hasty hangings were not done in a professional manner, and many a bad guy slowly strangled to death with a sizable audience to witness his dilemma.

Nonetheless, very few robbers, be they burglars or armed holdup artists, ever gave much thought to what might happen if they were captured. A smattering of them didn't seem to worry about being killed, as long as they got to take an honest citizen with them. This factor has changed hardly at all, from the early days of bankrobbing to modern times.

The Civil War, aside from its noteworthy effects on several other aspects of American life, had a titanic impact on bankrobbing. Gone were the days when the burglar or sneak thief was the most sinister threat to a financial institution. Now, hundreds of thousands of men were expertly trained in firearms, horsemanship, and killing. The country's social fabric had been torn, creating a byproduct of intense class and regional resentment. Many communities had been destroyed or rendered destitute, and among those who fought for Dixie were many young men who refused to accept that they had been defeated. Skill at arms, of course, was not the sole province of Confederate veterans. The forces of law and order—sheriffs, police, Pinkertons, or just plain citizens—had gained a hardened cadre of veterans with which to do battle with the desperadoes.

Some bank robberies took place during the Civil War itself, invariably Rebels robbing Union banks rather than vice versa, since no Yankee would put himself out to steal Confederate government currency. The South also retained little in the way of gold reserves. The most notorious heist of the war was perpetrated by John Morgan's Rebel raiders at the town of Mount Sterling, Kentucky, in June 1864. Morgan professed outrage at the crime, and many people believed him; however, three months later he was shot down by Union troops (who considered him more of a horse thief than a bank robber) and the crime remained unsolved. Banks were also the primary target of the Southern insurrectionists who descended from Canada on St. Albans, Vermont. In general, however, the Confederate army's patrician code of honor—best embodied by Robert E. Lee—prohibited criminal impropriety within its ranks. Things would be different after the war, when ex-Rebel riders would find their army disbanded and the country run by a president named Ulysses S. Grant.

There is a bit of history that must be resolved before we discuss the most famous of all bank robbers. The first armed bank robbery by a civilian—whose greed was unelevated by any larger cause—took place before the Civil War had ended. On December 15, 1863, in Malden, Massachusetts, Edward Green walked into the town bank, shot the banker's son in the head, and stole $5,000. After a short spending binge, the robber was captured. He was tried, convicted, and went to his eternal reward at the business end of a rope on the 27th of February, 1866. This hanging took place 14 days after the James Gang embarked on its infamous career. Mr. Green had already committed America's first armed bank robbery, been tried, and was executed for that milestone in history—before the most famous of all bank robbers had even been recognized for their first.

As we'll see in this chapter, the James Gang, the Youngers, the Daltons, the Doolin Gang, and others were pioneers in this field. Most people only know about these highly visible thieves of the Old West, but we will find additional desperadoes stealing huge amounts of money elsewhere in the country at the same time. Few people are aware of these other men and their influence on robbery. Several of these little-known culprits, in fact, were responsible for prompting countermeasures by the authorities that made the armed holdup more difficult and the bank burglary seemingly impossible for future aspiring criminals.

The stage is now set. The so-called godfathers of armed robbery are about to make their appearance. Bank robbery moved into high gear shortly after the Civil War, and this nation will forever reap the consequences.

FRANK & JESSE JAMES

The James boys, Frank and brother Jesse, have been referred to as criminal products of the War Between the States. Frank had ridden with Quantrill's Raiders during the war and Jesse was associated with "Bloody Bill" Anderson's band of Confederate irregulars. Quantrill and Anderson are considered two of the most ruthless—and daring— leaders to emerge from the Civil War. Their battlefield was the border state of Missouri where Union numbers were pitted against Rebel determination. One also needs to understand that these bands of commandos were highly trained specialists at engaging and eluding opposing forces. Their method of combat was rapid strike and scatter. Their raids were well planned and executed with little left to chance. After the war these raiders split up, heading in different directions.

Jesse had been wounded just before the end of the war and was not expected to recover. He went back home to Kearney, Missouri, to die in the arms of his family. Frank, unaware of his brother's condition, was in Kentucky, but when he learned of Jesse's condition he, too, returned home. At this point they were merely two ex-Confederate military men who had refused, like many others, to swear allegiance to the federal government upon their discharge. The outcome of their noncompliance was that they, along with hundreds of others, were identified as criminals by the Union government. Given their financial situation at the time, some of these men decided that if they were going to be branded as outlaws anyway they might as well engage in some illicit activity against their newly reunified nation.

Jesse and his brother Frank planned and executed the first organized daylight bank robbery in American history. This robbery, involving 11 men on horseback, was committed on the day before Valentine's Day, 1866. The target of the historic holdup was the little town bank of Liberty, Missouri. There has always been some question as to how much these robbers took. Some authors state that the amount was about $17,000. My research has uncovered a take of $24,316 in cash and about $40,000 in bearer bonds. Whatever the true amount, a more important statistic resulted from the crime: one innocent bystander was killed by the gang. All of the men were firing their weapons on their way out of Liberty, so who actually shot the hapless unnamed victim is clouded by the passage of time. Eight months later, at the end of October 1866, the same group attempted to rob the bank of Lexington, Missouri, but this robbery ended in failure.

The James boys and their gang, undaunted by their failure in Lexington, pulled off their second successful holdup in March of 1867. Two months later they relieved a Russelville, Kentucky, bank of $20,000. At the time of this robbery Jesse was still a teenager, 19 years old, and his brother was only 23. But they, along with their compatriots, had learned the finer points of guerrilla tactics very well. Most of the gang were exceptional horsemen and crack marksmen. Jesse was one of the few in the gang who couldn't shoot straight, but even he was capable of killing someone if the situation warranted it.

On December 7, 1869, this band of outlaws robbed the Gallatin, Missouri, bank of $70,000 and in 1871 they took a trip to Corydon, Iowa, relieving that bank of $40,000. Following their success in Iowa, they met with a dismal defeat, netting only $1,500 from a Columbia, Kentucky, bank on April 29, 1872. The gang headed back home with a short stop in Kansas City, Missouri. There they robbed the local county fair of an estimated $20,000, killing a little girl in the process. The following year, on May 27, they held up a bank in the community of St. Genevieve, Missouri. For the first seven years of their careers they had averaged one robbery a year.

This is where the group of outlaws was about to write another page in history. Assailing trains was something many guerrilla veterans like the James Gang had learned during the war. Early trains were equipped with small safes, usually secured to the floor of the baggage car and entrusted to the care of the baggage handler and conductor. Banks and businessmen had made it a regular practice to transfer funds in this manner, as did the railroad companies. Trains were little banks on wheels and naturally made attractive targets.

The James Gang committed their first train robbery on July 21, 1873. This heist, which took place outside Adair, Iowa (Chicago-Rock Island & Pacific Railroad), netted the gang $4,000 in cash and about $600 taken from the passengers. The band of thieves had missed a large gold shipment, valued at over $75,000, by only one day. Because the James Gang was already famous, this exploit received national attention and is considered by some to be the first of its kind. But it was the Reno Brothers who committed America's first train robbery, in October 1866, at Seymore, Indiana, netting $10,000. The Renos took the palm, but they lacked the great press coverage that gave bragging rights to the James Gang seven years later.

The last "old style" train robbery in the United States was committed by the Al Spencer Gang, outside Bartlesville, Oklahoma, 50 years later on August 20, 1923. This was a direct attempt to emulate the James Gang's success in robbing trains. Indeed, it was a sort of anniversary robbery, but all the men were arrested and did time for the crime. The James boys have remained a major influence on the criminal elements of American society, something we will see a lot of later on.

After the few bank robberies by the James brothers, things got out of hand. Other bandits saw just how easy it was to knock off a bank and bank robbers sprouted like weeds across the nation. Literally hundreds of heists were attributed to the James Gang, partly because bank employees preferred to believe they had been robbed by celebrities rather than more obscure low-life. The bank managers, however, did-n't care who all the outlaws were; they just took steps to protect themselves. Lawman Allan Pinkerton had formed a detective agency prior to the War Between the States and on one occasion had been instrumental in saving President Lincoln's life. Banks, as well as railroads, hired his agency to put a stop to the rash of holdups, which were costing businesses hundreds of thousands of dollars a month. And Pinkerton's, established in 1850, was only the beginning. Wells Fargo made a name for itself guarding stagecoaches starting in 1852, and the Brink's Armored Car Co., originally known as Brink's Security, was begun in 1859.

While agents in the employ of Allan Pinkerton were on the hunt for the James Gang, they succeeded in killing Frank and Jesse's nine-year-old half-brother. Archie Samuel died almost instantly when a surreptitiously thrown bomb exploded in the brothers' Kearney, Missouri, home. The blast also blew off the outlaws' mother's arm. The undercover agent thought to be responsible for this atrocity was later gunned down in cold blood by Jesse. Needless to say, this crime ralled moral and material support from the local citizens to assist the James brothers whenever and wherever requested. As far as the locals were concerned, the U.S. government was out to get their boys. And besides, in their view, the Yankee-owned banks and railroads formed a bigger nest of crooks than the good, honest town of Kearney.

During these first years of the Jameses' career their activities netted the gang a respectable amount of money. They also cost six people their lives. Some of the more romantic authors of the time have claimed that Jesse and Frank never intended for people to be hurt during the commission of their crimes. However, several of the deaths attributed to Jesse were simple, cold-blooded murders. Frank may have been a little more level-headed when it came to gunplay, but Jesse had no qualms about shooting to kill, either during a robbery or on any other occasion that arose. No bank-robbing death is attributed to Frank James.

Countless writers have embellished the myth of how good a shot Jesse James was. In fact, Jesse was a notoriously bad marksman. He was fast, but hardly ever accurate. On one occasion he fired at a bank teller at close range, using all six shots and missing all six times.

During his life, he killed between 9 and 12 people, depending on which of the legends you choose to accept. With the infamous Jesse James shooting his dual Springfield six-shooters at you, it was possible he might hit you with a lucky shot or miss you altogether. The people responsible for elaborating on his prowess as a marksman were the early pulp, dime novel writers of the 1860s and '70s. The truth is that Frank was an accomplished shot, though fortunately more restrained, while Jesse fired away more often. With the James Gang, you had one brother who was a calm marksman and another who was just a plain lunatic—not the kind of people you would want to see entering a bank.

The James Gang, not unlike a lot of the other roving bands of desperadoes at the time, robbed only on an as-needed basis. When the money ran out, which was not all that often, they went back to work. The gang remained intact for a number of years, its membership averaging between 8 and 12 men. There was, however, another group of bandits who threw in with the Jameses from time to time.

The Youngers, second cousins to the Jameses, lived in the same general area of Missouri and were also ex-Confederate guerrillas. There is little dispute that Jesse was the driving force and the brains of the outfit known as the James/Younger Gang. However, his role was challenged from time to time by Cole Younger, self-acclaimed leader of his own family of thieves. In a moment we will get to the robbery that set this gang apart from the rest of the run-of-the-mill crooks of the time, but first there must be a little technical background.

The style in which the Jameses pulled off a holdup was one of surprise—something which hasn't changed in over 150 years. Their usual drill was for one of the gang to go into the bank and ask for change for a $10- or $20-dollar bill. This first man was accompanied by one or more of the robbers. Another man was stationed at the door, one on the outside, and one or two men on the street. One member of the gang kept the unmounted horses gathered up for the escape. The point man, in the bank, would then size up the situation. If everything looked right, they would then initiate the holdup by pulling their weapons and informing the banker that this was a robbery.

The clothing the Jameses used was the duster, a long, canvas or linen coat, used extensively at the time by American ranchers. This coat came almost to the top of the wearer's boots and was convenient for the concealment of weapons. It was not uncommon for a holdup man of the day to carry either a shotgun or a Winchester lever action saddle gun under his duster. The duster is still available in thousands of Western shops and, along with its urban equivalent, the trenchcoat, is still used by modern-day bandits as a mode of dress and for the shrouding of weapons.

After the gang had gathered up the money they would break for the street and their horses. If the community wasn't aware there had been a holdup, they would certainly know it as the boys were riding out of town. Their customary exit entailed shooting in the air as they galloped full-speed down the town's main drag. Merely the sight of over half a dozen men in long gray coats, shooting wildly, was enough to keep the curious off the street. Of course a few people made the mistake of taking a shot or two at the fleeing bandits and paid for this impropriety with their lives.

Frank and Jesse always made it a point to have the finest horse-flesh they could afford. These horses even included the occasional registered racehorse. In some cases they kept fresh mounts along their escape route; this gave them a decided edge during their getaway, in the event a posse should give chase. This was a finer point that not all bank robbers of the time emulated. Needless to say, many of the would-be imitators wound up on the bottom end of three yards of the finest hemp rope or in "boot hill." (The local cemetery in many communities was called "boot hill" because a number of the inhabitants were buried with their boots still on.)

By the summer of 1874 both Frank and Jesse had taken wives, but were still engaged in the "banking" business. Three months after Frank's marriage, the boys robbed a bank in Huntington, West Virginia. Although it was a successful holdup, the take was very small.

The most spectacular event of the James Gang's career has become known to history as the Northfield, Minnesota, Raid. On the morning of September 7, 1876, nine men wearing dusters rode into the little community of Northfield with the intention of robbing both of the town's banks at the same time.

The operation, though well planned, fell apart quickly when one of the bankers couldn't open his vault because of a time lock. Meanwhile, the citizens of Northfield had seen the group of men split up and enter the banks. Two of the strangers were holding horses in the street. It didn't take a genius to figure out that the banks were being held up. The community of Northfield was predominately Swedish, and these people began taking up firing positions along the town's main street.

The robbery was a team effort between the James Gang and the Younger brothers. One group of men got the money from the first bank, but the other group had to leave the second bank empty-handed. When all the men came into the street, the townsfolk opened fire. By the time the smoke had cleared there were three dead outlaws and two others badly wounded in the thoroughfare. Frank James was hit along with one of the men in his group. The only man not wounded by all the flying lead was Jesse. The three Younger brothers, all wounded, were captured alive and ultimately sentenced to life in prison. Jesse, Frank, and their accomplice Billy raced their horses out of town with a posse hot on their heels. Billy later died of his wounds. Frank and Jesse headed southeast and after a month on the move had made good their escape.

This robbery, the James Gang's biggest disaster, has oddly enough inspired imitators over the years. The inspirational factor is that robbing two banks at the same time was something even Jesse James couldn't accomplish, so others have given it a try. Only one armed robber has ever pulled it off, and he was captured shortly after the act.

Although they were accused of many robberies committed by others, Frank and Jesse remained inactive for the next two years. They busied themselves instead with gambling and horses. Frank took a real job in Kentucky and Jesse kept occupied with different odd jobs in Missouri and Texas. Their next holdup took place on October 8, 1878, and utilized 11 men. The robbery was to be known as the Glendale Train Robbery (immortalized in the song "Dirty Little Coward"), and netted the gang $40,000. The remainder of the robberies committed by the James Gang were not of banks, but rather of a stagecoach, in September 1880; a government paymaster, in March 1881; a train in Winston, Missouri, in June 1881; and the Blue Cut train robbery in September of 1881.

Given their many successful robberies, it has always been a matter of speculation how much money the James boys earned from their nefarious, though colorful, vocation. Some estimates of their total take are in the neighborhood of a million dollars, but I feel the true number is closer to $350,000. There have always been rumors concerning the loot. These stories include caves where money was supposedly buried and other locations that may conceal vast caches of gold, silver, or currency. But the bulk of evidence indicates money was never buried by this bunch of outlaws; the gang members needed their share for their day-to-day expenses. Likewise, the gang's charity to the underprivileged citizens of their community has been grossly exaggerated. They gave away a few dollars to needy friends but, for the most part, their largesse was a form of insurance against informers "ratting" them out to the authorities.

Jesse James died while living in modest anonymity. He was murdered by a gang member, Bob Ford, for the reward money in St. Joseph, Missouri, on April 3, 1882. Frank surrendered himself to the governor of Missouri on October 15, 1882, and was tried and acquitted of his crimes. He continued his life as a model citizen, and passed away as "an honorable old man" on February 18, 1915. His post-bankrobbing life included officiating at boxing matches, grand openings, and selling stones taken from the grave of his infamous brother. His one-armed mother also engaged in selling trinkets to tourists who would stop by their Kearney farm, Jesse's final resting place. Stones were replaced as needed from a creek bed not far from the house. The Jameses' criminal career had spanned a little over 15 years, with just about that same number of major robberies to their credit.

There is little doubt that the Jameses were accused of more crimes than they ever committed, but in understanding their fame one must consider what factors played important roles in elevating them to legendary status. Surely the atmosphere in the country was a principal element. Most people hated the bankers and the business barons who owned the railroads, so the James Gang had the common man on its side. The press and dime authors—who had an Eastern audience rabid for exciting tales of the "Wild West"—embellished their deeds and made them out to be more courageous, romantic, and prolific than they ever were. In turn, the gang's notoriety may have caused lawmen to back off when looking for them. (Jesse is even said to have joined a posse in Kansas City to search for himself; nobody really knew what he looked like.) But the primary explanation of the James Gang's fame is that they were the foremost innovators of a new style of crime that had burst upon the American public. Their military-like approach to a stickup gave the James boys an edge, and neither Frank nor Jesse were every caught while pulling a job. The James Gang may not have been the first to rob a bank or a train, but they were the flashiest of the early practitioners. Elvis, after all, did not invent rock and roll.

And their legend lives on. The museum in Kansas City has an entire wing devoted to the Jameses. The house Jesse was killed in is also a museum. The community of Kearney still holds a summer play called "The Life and Times of Jesse James," which attracts large crowds. There is a rather loose fan club called "The James Gang" that holds conventions every summer to extol the virtues of the two outlaws. There are caves, in the Ozark region of southern Missouri, said to be hiding places of buried loot and these draw thousands of people every year. Jesse had a son who was arrested for robbing a train and later acquitted with help from some of his father's old associates. This son had a hand in the first Hollywood production of a movie about his famous father. It was a flop, however, and Jesse Jr. went on to become a well-respected lawyer and died on March 26, 1951.

In 1948 a man claiming to be one hundred years old, calling himself J. Frank Dalton of Lawton, Oklahoma, identified himself as Jesse James. Reporters from across the nation interviewed this man and could not disprove his claim. Until his death in 1951 Mr. Dalton appeared on TV and radio programs attesting to his authenticity. Of course, the living relatives of James were not convinced and, for the most part, considered this man an imposter.

In 1971 the remains of Jesse were disinterred at the family grave site in Kearney, Missouri. At that time there was still enough of him left to make a positive identification. But this was in the days before modern DNA mapping, so conclusive evidence was difficult to obtain. Rumors persisted, and in July of 1995 James was again removed from his resting place. This time scientists skilled in the forensic arts of DNA identification went after Jesse. All that was left of him by this time was the occasional hank of hair and piece of bone. The scientific community was now able to identify these scant samples of Jesse's mortal remains for the descendants, who would also be able to dispel, once and for all, the claims of J. Frank Dalton. The results of this testing were released on September 22, 1995. The scientists stated they were 99 percent sure that the remains in the grave were, indeed, those of the infamous bank robber. Jesse was reburied, with full Confederate military honors, on October 28, 1995. His "Stars & Bars" battle flag–draped casket made all the local television news programs.

Just how important were Frank and Jesse James? There is little question that their gang's career—and its accompanying legend—has had a profound influence on the business of bank robbery. Many of the outlaws we will examine in upcoming chapters attribute their early ambitions to an infatuation with the James Gang. Were they just misunderstood young men, hardened into a life of crime because of the fortunes of war, as a lot of writers have said? Most likely they were not. They were thieves and occasional killers who enjoyed robbing banks. When you scrape away the illusions many had about the two James men, it is difficult to come to any other conclusions. They were bright enough to take advantage of a discrepancy in the history of crime; their tactics were modified for robbing banks, but in the end they just did what came naturally for violent criminals. Jesse James may have had a few redeeming qualities but, the "Robin Hood of the Old West" was indeed a cold-blooded killer, thief, and bank robber—and an inspiration to thousands of such robbers to come.

THE RENO BROTHERS GANG

The Reno brothers—Frank, John, Simeon, and William—were for the most part burglars and highway robbers. As mentioned before, they pulled off the first train robbery in Seymore, Indiana, in 1866, and that loot included bank money. Their band of followers numbered about two dozen and were all known as ruthless and brutal killers. Also in 1866, they robbed a train outside Marshfield, Indiana, and stole $96,000, a huge amount for a robbery in that day.

This group of robbers and murderers was a prime target for the Pinkerton Agency and was hounded by them continuously, for much of the money they stole was destined for banks. Allan Pinkerton himself, with one of his private detectives, arrested John Reno at the Seymore train depot. Reno was hustled off by the agents on a waiting train but when the rest of the gang figured out what had happened they gave chase. The pursuit ended in Illinois, where Pinkerton gave John over to lawmen and he was sent to prison.

Pinkerton had another run-in with this gang in March 1868 and surrounded them at Council Bluffs, Iowa. All the gang members were jailed, but on April 1st they escaped, leaving the phrase "*APRIL FOOL*" painted across the side of the building. Three were recaptured by Pinkerton, but as he was transporting them back to Seymore, the train was flagged down by masked vigilantes who seized the three prisoners and lynched them from the branch of a handy cottonwood tree.

Pinkerton, undaunted, went after the rest of the gang, rounding them up in Indianapolis and Canada. Because of threats, the prisoners were placed in the county jail at New Albany, Indiana. During the night of December 11, 1868, 100 masked vigilantes took over the town. They hanged a man by the name of Carl Anderson along with Frank, William, and Simeon Reno. They did a poor job on Simeon and it took him over a half hour to strangle to death. The Vigilance Committee, as it called itself, notified the rest of the gang that if they continued to engage in their business in or around the community, they would be dealt with accordingly. The Reno Gang took the hint and disbanded.

Although this group of men were not bank robbers, their story does make several points. Banking concerns and railroads were frustrated with the turn of events following the James Gang's ventures. The Pinkerton Agency was a solution, but so were vigilantes. In some parts of the country citizens were willing to accept the Robin Hood aura of dashing desperados, but in other areas of the nation this sort of thing just wasn't allowed. The demise of the Reno Gang was a direct result of how the people felt about this brand of lawlessness.

GEORGE LESLIE

Unlike either the James or Reno gangs, bank robber George Leslie was an educated man, receiving his degree from the University of Cincinnati. This man could have made a successful career in almost any occupation, but Leslie liked to rob banks. Mr. Leslie possessed a very simple theorem: most criminals were too stupid to make crime pay to it fullest extent. George Leslie wasn't stupid. His gang's total take has been estimated at between 7 and 12 million dollars, and he has been credited with masterminding over 80 percent of the nation's bank robberies or burglaries between 1865 and 1884. His work was, for the most part, confined to an area east of the Mississippi River and the eastern seaboard. His consultation fee, charged to other robbers and burglars, ranged from $5,000 to $20,000, payable in advance regardless of the amount stolen.

George Leslie netted over 10 times the amount of money as the James Gang, but he didn't have their publicity. On the East Coast authorities had a good idea who was doing a raft of burglaries, but they couldn't prove it. They knew that the reality was that one man was very likely responsible for either pulling the jobs himself or for teaching a student who committed the crimes. His robberies were exercises in timing and daring. In a few of his robberies the takes were enormous; for example, from the Ocean National Bank at Greenwich and Fulton Streets, New York, he took $786,879. The Manhattan Savings Bank lost $2,747,000 to Leslie, but he had left over $2 million, in cash and securities, lying on the floor of the vault. The theory was that his bag was full and he simply didn't have room for the extra couple of million.

During his 18-year career, Leslie lived a double life. He had come from a monied Ohio family; his father was a Toledo brewmaster and had seen to it that Leslie received a good education. With the kind of money Leslie brought in he could afford to live the life he so enjoyed. His connections to elite New York social circles were all well established but the gregarious upper crust of New York had no idea what Leslie did for a living. Conversely, his connections to the criminal underworld were very low-key. His only real relationship to the murky side of the law was with the notorious Marm Mandelbaum. Considered at the time as "Ma Crime," she was the paramount fence of stolen goods in New York. All big-time thieves and scoundrels used her services and delighted in her spectacular reveries. Leslie was no different.

To get an idea of just how good this guy really was we need to take a brief look at something Leslie invented to make his work a bit easier. The object was a thin wire which he used to crack the combination on a safe or vault. A burglar would remove the dial from the safe and fit the wire into the recess of the opening around the dial. The dial was then replaced and the robbers left the bank. A few days later, the bandits returned, removed the dial knob, and the impressions of the tumblers were etched into the shape of the wire. In short, there were dents in the wire. True, you didn't have the combination, but you did know the approximate location of the numbers. Any burglar worth his reputation could figure the combination out in a matter of minutes. Leslie was so bold as to enter a bank building several times until the money was right, or at least was enough to make a heist worthwhile. It wasn't uncommon for Leslie to leave a vault with $40,000 or $50,000 in it and wait for a bigger haul. This special tool, the wire, was known as "The Little Joker," and it took authorities over a decade to discover how burglars were getting into vaults with it without using force. A man named George Bliss has also been considered the inventor of "The Little Joker," but this man lacked the necessary technical knowledge. Even if Leslie didn't invent it, he sure perfected its use. This tool kept the police on their toes well into the late 1800s.

The fact that George Leslie never spent a day in jail for his crimes would also attest to another facet of his philosophy: he paid off the cops and he kept a battery of very good criminal lawyers on the payroll. Leslie never spent any uncomfortable nights attempting to elude a posse in the sagebrush like his Western counterparts. Leslie inspired a number of bank burglars we will look at later. His attention to details and timing is what separated him from the rest of the herd.

Leslie's career was just a little longer than average, but his takes were tremendous compared to what the Western bandits settled for. He also accomplished his goals without bloodshed. He was one of the men who caused the banking business to reexamine its security. Back-welded, or attached, dial knobs are a direct result of men like George Leslie and his "Little Joker."

Although Leslie was a married man, he was also a social gadabout in New York, and this was his downfall. He had been keeping company with the wife of another thief and it probably cost him his life. Leslie was found shot in the head and, to make matters worse, he was interred in a pauper's grave. The theory at the time was that Leslie was going to meet the woman, and a jealous husband got there first. His murder had nothing to do with his banking activities, but "The King of the Bank Robbers," a title he had acquired during his lifetime, was dead just the same. Rumor had it that Leslie's widow took all his accumulated funds after he had been buried, and left the country. She changed her name and lived to old age in a life of luxury on the

European continent. Of course, there was also the supposition that Mrs. Leslie, aware of George's extramarital escapades, had him taken care of. There was never proof of this, but she was known to have a very violent temper.

THE OUTLAW'S OASIS

The difference between the career criminal and the ignorant amateur can often be more important than many bank robbers could know. In the Wild West, this could mean more than the amount of money you get from a bank job; it could mean your life.

In 1888, Salt Lake City, Utah, was the scene of a rather unique bank robbery. Two desperadoes strode into the bank at high noon, pulled their pistols, and ordered the bank manager to open the vault. The robbers' wishes were accomplished without bloodshed. The bandits filled up four saddle bags with gold coin, tied up the bank employees, and left town. The horsemen headed out across the desert, each with two saddle bags across the rumps of his animal. A posse was formed almost immediately to give chase.

A spirited ride across a Utah desert has only one requirement: water. Our outlaws had one canteen full of water between them. Now, with the added weight of gold coin, they couldn't make as swift an escape as they might have wished. The horses began to lather up, their mouths covered in foam, but the riders pressed on.

The posse, on the other hand, did not attempt to make a quick capture; they took their time. They stopped for water breaks for themselves and their horses. After all, the hoofprints were easy to follow with the additional weight the robbers were hauling. There was no real rush; where could the two men go?

Four days later, the posse came upon the carcasses of two dead horses. The saddle bags full of gold were nowhere to be found, but the tracks in the sand gave the posse a good idea which way the robbers had gone. The posse left the dead animals to the buzzards that had begun to circle and headed out at a canter. These men knew it would not be long now—the thieves had to be close by. As the sun was setting, the posse made camp for the night. The next morning would be soon enough to resume the search for the bandits.

In the morning the buzzards were again a dead giveaway. When the posse arrived beneath them, the birds were already feeding on one of the desperadoes and slowly walking around the other, waiting for him to die. Both men still had the saddle bags over their shoulders. A single pistol shot dispersed the birds and finished off the dying bandit. The posse filled their canteens at a little natural spring about five hundred yards from where the outlaws died. Both thieves were added to the collection of five other bank robbers who had been buried at the water hole on other occasions. The gold was taken back to the Salt Lake City bank and the whole thing was forgotten. The outlaws were never identified, but there once was a small stand of greenery around a natural spring in the Utah wilderness known to all the locals as "The Outlaw's Oasis."

THE "HOLE IN THE WALL" GANG

Willard Erastus Christianson, son of a Mormon bishop, was to become one of the few bank robbers who would go straight, after a riotous and reckless youth. One of the first things Christianson did as a youth was to change his name. It was just a bit long for an outlaw, so he became Matt Warner and, occasionally, "The Mormon Kid." Warner teamed up with a sidekick and saddle pal named George Leroy Parker, more commonly known as "Butch Cassidy," and the rest of his gang, "The Wild Bunch." Warner was just one of several dozen outlaws who made up this very loose criminal organization that executed their illicit activities in the western states in the late nineteenth century. His first bank robbery was the Telluride Bank of Colorado in 1889, with Cassidy and a man named Tom McCarty. They escaped from this holdup with $31,000.

Cassidy had an impressive group of men around him from time to time, with the likes of Bill Carver, Ben Kilpatrick, Harry Longbaugh a.k.a. "The Sundance Kid," "Black Jack" Ketchum, Harvey Logan, "Flat Nosed" George Curry, and several others. This gang, known for their daring, were soon referred to as "The Wild Bunch." After a few brushes with the law this gang found a hideout in the Wyoming high country known as "The Hole in the Wall." The location, almost impregnable from the outside, was to become part of one of their handles as a gang: "The Wild Bunch" was also known as "The Hole in the Wall Gang."

McCarty and Warner were arrested for robbing the bank at Roslyn, Washington. Butch Cassidy smuggled guns and tools to the men and they escaped. Although they were recaptured shortly, they managed to beat the robbery charge in their trial. Warner was again arrested in 1896 and "The Wild Bunch" paid for his lawyers. This time Warner lost and received five years for his crimes.

While Warner was in prison, Cassidy and his gang continued to engage in their line of work, but were getting too hot in the state of Wyoming. The gang members were not only bank robbers they were also efficient train robbers. The gang was capable of normal holdups on trains, but when they began to use explosives things got a little trickier for them. Just outside Tipton, Wyoming, in 1900, the bunch had separated the baggage car from the train and were attempting to gain access. Once inside they set their dynamite and moved down the line. The charge was too big, however, and when it went off it not only opened the safe, but also demolished the baggage car and all of its contents. The money turned into confetti and floated all over the prairie.

This was to be the last American robbery for Cassidy, Sundance, and his mistress, Etta Place. By 1901 the three were somewhere in Argentina, supposedly robbing banks. By the time Matt Warner had gotten out of prison, what was left of "The Wild Bunch" had broken up. Some authors have Cassidy and the Sundance Kid dying in a shootout with Bolivian troops, but there is another version of this story. Some writers have Butch coming back to the United States in the early 1900s and living to be an old man under an assumed name.

Warner moved to central Utah and became a justice of the peace and a deputy sheriff. He worked as a policeman in Prince, Utah, with a sideline as a bootlegger and died a well-respected man at the age of 74 in 1938. The tale of his involvement with "The Hole in the Wall Gang" receded into nothing more than a few colorful stories for the townspeople. There were some who believed that Butch Cassidy and Matt Warner continued their friendship secretly after Cassidy's return to America, but this is mere conjecture. Matt Warner would be remembered as an outlaw who went straight.

Butch and Sundance have been portrayed time and again in motion pictures. Butch Cassidy (George Leroy Parker) was never connected to a killing during his career, although he was a crack shot. The Sundance Kid (Harry Longbaugh), on the other hand, was a "shootist." Several killings have been attributed to him in the commission of his robberies. The movie released in the 1970s depicted the two men as a couple of fun-loving boys who dabbled in crime while raindrops fell on their heads. Movies have had a tremendous effect on the business of bank robbing because of their admiring portraits of criminals. This trend increased during the countercultural 1960s and 1970s as the public grew wary of "heroes" and actually became more drawn to "anti-heroes."

COFFEYVILLE & THE DALTON GANG

Twelve minutes after all the shooting started, it was over. Eight people were dead and three more were wounded; the date was October 5, 1892, and the location was Coffeyville, Kansas. Jesse and Frank James, along with the Younger brothers, had made a serious mistake earlier, when they attempted to rob two banks at the same time in Northfield, Minnesota. On this October day the same blunder was to be repeated by the Dalton Gang. Coffeyville residents knew these robbers well. They were the infamous Daltons—Gratton, Bob, and Emmet—with Bill Powers and Dick Broadwell. The gang's targets were the First National and C.M. Condon Company Banks of Coffeyville. Another member of the band, Bill Doolin, had a horse go lame on the way to town, so he turned back—a delay which saved his life. The members of the gang were well known as train robbers and petty thieves, not as bank robbers. They were also known by the local lawmen as a ragtag mob of want-to-be bad men.

At about 9 A.M. five of the men rode into town: Gratton, Powers and Broadwell went into the Condon Bank, while Bob and Emmet Dalton crossed the street and entered the First National. A man who recognized the Daltons, even with the false beards they were wearing, watched as they entered the banks. He sounded the alarm to the people in the street when he saw one of the robbers in the Condon Bank pull a Winchester from under his duster. The three men scooped up $3,000 in silver, then took the money from under the cages and demanded that the banker open up the safe. The banker bluffed by telling them the safe was on a time lock and wouldn't open until 9:30. The gang figured that wasn't a long wait; they would just stay until that time.

Suddenly, bullets began crashing through the windows of the bank. Coffeyville's townsfolk had armed themselves, some from the local hardware store, and were shooting at the outlaws. The other two members of the gang, across the street, were having better luck. They had already gotten all the money from the drawers and the vault, and now became distracted by the shooting. Using hostages to shield themselves, Emmet and Bob Dalton came out into the street.

When it was over, four of the bandits lay dead in the street and Emmet Dalton had been badly wounded. Four locals, including the man who had sounded the alarm in the first place, were also dead. Two other citizens had been slightly wounded and three pretty good horses were killed. The sight was photographed by the local newspaper shortly after the incident. (The little town of Coffeyville still has plenty of copies of this picture to sell to tourists. If you're so inclined to purchase them, there are also several photos of all the dead robbers, laid out in their pine boxes.)

Emmet was found guilty and sentenced to life imprisonment at the state penitentiary in Lansing, Kansas, in March 1893. He was only 21 years old. He would be almost 36 by the time he was released and would then team up with an elderly Frank James and attempt a stageshow of old Wild Western outlaws. The show was a flop. Emmet wrote a book condemning the ways of crime, but this too was not well received. He would occasionally be a guest speaker on the evils of a criminal career, but for the most part his remaining years and his show business career were dismal. The last of the Dalton Gang, Emmet died in July 1937 at the age of 66, stone broke.

The most often asked question about this attempted holdup is: what went wrong? Several things could have contributed to the disaster of this bank robbery. The idea of attempting to rob two banks at the same time would be one flaw. Staging a heist in a town where everyone knew them by their first name could have also been a problem. But lack of planning would have to be the foremost issue. This was a bunch of very inexperienced bank robbers, inasmuch as they didn't know how to handle this type of robbery. A gang of young men acting like kids, who wanted to succeed where the great Jesse James had failed, were surely going to run into problems.

While I was doing research for this book I interviewed several old-timers from Coffeyville. The story of the incident has been passed down from generation to generation so their accounts are as fresh in their minds as if the event happened yesterday. The shootout in Coffeyville that ended the careers of the Daltons on that sunny day in 1892 is still accorded a cherished place in the memory of the town's inhabitants. As train robbers and rustlers the Daltons had been moderately successful; however, as many professional bank robbers could tell them, it takes just a little more skill to crack a bank. The Dalton Gang should have stayed with what they did well.

BILL DOOLIN

After the massacre of the Daltons in Coffeyville, Bill Doolin went out on his own in the banditry business. Born in Arkansas, Doolin had also worked as a cowboy in Wyoming. He had formed his own gang, known as the Oklahombres, in 1891. For the most part, his mob was a fun-loving lot who delighted in taking posses on wild-goose chases through the Oklahoma badlands known as "Hell's Fringe." Odd as it may seem, Bill Doolin instilled in his men a code of conduct that did not permit shooting pursuing lawmen in the back. It was even said he saved the life of Bill Tilghman, the legendary lawman, in this very way when he surprised Doolin's men in their camp one evening.

Not unlike Jesse James, Doolin had the support of the local citizens in his part of Oklahoma. They provided him with shelter and, when needed, information concerning roving bands of lawmen. This help was a decisive factor in a shootout known as the Battle of Ingalls in September 1893. That gunfight took place about 10 miles east of Stillwater, Oklahoma, in the dusty little clapboard community of Ingalls.

Marshals from nearby Guthrie attempted to capture the entire Doolin gang in one fell swoop by surprising them during a heavy drinking spree. The lawmen had entered the town in a covered wagon and were waiting in an ambush for the gang. An informer notified "Bitter Creek" Newcomb, one of the Doolin gang members, that there was a trap. After a fierce fight the gang escaped Ingalls and made their way back to the badlands. This incident is recalled in the folk ballad "Rose of Cimarron," which glorifies Newcomb's part in the conflict.

There is little doubt that the Doolin gang were proficient in their trade. Banks, railroads, and the occasional small business fell to this raucous band of outlaws. Practice was their edge; they rehearsed each holdup carefully. Further, all members of the gang were crack marksmen and horsemen. It was well known that they all were good-timers unless cornered; then they shot to kill. In other words, they didn't go out of their way to murder anybody, but tangling with the Doolin gang could, and often did, end in a challenger's death.

After Doolin was married in 1894 the gang began to splinter because of deaths, captures, and just simple lack of interest. Doolin had every intention of settling down with his new wife, the daughter of a minister. But, of course, there was no way the law was just going to let Mr. Doolin slip into an easy retirement—he had committed far too many crimes for this to happen. After a horrendous hand-to-hand, half-hour battle with Marshal Bill Tilghman, in Eureka Springs, Arkansas, Doolin was captured. When he was led through the streets of Guthrie, Oklahoma, 5,000 people filled the streets to get a look at the famed bandit. Most of these citizens were attempting to get Doolin's autograph, ignoring the brave lawman Tilghman in the process. Shortly after Doolin's arrest, he proved that no jail was big enough to hold him: he escaped, freeing 37 fellow prisoners at the same time.

Doolin headed for New Mexico where, it was discovered over 40 years later, he was sheltered at the ranch of American novelist Eugene Manlove Rhodes. In 1896, Doolin and his wife settled in a small house in the community of Lawton, Oklahoma. For all practical purposes Doolin had given up his life of crime and running from the law—in part because of a bad case of consumption and an overall poor physical condition. The Doolins maintained a low profile and very few people even knew where he was.

Over the years several versions of Bill Doolin's death surfaced. One tale concerns the legendary Cherokee Strip marshal, Heck

Thomas. The story goes that Thomas encountered Doolin on a road and blasted him with a shotgun. Another story has Thomas busting into their cabin and finding Mrs. Doolin in tears; Doolin was supposedly already dead. Marshal Thomas knew there would be no reward money for a deceased Doolin so he shot the outlaw after he was already dead. He then concocted the account about a confrontation on the road. The yarn goes on to claim that Heck Thomas then gave the reward money, $5,000, to Doolin's widow, who had a small boy.

Thomas was one of a trio of lawmen known as "The Three Guardsmen." The other two members were Bill Tilghman and Chris Madsen. These three peace officers worked for Hanging Judge Leroy Parker, who operated out of Fort Smith, Arkansas. The three were well respected, even by outlaws, for being fair, brave, and thoroughly incorruptible. Doolin had gone straight for a time, so the story of Marshal Thomas's giving the reward money to his widow is not so far-fetched.

Whatever the facts are of Bill Doolin's death, there is little dispute that Doolin and his gang were among the early forefathers of territorial banditry. No real records exist of the amounts of money this group of outlaws got away with. Numbers vary widely and are subject to controversy. It would be safe to say that several dozen banks came under the professional handling of the Doolin Gang. Considering that Doolin had gotten his early instructions from the not-too-successful Dalton Gang, he and his band did very well for themselves. When we list the "immortals" in this line of endeavor, the Doolin Gang would rank right up there with the James Gang, if only by reputation alone.

HENRY "BEARCAT" STARR

Henry Starr, the supposed nephew of reputed "Bandit Queen" Belle Starr, was the last of the territorial bank robbers of the Old West. Starr's background in banditry extends all the way back to the Bill Doolin gang of Oklahoma and is even within the same time frame as the Dalton Gang. At least one writer has linked Henry Starr genetically to the Youngers, through a romantic tryst with Belle. Her career in crime was primarily confined to rustling cattle, although

Hollywood has managed to expound on her exploits to the point of making her a classic crime figure. The real story is less fantastic than fiction, and thus it is safe to assume that any connection between Henry Starr and Belle would be shaky at best.

"Bearcat" Starr, with a career spanning 1891 until 1921, is the first and most important modern connection to the old-time bank robbers. He had been successful as a cattle rustler and petty thief in the latter part of the nineteenth century, but had been sentenced to a few years at the federal prison in Columbus, Ohio. Upon recommendations of the warden, however, Starr received a pardon from President Theodore Roosevelt in 1902. At about the time Oklahoma became a state, in 1907, America saw an outbreak of bank heists. Many people felt that Starr was the scoundrel responsible for this new crime wave. In actuality, he was not all that good at robbing banks, but he didn't mind the notoriety he was receiving for the crimes.

Starr's reputation tended to make life difficult for him, with law enforcement focusing on him each time a robbery was committed. It didn't take an incredibly smart man to understand that things were getting just a little hot in Oklahoma, so Starr decided to head for California and try his luck out there. He only made two stops on his trek; he robbed the bank at Webster Groves, Missouri, and then another in Amity, Colorado. The Amity holdup was a bad idea. Starr was captured and sentenced to prison in Canyon City, Colorado, for 25 years. But Starr was again a model prisoner and, after promising never to set foot in the state of Colorado again, he was paroled after serving only two years.

In March 1915, Starr, with five associates, decided to try to make up for the mistakes of Jesse James and the Dalton Gang; they were going to rob two banks at the same time. After all, it had been 23 years since the Dalton failure and 39 years since the Jameses' blunder. There were so many new innovations in the business that Starr felt his scheme couldn't miss. His plan worked, but as the gang was making its escape Starr was shot by a 16-year-old and captured. A pursuing posse killed one of the robbers, two others were apprehended, and the other two escaped. One escapee was a 20-year-old punk named Al Spencer. Years later the Al Spencer Gang of Oklahoma was to become one of the most enterprising gangs in the nation and was also responsible for the last old-style train robbery in American history. For his part in the double robbery in 1915, Henry Starr was given 25 years in the prison at McAlester, Oklahoma. He was paroled at the age of 47, in 1919.

On February 18, 1921, in Harrison, Arkansas, Henry Starr pulled off his last bank job. He ordered the bank president into the vault but then the man suddenly pulled a double-barreled shotgun from a hiding place. Both barrels were discharged at the same time, effectively dispatching Mr. Starr into the somber recesses of legend. The other two men with Starr decided that it would be a good idea to head for parts unknown. This was by and large the last anyone heard from the old-time bad men of the Wild West days—but there was one more aspect to the Starr saga.

Starr bridged the gap between the horse-mounted robbers and men who arrived and departed the scene of the crime via a new mode of transportation, the automobile. Starr was the first bank robber to utilize a car in a bank robbery in the United States, reputedly a stolen Stutz Bearcat sports model that became the source of his nickname, "Bearcat."

Gone now were the days when robbers had to tie up their dusty ol' horses to the hitching post. Now the bandits could arrive in a suit and tie, walk into the bank, take care of business, then outrun whomever was inclined to chase them. Of course this didn't last long; the lawmen soon had cars of their own. But it was a beginning. From this point on, bank robbery was a whole different kind of business.

We have seen something of how the first century of bank robberies came about, and met some of the people who propelled this nefarious occupation into national prominence. The next three quarters of a century in our story will encompass what can be called the contemporary times in this business. Time and again, the men chronicled in these early days are seen to serve as role models for those who followed, even as technology in the twentieth century progressed.

Chapter 2

Packards and Thompsons

*"A criminal is a person with predatory instincts who has not
sufficient capital to form a corporation."*
—Howard Scott

The transition between the outlaws of the Old West and the modern
rogues spans about 40 years. What we will discover in this chapter is
the new breed of brigand, the kind that relies on a combination of
other outlaws' past deeds plus updated technology. As this technology
evolved so did the profession of robbing banks. Bandits needed to
keep up with advancements in building construction, security,
weapons, escape methods, and intelligence gathering. There is little
question that some of the robbers were up to the task.

As we encountered in the previous chapter, the post–Civil War era
featured a degree of emotional upheaval throughout the nation.
Mistrust of authorities and widespread melancholy assisted the bank
robber in his enterprises, even if only in the form of moral support. In
the same vein, a recession, beginning in 1918 after the First World
War, triggered a rash of bank robberies. Once again, people trusted
neither the banking industry nor, in particular, the bankers. Of course,
even during the war years bank robberies hadn't slacked off completely. The big difference, however, was the press' preoccupation with
reporting the war. The occasional robbery took a back page to war
news and people tended to view such crimes as trivial in comparison
to larger events. After the war, reporters still needed gripping news to
write about, and the bandits again took front page.

Journalists at the time knew how to beef up a story to catch the attention of the public. By and large the press gave these new robbers catchy names and exploited the events themselves to attract the reader. Not that there hadn't been yellow journalism in the newspaper business before; but now some of the correspondents took this procedure to an all-time high, fashioning crime stories into an art form.

During the war the use of the five-inch headline was standard. When you added the name of some flashy bank robber to the format, along with all the thrilling details of the robbery, you had the public's attention. The crooks once again had a public following, and the outlaws played it for all it was worth. In some areas of the nation individual newspapers had their own celebrity crime reporters. These journalists' work was often carried on wire services all over America, which placed some high-profile Chicago robberies into a reader's hands in Des Moines. Now subscribers could experience the excitement of a real bank robbery, by a big-time bank robber, in the sleepy little hamlets of the nation. There is no question that many of the reporters took some punk bank robbers and elevated them to star status, and it was the columnists who were responsible for the flamboyant nicknames added to many accounts. Most of these petty holdup men didn't have a nickname, or handle, until some enterprising and imaginative reporter got hold of their stories.

Succumbing to a mighty wave of moral rectitude, in 1920 the U.S. government instituted Prohibition, banning the sale of alcohol. Suddenly, millions of law-abiding Americans had a rooting interest in the criminal class, which was responsible for the bootlegging and maintenance of speakeasies that made continued imbibing of spirits possible. Given their new responsibility, gangs, of course, grew in size. The city of Chicago was practically run by them. Although smuggling alcohol was not strictly related to bank robbing, the effect of Prohibition was to enlarge the criminal class in America, and give it new status.

The 20-year period between the early 1920s and the 1940s saw a rapid increase in individuals willing to risk life and limb to get their money the easy way. Like the situation after the Civil War, a lot of men were wandering across the nation with little or nothing to do. The stock market crash in 1929, and both its ensuing poverty and anxiety, added to the problem. The combination of the Great War, the Roaring

Twenties, Prohibition, and the Depression brought forth a whole different kind of criminal.

Thousands of World War I veterans were aching for some excitement. Jobs were, for a time, impossible to find and crime was a viable alternative to working for peanuts. The war had added to this brew automatic and semiautomatic weapons; many of these had been combat-tested by the same jobless ex-servicemen. In short the method, means, and men were in the same place at the same time.

The Thompson submachine gun had been added to the arsenal of bank robbers and gangsters by 1928. This gun, capable of a cyclic firing rate of over 800 rounds a minute, became the favorite weapon of cops and criminals alike. At least half a dozen manufacturers produced variations of the firearm and soon there was a glut on the market. Many weapons were being sold as surplus by such companies as Sears & Roebuck. A man could get one of these very efficient killing machines for about $175 by mail order.

The Colt .45 caliber semiautomatic pistol had been combat-tested not only in the war but also in the Spanish-American conflict. This weapon replaced the six-shooter as the firearm of choice because it fired three more shots than the old-style gun did. As with the Thompson, there were any number of manufacturers worldwide willing to produce guns of this design. Hand grenades, the Browning automatic rifle (BAR), and advances in the handling of explosives were also new tools of the trade for the criminal. Firepower available to the newly armed outlaws made going up against them in a gunfight something to think about. No longer were they armed with only a couple of hoglegs and a Winchester; now they could be a force to reckon with. Lawmen, not to be outdone, girded themselves in like fashion.

Bank robbers needed to worry about additional innovations that weren't available in Jesse James's day. Police were now but a phone call away, and most banks had added electric alarms. Moreover, in the early thirties the Feds got into the act. The Bureau of Investigation in Washington, DC had been run by a crimestopper named J. Edgar Hoover since 1924. In 1933 it was reorganized into the FBI, an elite nationwide police force. That same year, Franklin D. Roosevelt created the Federal Deposit Insurance Corporation (FDIC) to protect depositors against their institutions being swallowed up by the Depression. It also protected that money against being pillaged by criminals. Every FDIC bank in the country had become a federal concern and bank robbing had become a federal crime. Hoover's FBI was empowered to go after the bank robber, and it quickly gained a reputation for getting its man.

Of course, now that community banks were backed by the government in Washington, bank robbing took on more of the aspect of a "victim-less" crime. Bankers had never been the most beloved of citizens; now the funds they held were guaranteed by the Feds. During the depression, foreclosures by banks were commonplace. Little farms were being sucked into the Dust Bowl in Oklahoma and Kansas. Weather would be the primary tormentor of men striving to support their families, but the final agent of death would be the banker brandishing his overdue notes. Is it any wonder that many outlaws of this period were born and raised in these drought-ridden areas? In the 1930s, Americans were so emotionally, as well as financially, depressed that nearly anyone who could put something over on a bank became a superstar.

Once again the nation was ripe for the picking, and now the harvesters carried machine guns. In this chapter we'll meet some of the big guns of the bank-robbing profession. We will also meet some of the colorful lawmen this era produced to go after its celebrity criminals. Many old-style lawmen made the conversion to modern times without difficulty. A few were employed by the FBI and attained legendary status. Some were ex-Texas Rangers, ex-state police, and retired sheriffs of crimeridden counties across the nation. Many of them had ridden on horseback, chasing robbers in the old days. They had gut feelings and years of experience to do the job; and, as we will see, they would need all of that and more.

JOHN ASHLEY & THE EVERGLADES GANG

Between 1915 and 1924 John Ashley and his Florida Everglades Gang robbed 40 banks and got away with an estimated one million dollars. This man and his group of outlaws were also renowned for their endeavors in truck hijacking and rum-running.

The Everglades in South Florida comprise roughly 4,000 square miles, and was the territory Ashley called home. Reputedly he could get around in this swamp as well as a city dweller could navigate the streets of any major municipality. Ashley would pull a job and then disappear into the underbrush and mire of his semi-tropical dominion. Lawmen considered it suicidal to go in after him. One posse made this mistake and several of the members had to be hospitalized and treated for gunshot wounds.

Ashley's exploits are still remembered clearly in this section of the country where he attained folk-hero status within his own lifetime. He has been compared to Jesse James, not only in his appearance, but also in the style and daring of that famed outlaw. Ashley and his gang were an assortment of men you just didn't mess with, unless you were looking to get killed.

This man's obvious lack of planning was a novel approach to robbing banks. In one case the gang didn't even have a getaway car. Ashley's reasoning was that they didn't need one; someone at the bank would have a car and they could hitch a ride out of town. On another job, Ashley's only preparation for the heist was to call the bank to make sure it was open.

An old-time resident of this area imparted a story to me concerning Ashley. A banker would see "them Everglades boys" drive up to the bank and would start placing all the bank's money into a burlap bag. He figured it was a whole lot easier than what would happen if he gave Ashley any trouble. When Ashley entered the building, there was a "tote sack" full of money ready for him. After a kind word to the banker, Ashley left the bank without incident. People were so terrified of John Ashley and his gang that just the sight of them rolling into town was enough to cause panic.

Ashley also took interest in the out-of-town rum-runners who worked the region. Most of these bootleggers were from "up north" and they were taking business away from local moonshiners trying to make a living. Once, when he escaped from prison, he made it a point to "see to them Yankee whisky peddlers," many of whom were Chicago or New York mobsters—not that this made much of a difference to John Ashley.

In 1924 Ashley and his gang committed the crime that would establish their national reputation. Ashley had been engaged in hijacking trucks full of booze heading north for some time. In fact, his

efforts along these lines had all but put the rum-runners out of business in south Florida. Ashley reasoned that if he could rob these guys
of all their money he could be rid of them altogether. This wasn't just
a spur-of-the-moment plan for Ashley, but a concerted effort to drive
the mobsters out of Florida. It's possible that he didn't really know
who he was messing with, but that's doubtful.

The rum-running business was relatively simple to understand.
Mother ships, loaded with illegal booze, were anchored outside the
three-mile limit of American territorial waters. Fast boats, called packets or "cigarette boats," would then transfer the booze and run it back
to the mainland and their off-loading port. This was similar to what
was happening on the Great Lakes along the American border with
Canada. It was also taking place on nearly every coastline of the
United States. Millions of dollars were made every month by gangsters
engaged in this business, and catching them was almost impossible. In
South Florida most contraband booze was not of the homemade variety but bonded whiskey from overseas bound for speakeasies up
north. For the Florida operation the little island of Bimini in the
Bahamas was the distribution and payoff point. This was to be the
location of Ashley's big 1924 strike.

Skimming across the Caribbean in a couple of fast boats, the
Everglades Gang surprised the mobsters in their lair. In a couple of
hours Ashley and his crew had relieved the bootleggers of about
$8,000 in cash, all they had on hand. This was accomplished the "old-
fashioned way"; namely, with a lot of physical punishment. They also
set fire to the storage buildings and the docking facilities, perhaps in
frustration because they had missed a fast packet boat heading for the
mainland loaded with $250,000 in cash by just a few hours.

The fact that one bunch of outlaws robbed another group is not
what put this crime into the history books. Its significance was that
this was the first time in over a century that an American privateer had
raided a British Crown Colony. Needless to say, not only did Ashley's
actions prompt an international incident, but local bootleggers got a
kick out of it. In public the authorities were furious, but privately they
were delighted that a band of riffraff had been put out of business,
even if by a rival band. Nevertheless, the British government began to
patrol the Bahamas' coastlines and the U.S. Coast Guard did likewise.
Bimini was no longer considered a safe harbor for bootleggers;

Ashley's raid had succeeded. But when the word got out that some hillbilly had put the big-time mobsters out of business, there were problems for John Ashley.

The Everglades Gang went back to something they knew how to do: robbing banks. About a month after Ashley's return from Bimini, the gang engaged in a running gun battle with lawmen outside Jacksonville on the Sebastian Bridge. The gang members were all killed in an immense salvo of police bullets. At least that is what the public was told. The shooting, even to this day, is subject to question. There is some evidence that the gang, including Ashley, had been handcuffed and then were executed by the police. Was this a retaliation for the Bimini raid by Florida cops who had been paid by northern mobsters to "get" Ashley? There were clear marks of manacles on the men's wrists after their bodies were returned to Jacksonville, but no witnesses ever came forward to dispute the word of the police. Local as well as federal authorities didn't really care how this gang died, but the general public in South Florida was sure the local folk hero had been murdered.

Judged by talent, Ashley should have never been a success in this line of work, but his personality was such that he couldn't fail. He was, without question, an enigma as a bank robber, but he certainly fulfilled all the requirements of a rogue. Although his criminal career spanned only nine years, his impact on South Florida remains. To this day, when conversations turn to crime and criminals of the old days, someone will bring up John Ashley and his Everglades Gang.

HERMAN K. "THE BARON" LAMM

A discredited German army officer came to the United States just before the First World War and became the most efficient bank robbery planner of all time. The officer's name was Herman K. Lamm, "The Baron." His belief was that a heist required all the planning of a military operation, including options in case of trouble. While he was in a Utah prison in 1917 for a botched holdup, he developed "The Lamm Technique." His tactics had all the precise timing needed to make robbing any bank a success. The James Gang, all ex-commandoes for the Confederate army, had a few thoughts along these same lines. Lamm just took the premise one step further.

The Baron would assign each member of the gang a specific job, which included a timetable for completion of each stage of the robbery. Lamm's planning was so complete that sometimes full-scale mock-ups of a bank's interior were constructed for dress rehearsals. Timing was everything; they were only going to be in the bank for so much time, regardless of how much money they got. Every possible obstacle and contingency was timed, from entry to exit. Stopwatches were used in practice runs until the proper results were achieved. All this, of course, after the bank's alarms, employees, hardware (safe and the vault) had been thoroughly cased.

However, with the Lamm system, this was only the first part of the plan. The second phase of Lamm's strategy was the getaway. To this end he used finely tuned, hopped-up cars, and drivers with racing experience. The escape routes, with alternates, were run time and again. Lamm would make a map of the routes and then attach it to the dashboard of the gang's car. Every turn was mapped out and then driven and timed. Dry runs on the roads and alternates would take days to work out. By the same token, practice runs on banks were also physically rehearsed. From the end of World War I until 1930, this gang accomplished bank robberies with a net take of over a million dollars. They quickly became the gang to watch when it came to getting it right during a heist. But if luck is the residue of design, even the Baron's string of fortune was due to end.

During a December 16, 1930, robbery in Clinton, Indiana, everything went wrong, with catastrophic results. The gang had picked up the money, $15,000, but the driver panicked when armed vigilantes headed toward his getaway car. He swung a U-turn and blew a tire trying to get the robbers out of town. He hadn't followed the Baron's plan, and from then on things only got worse. The gang abandoned the car and quickly stole another, but this one had a governor on the engine and they couldn't get any speed. They then stole a truck, but were finally cornered by approximately 200 police officers and vigilantes. Of the five robbers, Lamm and the driver were killed outright in a hail of gunfire. An older member of the gang opted to kill himself rather than be captured. Two others were arrested, tried, convicted, and sentenced to prison.

Jails are more than just places to spend a few years of your life, at least to criminals. A smart rogue will learn from the mistakes of others, and also from what he may have done correctly to have escaped prison up until then. Certain members of the famed Dillinger Gang, incarcerated for assorted crimes, were planning to break out of an Indiana prison at around the time of the Lamm debacle. When they discovered that a couple of men from the Lamm Gang were in the same penitentiary, they made them an offer. These two men could join them in their planned escape if they would divulge Lamm's secrets. This seemed a small price to pay for their freedom, so the two were included in the 1931 breakout. John Dillinger used the Baron's system extensively during his own career with the same military exactness Lamm had imparted to his first students. Luckily, Dillinger's vocation only lasted 11 months. During this period he robbed somewhere between 10 and 15 banks, as well as three police arsenals; he was also involved in three jail breaks.

The most notorious achievement of the Dillinger Gang was that they killed 10 men and wounded at least seven others. Despite these gruesome statistics, the press turned Dillinger into a national hero. Writers of the day even gave him the nickname "Handsome Johnny." Dillinger was not all that bright and, if it hadn't been for the Baron's procedure, "Handsome Johnny" would not have had such a long career in the bank-robbing business. Dillinger had little style and was on a very predictable collision course with the authorities. He was, however, another of our bank robbers whose childhood hero was the legendary Jesse James.

In later years, others employed the Lamm scheme for the removal of money from banking establishments. Most successful bank robbers knew that the greater the planning the more productive the heist. Herman "The Baron" Lamm affixed three very important elements to the business of robbing banks: planning, practice, and timing. Of course, in today's rash of bank robberies the Lamm technique is rarely used. Today there are no real plans short of the basics—get a gun, a car, and a bag to carry loot. Timing, technique, intelligence, practice, and getaway routes are not usually part of the strategy. As one FBI expert told me, "There are no more good bank robbers around today, just punks!" "The Baron" was notable because he took the time to devise the necessary strategy to successfully holdup banks.

HARVEY "OLD HARVE" BAILEY

Born and raised in Oklahoma, Harvey Bailey was one of those bank robbers who could have rivaled the Jameses in many ways. His career spanned better than 20 years and his takes in robberies were extraordinary. Although he only had a basic education, he was well read and was referred to as a gentleman bank robber by lawmen and associates alike. Bailey was also known as a cool-headed man who didn't care for gunplay during a heist, but he also knew how to get the job done. As we have seen, many bank robbers obtain a nickname after they have pulled a few jobs; Bailey was no different. Because of his composed attitude during a robbery, and his remarkable hauls, he was known during his lifetime as the "King of the Heist Men."

Bailey was about six foot tall with brown eyes and a sturdy build. He began his adult career as a salesman. During his peak years he was a bandit without peer, pulling off some of the biggest holdups in American history. Bailey robbed the Denver Mint, with Jim Ripley and a couple of others, in 1922, obtaining an estimated half million dollars in untraceable bills. In 1931, he also relieved the Lincoln National Bank, in Lincoln, Nebraska, of the largest amount ever taken in an armed holdup: $1,000,000 in cash and securities. Some estimate that this haul was more like $2,000,000 (even today banks are sometimes reluctant to disclose amounts taken in a robbery, which often leads to inaccurate claims). Bailey's reasoning was, the more he could get away with in a heist, the longer he could stay out of sight.

Just before he was arrested on a golf course in the Kansas City suburb of Mission Hills in 1932, Bailey was involved in a robbery with Ma Barker and her gang of cutthroats. J. Edgar Hoover had already referred to Ma Barker as a "veritable beast of prey." A vast number of people, thanks to great press coverage, believed that Barker was just what Hoover proclaimed her to be. Bailey's comments about her were somewhat different from Hoover's. In an excerpt from the 1960s book by L. L. Edge, *Run the Cat Roads*, Bailey says about Barker, "The old woman couldn't plan breakfast. When we'd sit down to plan a bank job, she'd go into the other room and listen to Amos and Andy or hillbilly music on the radio. She just went along with Freddie [Barker] because she had no choice. Freddie loved his mother and wouldn't leave her to fend for herself."

The robbery that May was not in the old tried-and-true Bailey method; it was a complete mess. The bank in Fort Scott, Kansas, was the target. Such notables as Freddie Barker, Alvin "Old Creepy" Karpis, Larry DeVol, Tommy Holden, and Phil Courtney were Bailey's teammates for the job.

Very early in the robbery, someone in the bank hit the panic button and Freddie Barker came unglued. He threatened to shoot everyone in the bank if they didn't shut up. The robbers gathered up $47,000, seized three women from inside the bank, and headed for the door. They then placed two of the frightened young ladies on the running boards of the car (the other girl had fainted), and their escape was on! Lawmen were hot on their heels, but a burst from Barker's "tommy-gun" out the rear window persuaded the cops to back off. The business of placing hostages on the running boards of the getaway-car was standard operating procedure. The theory was that the cops would not shoot at the gangsters if they had to shoot around innocent citizens; in most cases, the outlaws' thinking worked.

The girls were released a few miles out of town after the bandits had lost the police. The robbers then split up the loot; Bailey's cut was about $4,000. Not the kind of money he'd been used to, but at least he was done with the Barker Gang. Bailey then went on to Kansas City, Missouri, where he was well known. While playing a round of golf at the Old Mission Golf Course, Tommy Holden, Francis Keating, and he were arrested without incident; all three men were unarmed. There was a fourth rogue in the party, the sometime partner to Bailey, a man named Frank "Jelly" Nash, who managed to escape. Bailey was convicted for the Fort Scott robbery and sentenced to the state penitentiary at Lansing, Kansas. But there is a lot more to the story of "Old Harve."

Harvey Bailey took part in a major breakout of the Lansing facility on Memorial Day, 1933. His escape was facilitated by his bank-robbing partner Nash, who managed to smuggle guns into the prison. It was reported that Bailey was wounded in the leg while going over the wall with 10 other convicts. One of the men who fled with Bailey was Wilbur Underhill, a known murderer and cop killer. Word had it that Underhill and Bailey were ringleaders of the escape. With the aid of a few well-placed connections in Kansas City, Bailey's group of five managed to make it to the hills of Oklahoma shortly after the breakout. They were heard from again on the morning of June 17, 1933.

Bailey, along with Wilbur Underhill, Bob "Big Boy" Brady, Jim Clark, and Ed Davis—all fellow escapees—were seen at the Union Station building in Kansas City. "Jelly" Nash had been arrested in Hot Springs, Arkansas, the day before, so federal agents with the help of local cops were transferring him to the prison at Leavenworth, Kansas. Nash had escaped from this institution three years before, so naturally he was familiar with Kansas City. Bailey and his men were there to free Nash from the lawmen.

At 7:15 A.M. the train from Little Rock entered the station. Unknown to the police escort, a contingent of heavily armed men waited in ambush for it. When the officers, with Nash in tow, crossed the parking lot of the station at least seven gunmen opened fire. This incident became known as the Union Station Massacre and cost the lives of four lawmen and the prisoner, Frank Nash. Bailey, somewhat out of character, was observed firing a .45 caliber Thompson into the group of lawmen from an automobile stationed behind the officers' car. Credible witnesses identified one of the other killers as Underhill.

Due to corruption in the administration of "Big Tom" Pendergast, Kansas City's powerful political boss, the official facts surrounding this event were changed. Although almost all investigators knew that Bailey and several of the escapees were in the killing party, the incident was blamed on someone else. Local Kansas City mobsters blamed the killings on outside gangsters, and the FBI director, J. Edgar Hoover, went along with this fairy tale. Hoover assigned the guilt to Adam Richetti and his well-known partner Charles "Pretty Boy" Floyd, both of whom happened to be in Kansas City at the time. In reality the shooters were the Lansing escapees and three or four local assassins.

Following the incident in Kansas City all of these men headed for parts unknown. Bailey went to a regular gangster hideout known as the Shannon Ranch. The head investigator of the Union Station Massacre, Gus T. Jones, an ex–Texas Ranger, knew that Bailey was one of the gunmen and set out looking for him. The Shannon Ranch, owned by the stepfather of Katherine Kelly, wife of George "Machine Gun" Kelly, was also where some gangsters had chosen to hide after kidnapping oilman Charles Urschel a few days before. Bailey had chosen to hide in an area of Texas crawling with lawmen looking for the kidnapers and the Kansas City killers.

While "Old Harve" was taking a snooze, holding a .45 automatic on his lap, Gus Jones slipped up behind him and held a cocked Colt .45 Peacemaker to Bailey's ear. "Get up, Harvey!" he said. "If you try for the gun, I'll riddle you." The ex–Texas Ranger, turned federal agent, had the drop on Bailey and this veteran criminal was no fool. He surrendered without a fight. In his pocket was $500 of the Urschell ransom money that had been given to him by George Kelly as spending money. As a result, he was arrested for being part of the kidnapping plot. Of course Jones was familiar with Bailey and knew he was uninvolved with the kidnapping, but also knew he was one of the Kansas City killers. Jones would go to his grave several years later believing that Bailey was not only one of the assassins but one of the masterminds of the massacre.

Harvey was taken to the Dallas jail, but in just two weeks he enlisted the help of a greedy guard and managed to saw through the bars of his cell. On September 4, 1933, he slipped out of the "escape-proof" Dallas jail, stole a car, and headed back to the Cookson Hills of eastern Oklahoma. Bailey only made it as far as Ardmore, Oklahoma, and was returned to Dallas under heavy guard.

Although he had been on the first indictment handed down in the massacre case, Bailey was never charged with this crime. He was, however, convicted of the Urschell kidnaping—something that nobody believed he had done. His Dallas escape, along with several other offenses, was added to his sentence and the "King of the Heist Men" was destined to serve the next 36 years of his life behind bars.

When Bailey was released from prison, he married the widow of one of the convicted co-conspirators in the Union Station Massacre case and died an old cabinetmaker at the age of 96. True to the code of the criminal community, Bailey never revealed the circumstances of his involvement in the massacre. Of course, the lack of a statute of limitations on murder would have been a good enough reason not to talk.

BONNIE & CLYDE

These two Americans, although considered by some to be romantic figures, were less than admirable individuals, and at best might be considered Romeo and Juliet from hell. Press reports and a far-fetched movie have concealed much of the truth about their lives, so we need to set the record straight about Bonnie Parker and the psychopathic Clyde Barrow.

Bonnie Parker was born in 1910 just off the Old Dodge City cattle trail in Rowena, Texas. Though an above-average student, she was very dependent on her mother for emotional support. As a young lady she engaged in violent fights with other classmates and was married at 16 to a petty thief. Before the marriage ended, Bonnie moved to Dallas with her mother and husband, and worked on the city's outskirts as a waitress at Cafe Morco's, a cheap hash house. A mere wisp of a woman, she was four-foot-ten-inches tall, 90 pounds dripping wet, and able to fit easily into a dress size of about two. Naturally, she was hardly an imposing figure.

Clyde Barrow was born on March 24, 1909, outside Telico, Texas, to a very poor, dirt-farmer family. His emotional escape was going to the movies and watching Westerns. His paragons were Jesse James and Cole Younger, and the two men occupied a lot of his daydreams. Barrow was also impressed with people like Henry "Bearcat" Starr, who had been gunned down in Oklahoma when Clyde was only 12 years old. And Clyde was a problem with the local lawmen even before he was a teenager; during his early years in Texas he amassed quite a juvenile record. Most offenses were trivial, but others included break-ins, auto theft, animal mistreatment, and several charges of torturing children. There is a question as to whether he even killed a child or two during this time, but there is no proof, only suspicion. Clyde's older brother, Buck, was sentenced to five years in the Huntsville Prison for burglary—a safe-cracking crime Clyde must also have been involved in.

Clyde and Bonnie began dating on a regular basis early in 1930. Clyde was soon arrested for a minor offense and thrown into the Waco, Texas, city jail. Bonnie smuggled a stolen .32 caliber pistol to Clyde and he escaped, only to be recaptured a week later in Ohio and returned to Texas where he received a 14-year sentence in the same prison as his brother. Clyde was released in February 1932, however, and rejoined Bonnie. But now there was something a little different about Clyde, a change Bonnie Parker was soon to discover.

Clyde's problems with abusing children had not endeared him to some of his fellow prison mates in Huntsville. The young man was raped while in prison by a number of older inmates. As a result, Clyde had developed a liking for male lovers. Although this aspect of his background is rarely mentioned, he was, in fact, a bisexual with leanings toward homosexual encounters. For the most part he was impotent when it came to Bonnie Parker.

Bonnie and Clyde's first big adventure into the world of crime occurred shortly after a car theft in which the two of them, with an accomplice, were chased by lawmen over some rough Texas countryside. Clyde, ever the gentleman, abandoned Bonnie in a barn and struck out on his own. Bonnie was arrested and taken to jail; she was released to her mother after swearing she would never see Clyde Barrow again. But Bonnie joined Clyde when he came for her. They were involved in their first murder outside Dallas in April 1932; the victim was a county deputy. The second shooting and murder attributed to the twosome was in Stringtown, Oklahoma, where a deputy sheriff and another man were killed.

By late 1932, Bonnie and Clyde had formed a small group of other misfits into a haphazard criminal ensemble. By and large, the Barrow Gang was nothing more than a controlled panic. There is little doubt that Clyde Barrow had a psychological hold over the impressionable and malleable Bonnie, and Miss Parker loved the excitement. The duo were accused of their first bank robbery, although evidence does not support this contention, in Ceder Hill, Texas, on October 8, 1932.

Even the lawmen of the day didn't consider Bonnie and Clyde professional robbers, but rather cheap, thrill-seeking murderers and thieves. By this time Clyde could be connected to at least five, and maybe six, deaths. Bonnie was present for at least two or three of these killings. Most of their victims were unarmed citizens who happened to be in the wrong place at the wrong time. For the most part, their robberies had been small takes at gas stations and country stores. The first bank robbery that could definitely be attributed to the Barrow Gang was at Orange, Missouri, and their total take was $115—hardly the stuff of legend.

On January 6, 1933, Clyde, with a new accomplice, W. D. Jones, shot and killed Temple, Texas, Deputy Sheriff Malcolm Davis in the nearby town of Grapevine. Bonnie was nearby in the car at the time of this killing. And now, after release from Huntsville prison, Buck Barrow joined his famous brother and Bonnie in Fort Smith,

Arkansas. Buck's wife, Blanche, became a somewhat unwilling member of the gang at this time. Friction was soon evident between Blanche and Bonnie, and their catfights fast became a problem for the men. In addition, there were too many lawmen looking for this group of people in Arkansas, so they moved on.

The gang had taken refuge in an apartment outside Joplin, Missouri, when, on April 13, they were surprised by a quartet of police officers running a routine check for some suspicious neighbors. The ensuing gunfight left two officers dead and W. D. Jones and Clyde both slightly wounded. Again the group of outlaws headed for the hills. Life on the run for this desperate gang of thieves and killers was ultimately trying. When the money ran out they were forced into petty holdups, and these included the theft of gasoline, food, and the occasional handful of cash. Their next bank robbery was in Okabena, Minnesota, and the take this time was about $2,500. The heist started out smoothly but when they exited the bank, the whole town seemed to know what was going on and started shooting at them. They escaped, somewhat shaken, and took to country roads.

During one of their trips into Arkansas, Bonnie was burned in an auto accident. While she was being tended by her sister, brought from Dallas to Arkansas, Clyde stayed by her side during the recovery period; therefore, W. D. Jones and Buck Barrow had to take care of business. W. D. and Buck robbed a Piggly Wiggly grocery store, but the theft degenerated into a gunfight with lawmen. One officer was killed and another wounded in the skirmish. The newspapers quickly attached the handle of the "Piggly Wiggly Bandits" to the caper and the villains. There may, indeed, be some question whether the lawmen even knew they had tangled with elements of the Barrow Gang. It would have been hard to determine at the time since the loot for this intended holdup was food, bandages, and a little traveling money. The peace officers thought they had had a run-in with a bunch of gun-crazy punks.

The next time we come across this bunch is in their hideout in Platte City, Missouri. On a July evening in 1933 the cabins where the outlaws were sleeping were surrounded by a posse of lawmen. The officers, unsure of who was really in the buildings, took the time to walk up and knock on a door. Clyde, knowing that something wasn't right, opened fire with a Browning Automatic rifle. The surrounding police opened fire. Bonnie was wounded and was quickly hustled into the backseat of the gang's recently stolen V-8 Ford. Buck was wounded, too, so he was placed in the rear of the car with Bonnie. Another shot from the lawmen hit Blanche and she was also thrown in the backseat of the Ford. As the gang made its escape, police bullets poured into the car.

Clyde drove to Dexter, Iowa, 25 miles from Des Moines, with his three wounded confederates. The group ended up in a farm field, and while Clyde and W. D. Jones attended to their chores, the injured licked their wounds as best they could beside a small campfire. Soon the wounded and the two uninjured men fell asleep. Meanwhile, thanks to a local farmer, the police had been notified about a band of people camping on the outskirts of town. The locals and the entire nation had already heard about the Bonnie and Clyde shoot-out in Platte City, so everyone was a little edgy.

The next morning, as the campers were preparing breakfast, a sudden stirring in the brush alarmed Bonnie. Buck was near death and unable to move when lawmen entered the clearing. The term "all hell broke loose" would perhaps be an understatement. Mass panic would be more like it. Clyde was wounded in the arm, Bonnie was hit by shotgun pellets, and W. D. was wounded twice. Buck drew fire from the lawmen and was wounded several more times; a few days later, he died of these wounds. His wife, Blanche, who had been wounded during the escape from Platte City, was taken into custody, but Bonnie, Clyde, and W. D. slipped into a creek and eluded the lawmen. Later the three stole a car and got away. There is a picture of this raid, taken shortly after the confrontation, showing Blanche being arrested. Buck is lying on the ground, mortally wounded, with cops all over the scene. This photograph was published in most of the nation's newspapers, further adding to the contrived titillation that surrounded this group of killers.

At this time, the general public believed that Bonnie and Clyde were just a couple of star-crossed lovers. People wanted to believe what they'd read in the papers and the papers sure weren't telling the truth about the two. For the fugitives, their movements started to become a blur on a day-to-day basis. In September 1933 Bonnie and Clyde, with Jones, returned to the area around Dallas; but even their own home state was not safe, so they didn't remain long. Around the town of Clarksdale, Mississippi, W. D. Jones decided he was tired of the gang's lifestyle, and simply walked away. After all, most of the time, this group of bank robbers didn't even have enough to eat. Jones was arrested by Houston police on November 15, 1933, and almost immediately began to provide the authorities a song-and-dance about his days with the Barrow Gang. Jones was, of course, only 17 and insisted that Clyde Barrow had forced him to take part in the crimes. The cops did, however, get some good information from Jones and they planned an ambush for November 22. Again, in a hail of bullets, the deadly duo outran the Texas cops. More press coverage, nationwide, glamorized their daring escape from predatory lawmen.

Bonnie and Clyde's next robbery, after Jones deserted them, was the 1933 daylight holdup of an oil refinery in the small community of Overton, Texas. This netted the gang, which again consisted of three people, about $3,000. Some say the second man in this holdup team was Ray Hamilton. Bonnie Parker drove the getaway car.

In January 1934, Bonnie and Clyde assisted five convicts to break out of Huntsville Prison. One guard was killed and the fugitives, along with a new woman, then rearmed themselves at a local armory. They next entered the town of Lancaster, Texas, and withdrew between $2,400 and $6,700 from a bank where they had no account. On April 6, three lawmen were murdered and another officer wounded when they confronted the killers during a routine check of suspicious individuals on a Texas back road outside of Dallas. These were cold-blooded killings, and in no way were the gang members attempting to defend themselves. Bonnie shot one officer with a shotgun while he lay on the ground wounded. When asked why she had done it, she was quoted as saying, "I just wanted to see his head bounce." This is also about the time Bonnie posed for the infamous photograph in which she is holding a shotgun and sucking on a cigar. The photo went a long way toward promoting her image as a rough, tough, gun-toting moll, even though she didn't smoke.

On May 23, 1935, a small, six-man posse, led by ex–Texas Ranger Frank Hamer, ambushed a tan V-8 Ford driven by Clyde Barrow outside Arcadia, Louisiana. When the shooting ended, both Bonnie, 23 years old, and Clyde, 25, were dead. There had been 167 bullets— about 28 for easch posse member—pumped into the automobile and at least 50 rounds had hit the couple. The firing was so intense that Bonnie's hand was completely severed from her wrist and Clyde's head was unrecognizable.

The information for this ambush had been obtained from ex-partner W. D. Jones. With it, Hamer had been tracking the two desperadoes for over a year and a half. Solid police work and a nose for following up hunches brought an end to Bonnie and Clyde's reign of terror. Years later their car went on tour throughout the United States. Earlier, trophy seekers also attempted to take souvenirs off the bodies of the slain killers.

Bonnie and Clyde's career as bank robbers accounted for three confirmed bank robberies and one they may have done. Other heists committed by this pathetic group of killers were petty. It would almost be untrue to say these two were bank robbers, because in this profession they were hardly more than amateurs. What the two lovers were really good at was wanton murder. Robbery was merely a way to keep them in gas and food; murder was their prime enterprise. In the 1960 movie *Bonnie & Clyde*, Faye Dunaway and Warren Beatty looked good as the two wretched psychotic butchers, but the movie didn't even get close to the real story. The idea that these two were just "misunderstood youngsters" is sorely mistaken. They were psychopathic killers. Their total take, from all their robberies, didn't amount to $20,000, but the body count was in excess of two dozen.

Bonnie and Clyde were among the high-profile breed of killer robbers who flourished during the 1930s. And the public was duped by the press into believing these two people were something they were not. Even in his day, Clyde Barrow was regarded by lawmen as a mass murderer. Nor was Bonnie Parker a hapless waif; she was implicated in several murders and the nation's lawmen considered her as dangerous as Clyde. Historian L. L. Edge, in his book *Run the Cat Roads*, comments: "The glamour of an individual criminal who happens to catch the public fancy is rare today. That period of the thirties when even minor bank robbers gained certain stature among the American public was a one-time thing in history. It'll never happen again." Perhaps it couldn't have happened at all without the assistance of the press, who glorified two murderous criminals into superstar status for no legitimate reason.

RAY HAMILTON

One of the members of the loosely structured organization known as the Barrow Gang was Ray Hamilton. A childhood friend of Clyde's, he would only be linked to the gang on a few jobs, but there was a bit more to his story than that. We've previously seen what happened to Clyde in prison. He became a bisexual and was by and large worthless to the lovely Miss Parker as a sexual partner. Bonnie, to put it politely, was a nymphomaniac. Enter Ray Hamilton. During the times the three of them spent together, Hamilton took care of the sexual cravings of Bonnie Parker; Clyde liked to watch. With a psychopath like Barrow, Hamilton needed to keep his arrangement with Bonnie really "open."

Hamilton may have been just the thing for the sexually depressed Bonnie, but he was also no lightweight in the field of robbing banks. His crime binge lasted only three years, from 1932 until 1935, but he got a lot done. With the help of talented accomplices he held up seven banks, a dozen or so other concerns, and two oil refineries. Add to this the robbery of a post office, a packing plant, and the National Guard Armory in Fort Worth, Texas, and you get an idea of what kind of guy Hamilton was. Arrested on several occasions, each time he was able to break out, once with Clyde's help. Further, he was also responsible for a couple of murders and suspected in others. For assorted crimes against society he was executed on May 10, 1935.

Clyde's boyhood relationship with Hamilton, or Hamilton's own record for violence, may have been all that kept Clyde from harming his sexual surrogate. Like many other aspects about the lives of Bonnie and Clyde, Ray Hamilton was not included in the 1967 movie.

Because of the famous exploits of Bonnie and Clyde, one line of work that prospered for a short time during the heyday of the gangsters was the bank-robber bounty hunter. "Wanted" posters, with text as seen below, were circulated by the Texas Banker's Association, in the hopes of reducing the number of bank robberies:

REWARD

$5,000 FOR DEAD BANK ROBBERS

"Not One Cent for Live Ones"

Such simple enticement was enough for many would-be law-enforcers to join the hunt for outlaws like Bonnie and Clyde. Other states waited to see if this approach would work, but it was discontinued before any bank robbers were captured or killed. Most deaths attributed to posters of this sort were either petty criminals or innocent bystanders. But the policy did demonstrate just how frustrated the bankers of America were becoming with the increase in holdups during this period of American history. The lawman responsible for putting an end to the practice was Frank Hamer, the ex–Texas Ranger who finally got Bonnie and Clyde.

CHARLES "PRETTY BOY" FLOYD

Charles Arthur Floyd was born on February 3, 1904, near Folsom, Georgia, to a family of hard-working, law-abiding farmers. No one could know that this little 10-pound baby boy would go on to become the nation's Public Enemy Number One before he turned 31 years old. "Pretty Boy" Floyd would become one of those larger-than-life bank robbers, a legend in his own time.

When little Charlie Floyd was about seven, in 1911, the family moved to Sequoya County, Oklahoma, near the town of Hanson. For the youngster this was real cowboy and Indian country. In earlier days of Oklahoma's history this section of the state, the Cookson Hills, was known as the "Robber's Roost."

While he was growing up Floyd heard stories about the local hero and territorial bank robber Henry "Bearcat" Starr, the reputed nephew of the "Bandit Queen" Belle Starr. Henry Starr was still an active "Old Western outlaw" when Floyd was a child. Floyd also relished hearing about the exploits of Frank and Jesse James. The Youngers, the Daltons, the Bill Doolin Gang, and Al Spencer were all important idols for the young Floyd. But far and away Floyd's all-time hero was Jesse James, the "American Robin Hood." Is it any wonder that when he was nine years old he was apprehended during his first daylight robbery for stealing a box of cookies from a local general store?

Jesse James, a man who stole from the rich and gave to the poor, was someone a little boy could really identify with. All these desperadoes had done business at one time or another in this area of Oklahoma and Charles Floyd ate it up. But these feelings were not something Floyd put away as he grew older. He cultivated images of the thrilling tales of outlaws and, during his daydreams, envisioned himself in a similar role. These visions of helping the downtrodden would add to his own legend. But during his youth he had his chores, and working in the cotton fields and on the family farm took almost all Floyd's time and energy.

As the late teens and early twenties brought their style to the American scene, things were changing for Charles Floyd. Jazz bands, hot-rod cars, flappers, and Prohibition would follow one another after the Great War ended. By 1919 Floyd had done all the farming he wanted to do and decided to hit the road to adventure. He headed west and in 1921 we find Floyd in the company of a known Wichita, Kansas, gangster named Callahan. Floyd found employment as a driver for Callahan's thriving bootleg business, where he gained a new kind of education, in the underworld.

In the late nineteenth and early twentieth centuries, Oklahoma led the nation in bank robberies. Social banditry was not frowned upon in the Oklahoma Territory; it was an accepted way of life. During the twenties, 60 to 70 banks a year were robbed in the state of Oklahoma. In Floyd's mind Henry Starr was, without a doubt, the reincarnation of Jesse James. Starr was finally killed in a holdup in Harrison, Arkansas, in 1921, when Floyd was 17 years old. His death would have a profound effect on Charles Floyd.

Sometime in 1922 Floyd, along with a couple of friends, committed his first crime as an adult, a burglary. They stole about $350 in pennies from a store that doubled as a post office. Fearing capture, they disposed of the loot down a farm well. This brief beginning was the end of Floyd's criminal career for a time. He married a local girl in 1924 and, for the most part, lived a law-abiding life, although his thoughts of an outlaw's existence still smoldered.

Floyd's first armed holdup took place on September 11, 1925, in St. Louis. He and two others relieved a courier of $11,929 in payroll money bound for a grocery and baking concern. Floyd was captured along with his colleagues. He was tried, convicted, and sentenced to five years of hard labor in the state penitentiary at Jefferson City, Missouri. Floyd studied the moonshine racket while in jail; in other words, he began to learn tricks of the trade from experienced teachers of the day, his fellow inmates; and Floyd learned well. This first incarceration provided Floyd a wealth of information.

Released from prison on March 7, 1929, after serving three and a half years, Charles Floyd now had a valuable education, as well as a divorce from his wife for nonsupport. Floyd took the train from Jefferson City and headed west. Kansas City, Missouri, in 1929, was a wide open town. This community of about 400,000 people was run by "Boss" Tom Pendergast. It had a rough-and-ready reputation and was known for its corruption as well as being a city where a person, looking for a little action could find anything he pleased. Criminals were welcome if they caused no trouble for the city's rulers. In the parlance of the day, Kansas City was a "safe town."

Two days after his release from prison, Floyd was arrested there and held for investigation. Police cleared him of any criminal wrongdoing and told him, in no uncertain terms, to go back to Oklahoma. He took their advice, thinking that perhaps he could find an honest job. Nevertheless, despite an oil boom, he still had a hard time finding work. Growing tired of job seeking, he went back to Kansas City and the good life he thought was there. On May 6, 1929, he was again arrested, this time in Kansas City, Kansas, for vagrancy and suspicion of highway robbery. Released the next day, he again headed west.

Floyd was arrested two days later in Pueblo, Colorado, most likely for running booze from Kansas City into the state. Fined $50, he got to spend the next 60 days in a Pueblo jail. He would be arrested a couple more times in Kansas City, Missouri, upon his return to that community. His luck was simply not good when it came to trying to make a living in that town. He didn't have the right connections—but this was all to change. With the help of a limo driver for Johnny Lazia, Kansas City's mob lord, Floyd was soon considered a player in "River City." The driver, James Henry "Blackie" Audett, showed the hillbilly "Okey" the ins and outs of crime in Kansas City.

It was in this town, late in 1929, that Charles A. Floyd acquired the sarcastic moniker "Pretty Boy." This name, given to him by a local girl named Beulah Baird, was to remain with him for the rest of his life. Also late in 1929, Floyd had another run-in with Kansas City cops; it was time to move on. He and a couple of associates ended up in the community of Akron, Ohio.

"Pretty Boy" Floyd's first bank robbery occurred on Wednesday, February 5, 1930, at the Farmers & Merchants Bank of Sylvania, Ohio. After the holdup things went awry. A police officer was killed attempting to arrest the suspects. Floyd was captured, convicted of bank robbery, and sentenced to prison again. While on his way to the Ohio State Penitentiary, Floyd overpowered a guard and leapt from the moving train to freedom. This was the last time "Pretty Boy" Floyd would ever be in police custody.

Floyd was soon involved in two shoot-outs with police and was a suspect in at least one murder in the Kansas City area. A wanted man, Floyd went back to the Cookson Hills in the summer of 1931. During this time he continued to rob banks and became proficient with a machine gun as well as handguns. Late that summer, Floyd teamed up with another bank robber named George Birdwell. Their first bank robbery together was the Bank of Erlsboro on August 19, 1931, and they liberated $3,000. Birdwell and Floyd held up at least six banks in Oklahoma between August and December 1931.

The following year things picked up for the pair and they robbed bank after bank. Floyd's new name, "Pretty Boy," was starting to get attention in the nation's newspapers, as were the duo's feats of der-ring-do. Although Floyd didn't care for the handle, it did give him sat-isfaction that he, too, was becoming a household name around the country, like his idol, Jesse James.

Floyd's family, his ex-wife, and most people from his hometown never believed that Floyd was a cold-blooded killer. History notes that Floyd was not a hired assassin and did not kill just for the thrill of it. But he had made it clear, after his escape from the train in Ohio, that he would not be going back to jail. The implication was that trying to take Floyd by force could be fatal; in some cases, it certainly was.

Amounts stolen from banks during Floyd's career are difficult to follow. Estimates range from a high of $1,500,000 to a low of $250,000. Whatever his income, Floyd was good at robbing banks. The number of banks robbed is also unclear, but the consensus is somewhere between 60 and 70. He managed to stay cool when the pressure was on and he was not trigger-happy. For the most part, dur-ing his robberies, he was polite, but firm. Random violence simply didn't happen when Floyd robbed a bank. However, it did sometimes erupt as he was leaving. If he was confronted by armed men who made the mistake of shooting at him, Floyd would respond in kind.

By late 1932, the legend of "Pretty Boy" Floyd had begun to grow. There were stories about how Floyd would take mortgage records of small-town banks he robbed and destroy them. He gave money to poor dirt farmers who aided him with kindness. In this way the role he had so much admired in Jesse James began to be associated with him. In his own mind, and in the minds of many down-and-out farmers, he was the "New American Robin Hood."

In late 1932 George Birdwell, Floyd's right-hand man, was killed while pulling a job on his own. Floyd then teamed up with an Oklahoma-born alcoholic and psychopathic killer named Adam Richetti. The two continued in the bankrobbing business through the end of 1932 and into the early months of the new year. On June 16, 1933, the two were cooling their heels in Kansas City. That night, Floyd and Richetti were approached by a local tough guy and hired killer named Vern Miller. Miller was looking for help in freeing a federal prisoner, and close personal friend, who was being escorted back to the penitentiary at Leavenworth, Kansas, the next morning. The two Oklahoma bandits met with Miller at his house the evening of the 16th, but they turned Miller down and refused to participate in the rescue attempt. We have already seen what happened at a little after 7:15 A.M. on the morning of June 17, 1933, at the Union Station in Kansas City, Missouri.

Almost immediately after the Union Station Massacre was finished, Floyd and Richetti were named as two of the half dozen gunmen whom witnesses identified as being involved. Their names were added to the list of suspects by J. Edgar Hoover in order to garner more power for his yet little Bureau of Investigation, which would become the FBI only a month later. A few days later, Richetti's fingerprints were said to be found on a beer bottle in Vern Miller's house. This, according to Hoover, was enough proof to implicate Floyd and Richetti in the mass murder. The conjecture was that Richetti and Floyd had spent the night with Miller. The only serious flaw in this logic was that an active alcoholic isn't going to drink just one beer during the course of an entire evening. Another way to look at it is that it took only one beer to turn Miller down. The fact is, there was no way to tell whether these two men had been there before the incident at the station or after. Regardless, Hoover said they were guilty and that that was enough to place them on the top of the list of suspects.

Although Floyd and Richetti were not named in the newspapers until the next day, in all likelihood they left Kansas City on the night of the massacre. The underworld grapevine worked a lot faster than newspapers, so the men would have been informed early on the day of the massacre to get out of town. This information would have come by way of Johnny Lazia's paid police force working with the federal investigators on the case. After a short run through southern Missouri, Richetti and Floyd, with two women, ended up in Buffalo, New York. Aside from a couple of trips out of town, including one back to Oklahoma, this foursome remained in their apartment for the next 16 or 17 months. Reporters had Floyd wounded in the massacre, yet robbing banks all over the nation at the same time. Within that time almost all of the men actually involved in the slaughter in Kansas City were either killed or captured. However, Floyd and Richetti remained at the top of the FBI's Most Wanted List for the crime despite the fact that they hadn't even been indicted.

On October 18, 1934, Floyd and his traveling companions bought a Tudor Ford and began a trip back to the Cookson Hills. When Floyd, driving, skidded into a telephone pole outside Wellsville, Ohio, both Richetti and Floyd thought it better to let the girls get the automobile repaired. They left their heavy weapons in the car and took refuge in a thicket along the roadway. There has always been some question if Floyd had a machine gun or not; none was ever found; but then, it would have been a great souvenir.

A man saw the two hiding in the brush and called police. When they arrived Richetti went for his gun and started shooting; he hit a posse member. Richetti was captured but Floyd got away. Richetti was taken to the Wellsville Police Station, where his identity was soon established. Richetti did not give up Floyd's name to the police; he may have been a killer and a drunk, but he wasn't an informant. Immediately a call went out to the FBI in Washington that Richetti had been captured. Hoover's logic was simple: "Wherever Richetti is, so is Floyd!" Hoover dispatched Melvin Purvis, one of his special agents from the Chicago office, by plane to Ohio with a contingent of armed agents. Purvis set up his command post in a hotel in the town of East Liverpool, Ohio. On Monday, October 22, Floyd was once again spotted on a small Ohio farm.

"Pretty Boy" Floyd was shot to death by a local posse and federal agents. He was 30 years old. Sixty years later, I discovered that J. Edgar Hoover had given Purvis orders not to bring Floyd back alive. The best conjecture is that Purvis had ordered one of his men to finish the wounded Floyd and the agent refused. Purvis then pulled his own .38 caliber revolver and shot Floyd twice in the chest; there were witnesses to this event.

Purvis's shots ended the criminal career of one of the nation's most notorious outlaws since Jesse James. Richetti was convicted for his part in Kansas City's Union Station Massacre and for two other murders in Columbia, Missouri. The conviction was obtained with the coerced testimony of only one witness, plus three FBI agents who perjured themselves. Richetti was executed in 1935. Richetti and Floyd would be cleared of any involvement in the Kansas City Massacre by the FBI, unofficially in 1939, officially in 1957. Richetti would also be cleared of both Columbia killings at the same time.

The end of Floyd's gang of partnerships signaled the true beginning of the FBI as a viable law-enforcement entity. Hoover, the organization's leader, became a virtual zealot when it came to ridding the country of its bank-robbing plague. Floyd was famous for occupying Hoover's list of Ten Most Wanted, but also included were big names such as Dillinger, Karpis, "Baby Face" Nelson, the Barkers, "Machine Gun" Kelly, and a host of other pesky bandits. Hoover's often-quoted statement was: "These people need to be exterminated and it needs to be done by us." Once his agents were officially armed, the orders went out from Hoover's office. He didn't care how the thieves and killers were taken off the street as long as it was done quickly. Years later, he would concentrate his efforts and those of his organization against the so-called "Red Menace" in the United States; however, his early days in office were devoted to tracking down and catching bank robbers.

Hoover's instructions were simple: his agents were told to keep running after the culprits until they were either dead or arrested. Many Americans are familiar with the massive shoot-outs between agents and outlaws that graced the headlines of our nation's newspapers during those earlier years. About that same time, the "Robin Hood" aura of many of these desperadoes found its way into the lexicon of American folklore.

Those early days of the newly formed federal agency brought out the best and the worst of Hoover's innovative approach to crime fighting. Most of his early agents had been involved in catching car thieves, so bank robbers were a different breed of criminal than they were accustomed to. For this reason, Hoover employed a number of ex-lawmen from across the nation to augment his own forces. Included among these were ex–Texas Rangers, county sheriffs, deputy marshals, and ex–police officers. Many of the men were holdovers from the days of the Old West, so they knew how to take care of bank robbers in the way Hoover intended—with no mercy.

Regardless of Hoover's arguably demented thinking, his agency made massive strides when it was employed in the hunt for bank robbers. During the rash of robberies and heists in the 1950s and 1960s, the FBI continued its fight with this criminal element—to varying degrees of success. The well-known phrase "The FBI always gets its man" was common even among the criminal circles of the nation. There was little doubt that if a thief robbed a federally insured bank, for example, he would not only have to contend with the local cops but would have the ruthless FBI on his tail even if he left the city or state where the crime was committed. The successes of the agency earned front-page headlines in the newspapers, while its failures were usually conveniently shuffled to the back pages or not printed at all. There was no reason to let the robbers see any weakness, of course, and public relations was definitely crucial for this.

The marked increase in bank robberies today has piqued the FBI's interest in such crimes once again, though scarcely to the level of the early Hoover days. The chief's orders of "Shoot first and investigate later" have been replaced by tamer policies, and this has helped develop the FBI into one of the most prestigious investigative agencies in the world. The six-shooter mentality has been thankfully replaced by scientific methods that Hoover probably never even dreamed of, much to the benefit of crime fighters everywhere.

During his lifetime, Hoover was certainly a force to be reckoned with. Not only did he elicit fear in the hearts of private citizens, politicians, and even presidents, but he also had bank robbers running for cover too. The early days of the FBI set the tone for decades to come, and J. Edgar Hoover was the driving force behind it all.

THE NEWTON BOYS

Shortly after the turn of the century, four brothers emerged from South Texas into the profitable business of robbing banks. Jim and Juanita Newton had no idea that their little boys—Willis, Jess, Doc, and Joe—would become four of the most enterprising bandits of their time. And, although the boys' active career only lasted about five years, they were a force to be reckoned with. In the brothers' minds it would at least be more lucrative than bowing down to the only cash crop in their part of the state, King Cotton. The Newton Boys certainly would not spend their lives picking cotton, of that much they were sure.

There was some question about the mental stability of Doc because of an animal bite in childhood. He had been attacked, some said, by a coyote, and bitten on the face and head. From that time on his behavior was unpredictable. Willis, on the other hand, was the brains of the gang and did most of the actual planning. Jess and Joe were the muscle and they did most of the grunt work. Specializing in opening square-shaped vaults, they were masters of using nitroglycerine. Over 60 banks fell to their talents during their short career—including one double robbery in 1921 in Hondon, Texas, that was not unlike the one attempted by the James Gang. The Newton Boys also hold the distinction of being the first American bank robbers hunted by aircraft.

But to understand the Newtons, one must look to the chronology that brought them into the spotlight in the first place. Willis had done time in prison for an early infraction and was released in 1914. His education in the fine art of bank robbery was at the hands of fellow inmates, not unlike hundreds of amateurs before him. His criminal hypothesis was simple to understand: "Take the money and don't hurt anyone!" For this reason the Newtons' vocation was free of homicides. This isn't to say that the men didn't use weapons, because of course they did. When Willis was released from prison a second time, in 1919, after another run-in with the law, he immediately used that knowledge to execute a robbery in Arma, Kansas.

The Newton Boys would case banks during the summer, and when the leaves began to fall, so did the banks. The early legwork provided the men with information about their intended targets throughout the autumn and winter months. Escape routes were noted, as were particular assets and liabilities of the banks themselves. Not unlike other early robbers, they discovered that cutting the phone wires in and out of the community was a good idea. Their choice of only going after banks with square vaults was not some random decision either. These safes were easier to "pop" than the round ones with interlocking round doors. And this "popping" would be necessary, of course, if they intended to take the bank during night-time hours. Should this be impractical, they would hold up the bank during business hours with their weapons drawn.

In July 1923, the gang moved their operations across the border to Canada. Here they managed to relieve several Toronto banks of their funds. After a short stay, they then relocated to the Chicago area and teamed up with a man named Fehy. In June 1924, they took an estimated $10 million off a train about 30 miles outside of Chicago. During another train robbery in the same general area, after scoring another $3 million, Doc was killed. After his death the three remaining brothers moved their base of operations back to Texas. There, over the next few years, the boys pulled off several burglaries and a couple of armed holdups. At this point in their career they had amassed several million dollars in stolen money, mostly from banks. The three men, however, were arrested during a botched holdup and all three went to prison. Given their age, the Newton Boys were officially out of the banking business—by the time they would have been set free, they would have been too old to continue.

The three Newtons were all released in the mid-1940s and took up another line of work as beekeepers. Jess Newton died of medical complications in the early 1950s, but Willis and Joe would continue a peaceful life until they died as old men—Willis in 1979 and Joe in 1989.

Before their deaths, these two men were interviewed on film together. Neither of them expressed any remorse for their lives of crime. They were bank robbers and were proud of what they had accomplished, whether it was lawful or not. They had been good at what they did and the fact that they hadn't killed anyone went a long way toward enhancing their public image.

The Newtons felt that the only reason they were successful bank robbers was their extensive planning. Willis made it very clear that had it not been for their technique they would have spent many more years in prison. In short, they got away with a lot more than they were ever convicted of. There is no question that the Newtons were consummate professionals in the business of robbing banks.

The bank robber of the 1920s and 1930s was learning that technology and newer methods were appearing that could help him accomplish greater feats of larceny than ever before. Naturally, this meant that banks, too, had a responsibility to resist the onslaught of predators with technology of their own. This seesaw battle is what we will examine now, as the bridge between the traditional and modern bank robber is formed nearly halfway through the century.

Chapter 3

The Banks Fight Back

"The surest way not to fail is to determine to succeed."
—General Phillip Sheridan

Literally thousands of quick, straightforward bank heists have remained unsolved throughout American history. In most cases, they were not particularly complicated or ingenious robberies, but all had one common denominator: there were simply no clues to go on. Either surveillance photographs were inconclusive, no fingerprints were left behind, or credible witnesses provided grossly inaccurate information based on their own perception of what happened. Add to these problems the fact that the stolen money never turned up, and one can understand how frustrating some robberies can be for investigators.

Nevertheless, 78 percent of all bank robberies are solved in a very short time. Only a small number of repeat bandits ever elude capture for an extended period. Most bank robbers commit just one crime before being caught and thus never learn how to do a robbery correctly or how to circumvent the multitude of security measures that banks take to protect themselves.

The lucky amateur thief who does escape from a robbery with stolen money can generally attribute his success to several factors, which in turn appear as challenges to the investigator handling the case. First, he does not have an established modus operandi since this is likely to be his first robbery; likewise, the investigator has a difficult time locating him because he can't base anything on where he has operated in the past. Furthermore, surveillance photographs, like most shown on television, cannot distinguish prominent features. The bandit may not have any characteristics that stand out particularly to the witnesses, such as hair color or vocal accent. Also, a robber may not have left any fingerprints at the scene, or, if he has, they are not on file. And last, the brigand has to consider how he spends his money, just as the investigator will be on the lookout for any odd purchases that may occur shortly after the robbery. Many times, both the thief and the investigator rely on one simple fact of life to either assure freedom or gain capture: pure, blind luck.

Thankfully for the police, the single biggest factor in the rapid capture of a criminal is the myriad stupid mistakes that amateurs tend to make during the course of an incident. These almost predictable blunders are what make the investigation of most bank robberies uncomplicated. Only witless providence keeps hundreds, if not thousands, of criminals—and bank robbers especially—out of prison. These robbers tend to fall through the cracks of justice, so to speak. Also, most bank robbers will only commit one robbery in their whole life; and even then, the take usually never amounts to more than a few thousand dollars.

It is, therefore, not prudent for an investigator to devote hundreds of hours chasing his tail while looking for that proverbial needle in a haystack. On many occasions, once all of the evidence is assembled, it doesn't take too long before the case ends up in the dead file. On the off-chance that something may turn up, the case will remain entombed deep in the filing cabinets of the police station and become merely another statistic for the yearly national crime report.

To prevent robberies from becoming lost in the rapid pace of new crime, banks decided long ago to use every available deterrent to ensure that robberies never happen in the first place. This chapter deals with some of the security measures that banks as well as law enforcement have taken to stop robberies altogether. Of course, the information here is not intended to assist bank robbers in their undertakings. Keep in mind that what you are about to read are naturally only a few of the many obstacles to a successful heist. Many others are not listed. What's more, bank robbers are very adaptable and creative; as such, they have managed to defeat every variety of deterrent listed here.

Although this chapter will deal with the physical obstacles that need to be conquered before there can be a successful bank heist, it does not include the emotional barrier a bandit must conquer to get up the nerve—which can be a very viable deterrent. Last of all we will examine the prison system and its effect on professional criminals.

IRON & STEEL

One of the first major impediments to robberies was the advent of iron safes and reinforced doors on bank vaults. This precaution began in the early nineteenth century, when most banks were small neighborhood buildings that took care of money for investors and depositors of their town. Security metal available at the time was forged iron or wrought iron. Safe locks were primitive affairs, not unlike the heavy door locks on the building itself. The iron of a safe was held together with bolts or rivets.

These early safes were hard to saw through because of the thickness of the iron. In those days there were no cutting torches; black powder explosives were the keys for crooks. With the advent of the armed holdup, in the middle to late century, there was no need to blast open a safe. But the robber intent on taking money at night or through stealth had a problem: explosives had drawbacks. Butch Cassidy and his gang almost blew a railroad baggage car to smithereens with a little too much dynamite. There are other examples of where too much explosive caused considerable damage to safes, vault, and bank buildings themselves. A case or two exists where even the robbers themselves disappeared in a cloud of dust and currency.

To avoid these dangers, or if noise was a problem, the box man was the solution. In early days, the rip-and-peel burglar accomplished his job with levers and hand tools. He was the guy who made the bankers almost go crazy. His attack began either on the door hinges or the back seams of the safe. After one bolt or rivet had been cut it was a matter of time until the rest could be removed. By means of cold chisels, and in later years hacksaws, the panel could be pried off with levers and crow bars. It was, of course, a time-consuming task and demanded considerable physical strength. By the mid-1800s the tumbler locking mechanism, or combination dial, was added as a deterrent. We've already seen where the "Little Joker" came in handy to get around this gadget. There were a few burglars, however, who could feel the tumblers in a combination lock and open the door to the safe. Basics of these combination locks were all about the same, regardless of manufacturer, although some were easier to open than others.

The first real safes were round objects with a locking door fitting into channels in the body of the safe itself. After burglars figured out how to open these, the manufacturers added sliding steel bars to the mechanism. Then burglars discovered that knocking out the mechanism would also take out the retaining bars. After removing that little blockade, it was easy work to get to the money.

Of course, in some cases a safe was so small that if the burglars couldn't open it on site, they merely threw a rope around it and dragged it off to work on at their leisure. In the 1800s, bankers bolted their safes to the floor to prevent that sort of theft. But bolts were just as easy to cut as rivets, and a lot of open safes were still found dragged away. That method of robbery may sound archaic, but even today ATMs are robbed in a similar manner. Bankers next went in a different direction; they had safes built that were so heavy they couldn't be dragged off. This, of course, brought the burglars full circle. They were back to opening the safe in the bank building itself.

When confronted with this problem, burglars had to get more creative. Toward the end of the Civil War, a Swedish scientist named Alfred Nobel had perfected an explosive utilizing a substance known as nitroglycerine. This compound is made up of nitric and sulphuric acids, and of glycerol, which appears as an oily colorless liquid. After years of experimentation, he received a patent in 1867 for a product he called "dynamite." We have already seen the awesome power of dynamite that Butch Cassidy discovered in his mail car disaster, but even that pales in comparison to the power of nitroglyercine.

For well over 100 years, burglars have been using nitroglycerine to open safes and vaults. However, bank robbers couldn't simply buy nitroglycerine off the shelf of their local hardware store—they would have to make it themselves. To complete this procedure, one must boil dynamite and wait for the glycerol and acids to float to the top, where it can be carefully removed and placed into a safe container. The danger comes when it is handled or transported: the slightest bump, friction, or electrical spark can set it off. It would almost go without saying that several would-be burglars never got the chance to use this product on a safe or vault. In most of these cases of juvenile chemistry, there wasn't even enough of the men left to bury after the experiment went awry.

The technique, however, could and does work in the hands of an expert. Over-zealous amateur robbers sometimes use a little too much and the results are awesome. Not only does it open the safe, but it also opens parts of the building and, in a few cases, parts of the neighborhood. As a result, at the turn of the century banks began upgrading their security with steel vaults.

Steel could be mixed with alloys to make the product harder to cut through. Then the fireproof vault came into existence: two sheets of steel with a center section of concrete. Although the advent of the diamond drill bit cut down some of the time going through the first sheet of steel, the robbers then had to chisel through the concrete and again go through a second sheet of steel. It was time-consuming and messy. Bankers now felt secure. In reality, however, at the turn of the century there was no safe which a determined robber couldn't get into. As years passed, the steel industry developed cold-rolled steel alloy. This stuff, bankers believed, was really going to be a deterrent. But though it took longer for the burglars, they got into it just the same.

The biggest boon to the burglar was the oxygen/acetylene cutting torch. It was highly effective in cutting through even the hardest steel, regardless of thickness. It was portable and quiet. For many years this was how entry was accomplished, and even in some cases today thieves still use it to gain access to the loot.

Then the construction business came up with the mother of all tools for the bank robber: the core drill. This monster came in several sizes, but needed water as a coolant. The core drill was attached to a heavy-duty motor and, depending on the size of bit used, was big enough to cut through steel and concrete. What's more, several holes could be drilled and a man could enter the vault. The only real drawback to this device was the massive amount of water needed to cool the drill. If a thief had access to this tool, as well as a good water supply, it was a fairly quick job. Core drill jobs have almost always been the work of the professional thief.

The bankers, not to be outdone, again changed the rules. Builders began constructing very thick-walled safes to defeat the cutting torches and the core drills. Once more, however, the construction industry had just the tool to get through these massive concentrations of steel: the burning bar. This is one of those contraptions that necessitate the hands of a professional. The idea of the burning bar is very simple, but it can also be very dangerous. Several cutting rods are placed inside a tube of steel and then electrically ignited. It's the same principle as an electric cutting torch that uses cutting rods, only a lot bigger. The rods burn at an intense temperature and are fed into the area which needs cutting. The operator must be clothed in a fireproof (asbestos) suit and gloves. This method can be time-consuming but in some cases it's the only way to get through one of these heavy-duty vaults. Fire and toxic gases emitted during the cutting process can be a problem. When authorities walk into a freshly robbed bank and discover that a burning bar or a core drill has been used, you can bet that most of the money is gone too. Bankers and lawmen know that someone who is willing to go through all this trouble can't be stopped by conventional methods.

The only way to stop burglars and robbers of this caliber is to catch them in the act. However, people this dedicated to robbery are not the kind you are likely to catch pulling the job, unless by luck. This is where planning pays off for the robber. Every detail of the job has been researched long before any tool is ever laid to steel. These guys are the true professionals in the business and, in most cases, the rewards they reap from vaults are well worth the trouble. As we will see in an upcoming chapter, several of our bank robbers fall into this expert class. They made few mistakes and they got away with a considerable amount of money.

REINFORCED CONCRETE

From the characteristics of safes and vaults let's turn to the characteristics of the buildings in which they are housed. In the beginning of the bank-robbing "business," most banks were simple wooden structures: getting into the building was a job for standard woodworking hand tools. Concrete only came into its own as a building material in the late nineteenth century. Slab concrete walls were a marked improvement over wood but not much of a deterrent for the bank robber. The big change came when some bright engineer added steel rods to the wet concrete (rebar). When there was a crosshatch of steel rods in the walls, floor, and ceiling of a building, it made knocking a hole in the structure a bit more complicated.

All that this engineering advancement accomplished was to slow down the forward progress of the thief. He would need to remove up to a foot of concrete, then cut through several closely spaced steel bars, then remove another foot of concrete. The burglar discovered that explosives were the best way to take care of a problem like this; that is, if noise was not a problem. A dynamite charge placed on the bank's ceiling would do the job. By placing a stack of sand bags over the charge the blast was concentrated downward. Then all the robber needed to worry about was cutting through the bars. Hacksaws or cutting torches were good for this.

Another method, without appreciable noise, was using drills, chisels, and hammers. This was a time-consuming venture but got the job done. Approximately 80 percent of all bank buildings built before 1975 were made with reinforced concrete. These banks are still considered hard to get into, but not impossible.

Advances in this tried-and-true method of construction have thrown robbers yet another curve. Today the use of reinforcing steel bars in the construction of concrete bank buildings has been replaced. Case-hardened steel mesh is now placed into the wet concrete, sometimes in several layers, to discourage burglars. A single blast will not blow a hole clear through this stuff, as it did in the old days. And instead of having to cut a crosshatch of steel rods, the robber has one or more very difficult steel screens to cut. To make matters worse, some construction utilizes both products in the building. Not only could there be steel mesh but also rebar. This makes the invasion of the bank building a time-consuming project—and time is something the burglar really doesn't have a lot of. The bankers may be winning on this count.

ALARMS

Alarms have been around for almost as many years as bank robbers. Bankers discovered that if they could get the word out to people on the street there might be a chance of catching the scoundrel. In the early days it could have been nothing more than a big cowbell attached to a rope. When the robbery was taking place or, more prudently, shortly after, the banker could tug the rope and alert the town. The introduction of electricity simplified this alarm business and again gave banks another barrier to robberies. By the early twentieth century almost every bank had one of those big iron bells on the side of the building. The bell would occasionally go off accidentally, much to the displeasure of local townsfolk. In the early days false alarms were a common but accepted inconvenience to the serenity of the community. The bell ultimately more than paid for its nuisance. During the time between the turn of the century and the late 1930s, armed citizens foiled more than a few bank robberies thanks to the bell. When people heard it go off and saw unfamiliar cars in front of their bank, they knew what was going on.

All of our early robbers, at one time or another, encountered armed citizens or lawmen shooting at them as they fled. In some cases small towns did not have organized law-enforcement personnel who could respond to criminal behavior. Even in many urban areas vigilance committees assisted the local sheriff. Either way when the bell went off during banking hours, people paid attention; because of this, Bonnie and Clyde, Herman Lamm, and others all ran into gunfire as they were engaged in robbing a town's bank.

That was the effect of the bell on armed holdups, but there was also another kind of robber to consider. If the only alarm was a panic button, then it would only work during business hours. Something had to let people know that someone was breaking into the bank during off-hours. Several early engineers figured it out. If an electrical circuit was interrupted or broken, it could activate an alarm. Bank robbers soon also realized, very quickly, that it didn't take much time and trouble to disable this big bell. In the early days all that needed to be done was nothing more than cutting the wires to the alarm. Bankers then, reasonably, began hiding the wires. Of course, the robbers found them eventually.

It wasn't long before banks had alarms on doors, windows, and vaults. Needless to say, this also multiplied the chance of false alarms. Clever crooks discovered that these frequent false alarms could work to their advantage. People who lived around the bank got so used to hearing them they didn't bother to call police. There was even one case where the robbers set off the alarm every night at the same time. Every night for a week the cops showed up to see what was wrong, and discovered it was a false alarm each time. The night of the robbery, an accomplice caused a diversion in another part of town. The entire police force (two cops) responded, and the bank alarm sounded at the same time. Everybody assumed it was just another false alarm and went on about their business. It only took the robbers about a half hour to pull off the caper; they got away with $72,000 and the robbery wasn't detected until the next morning. When it was discovered, it was found that the burglars had simply kicked in the door to the bank.

To this day, burglars still use these alarms to test whether they have actually foiled the townspeople. Once the wires are located, a test is run to see if the bell would go off before proceeding with a robbery. This is also a good way to examine the response time of local constabulary in the event that the bell does ring. In our previous example the response time of the two-man police force got longer and longer as each night passed. The robbers had figured human nature very well and, for this reason, the robbery was a success. The cops' failure to stake out the bank building for a few nights and see what was causing the alarm to go off was also a mistake.

Alarms then fell into two distinct categories: internal (or silent) and external. The external system sounds either within the building itself or, more often, just outside the bank. Other than the big iron bell there are also sirens, buzzers, and horns. A lot of these devices are triggered with a button, or foot-peddle, located under the counter by the teller's cage or by a bank officer's desk. This kind of alarm can work in the event of an armed robbery if the robber doesn't see the person trip the trigger. One of the first orders of business in an armed bank robbery is to get all employees away from the counters, ergo the buttons. Bank employees have been killed while attempting to set off some sort of alarm.

For several years bankers used to put alarm buttons in the ladies restroom of the bank building. Why? Some people who rob banks aren't all that sharp, and several have locked women employees in the ladies room to get rid of them during the robbery. The surprise comes when the robber is confronted by a squadron of cops at the front door and no one in the lobby pushed an alarm. Silent systems, on the other hand, also have advantages. No buzzers, whistles, or bells go off around the bank when the button is pushed. The alarm registers instead at the police station or some other monitoring depot. It's a lot safer for bank employees and aids law-enforcement people in apprehending culprits in the act. Alarms have foiled literally thousands of bank robberies before they ever got going. Alert bank personnel familiar with a holdup suspect's profile have triggered alarms even before robbers have their guns out.

There is another group of systems used: the passive apparatus, or sensor. This alarm is triggered by the robber and can either be silent or audible. Sensors on windows and doors have been around for a long time, as have unseen triggering mechanisms on vaults and safes. But sensors can also be built into walls, ceilings, and even floors of the building to protect the bank from the burglar kind of robber. Bankers, not content with physical pressure-sensitive devices, have also installed photo-electric devices that sense any movement in a room. Then there are infrared beam sensors, which can only be seen by using special glasses. And if this doesn't seem like enough, the latest device sounds an alarm if the temperature changes in the room. Just the body heat of a human being is enough to set it off.

In the old days, electrical equipment was run on direct power. Logically, knock out the power source to the gizmo and the gizmo won't go off. Today almost every system has a battery backup to take over if power is cut off, or to sound the alarm if power is even briefly interrupted. So, can these sophisticated alarm systems foil any bank robber intent on gaining entrance to a bank? Absolutely not. With the right kind of know-how, and about $25 worth of electrical mechanisms, these systems can be defeated.

Since the advent of the alarm system there have been those specialists whose only task during the robbery is to get past the alarms. These specialists know what to cut, cross, freeze, or foul up to take the system out of commission. There have also been bank robbers who only employ accomplices who know how to install alarm systems in the bank in the first place. If for one second the banker thinks that the robbers aren't keeping up-to-date, he had better think again. Time has demonstrated that the only thing alarms achieve is to slow the robbers down temporarily—either in getting into the bank in the first place or getting away from it after the robbery. As of this writing there is not one alarm system which has not been defeated at one time or another by a skilled bank robber/burglar.

SURVEILLANCE CAMERAS

Along with alarms, another kind of security device has been in place in most banks since the late 1950s: movie or television surveillance cameras. The problem with television in the early days was that it was only live; there was no way to retain the image transmitted and have it for viewing later. Early kinescopes were a crude form of videotaping, but they weren't very effective in maintaining a clear image for an extended period of time. Surveillance cameras began to be utilized in many industries for the protection of property and personnel in the 1950s. The key factor in this kind of setup was that there needed to be someone there to physically monitor the picture. All he or she could do was watch what was going on; there was no way to keep the picture and play it back later—not a very efficient use of money or manpower. For a while a number of banks used guards to watch TV monitors in a back room as part of their security procedure.

The first known application of a surveillance camera, in this case a 16mm movie camera, was employed in the spring of 1957. The St. Clair Savings & Loan Co., of Cleveland, Ohio, installed this camera to circumvent armed robberies. It paid off during a 1957 event when the pictures aided in the capture of the three bandits within 36 hours of the robbery. It became obvious to bankers and lawmen alike that this new tool could deter bank robberies. Merely the fact that there could be cameras mounted in prominent locations, around tellers cages, vaults, lobbies, and the like, would add to overall security of the establishment. It also became clear to robbers that cameras were going to be a problem.

Just like small children with new toys, bankers went nuts with surveillance cameras. At one time it wasn't uncommon to go into a bank lobby and see a dozen cameras stuck to walls. Today you are more likely to see one or two in the corners and maybe one or two over the tellers' cages. All these cameras are now hooked up to video-

tape machines that record everything the camera sees. Some of the
cameras are in fixed positions while others are in constant motion. A
few banks have security cameras located within their vault. Most burglars know this and disable these cameras as one of their first orders
of business. This aspect of the robbery is handled by the same guy who
takes care of the alarm systems. Very few burglars have ever been
caught on tape.

To the armed robber, the camera is like having an eyewitness to
the robbery. It would be in his best interest to either take out the camera or disguise himself so that he can't be recognized. But the cameras,
too, have become disguised. Sure, the robber saw the camera over the
tellers cage, but did he see the "pinhole" camera in the clock behind
the counter? Did he notice the sprinkler head on the ceiling? That odd-
shaped brick by the door? All the images recorded will be used as evidence if the rogue is captured. Many armed holdup men have no
qualms about taking a shot or two at a surveillance camera. Some robbers carry little cans of spray paint to coat the camera's lens. It's also
not uncommon for a robber to take a broom handle, or a gun stock,
and push the camera into an ineffective position. Although cameras
out in the open are working, they are also expendable. Other cameras,
the ones the robber can't see, are taking the pictures which will be
used at his trial.

To make matters worse for robbers, the pictures themselves are
better than in the old days. Not only are they in color but they can be
computer enhanced for clarity. Individual aspects of the image can be
isolated from the overall photo and enlarged to pick out finer details
of the suspects. A fancy watch, a tattoo, an uncommon facial feature,
a ring, or in one case the license number of the getaway car. Next time
you go to your neighborhood ATM, notice that little black dot on the
front of the machine—it is a camera. Little black dots are now in a lot
of bank locations.

The video camera has been a pain to robbers. Not only can these
systems be used to convict, which is very common, but also to educate.
Bank employees can be shown just what they did wrong during a robbery, and maybe down the road save an employee's life in another robbery. It's a Monday-morning-quarterback scenario. If you can identify
problems in the bank, then you can take steps to correct them before
the next crime is committed.

MARKED MONEY

The use of die packets and marked money came into its own in the late 1970s as a deterrent to armed, and unarmed, robberies. This device is concealed within a packet of bills and placed in the teller's drawer. During a holdup few robbers notice what the money looks like because they're naturally too busy thinking about every other security concern.

The pressure-sensitive triggering mechanism is concealed within the money and the teller activates this when handing over the cash. The delay can range from a few minutes to up to an hour and is pre-set. All the bank teller needs to do is to give it a little squeeze while complying with the robber's wishes. After the bandit gets out of the bank and down the road this device goes off in the bag or wherever the robber has chosen to stash the cash. The contraption is not intended to injure the robber, but it can have comical aspects. The packet of bills conceals a pouch of very visible dye, usually violet in color, that covers the money and, most likely, the robber. What the thief has is a whole bag full of worthless money, and very possibly a violet hue that can be hard to explain. If, for some reason, a thief is smart enough to go after the big money in the vault, he can still get a packet to take with him. Bankers have seen to it that one of these little surprises is lying on the shelf with the rest of the currency—but activated only if the robber requests assistance from a bank employee.

The story of an actual bank robbery in Kansas City, Missouri, will illustrate how effective these devices can be. When I use the term amateur bank robber, I generally mean it. This particular man's getaway vehicle was a city bus. The bandit got the money from the tellers and headed for the door. The timing was perfect: his getaway bus was standing at the curb. He no sooner got on the mass-transit conveyance than the packet went off. If the ski mask in August hadn't given the other passengers something to think about, all that purple dye sure did—the stuff was billowing out of his baggy pants where he had chosen to hide the money. While the bandit was trying to figure out what was going on in his trousers all the passengers and the driver got off the bus. The robber, too, got off the bus and made a run for it. A light purple contrail followed the gentleman down the street. He ran about three blocks and entered a grocery store.

There, the man attempted to blend in with customers but there were a lot of descriptions to draw from. He was about so tall, and about so heavy, wearing a ski mask, brown pants with $20 bills around the waistband, a white shirt, and he had a very pronounced violet cast about him. Oddly enough he was the only person in the frozen food isle who answered that description and was therefore in cuffs 20 minutes after his robbery. I got there about the time they were placing him in the paddy wagon. To say the least, he looked a little beat. This is just the kind of robber the dyed money packet was designed for and it did its job that day.

And then there is marked money. Bundles of bait money—$20s, $50s, and $100s in many cases—have had their serial numbers recorded. These packets of bills are left in the vault to be included in the event the robber goes for the big bucks. Shortly after a robbery these serial numbers are given to local merchants in the hopes that whoever is passing the money can be identified. It's a long shot, but with the rash of snatch and grab robberies it pays off from time to time. In the event of a major holdup, be it armed or otherwise, the hundred-dollar bills and sometimes the fifties have aided in the capture of the bandits.

Needless to say, a lot of robbers have no idea how to lay off their take to a fence or launder the money through a middle man. Far too many amateurs figure they can spend their take the next day and everything will be okay. As in days of old, these guys are arrested shortly after their big robbery. Either the marked money is spotted or someone notices that what's-his-name, the guy who's been broke for months, suddenly has paid off all his bills. In some cases the robber's friends turn him in to the authorities. The real professionals liquidate their hot loot through a fence, not on the street. Fences are important to the skilled bank robber intent on getting the most money with the fewest problems, so they deserve a short definition here.

Fences fall into four general categories: the local, the specialist, the outlet, and the ethnic. A local fence operates at the bottom of the distribution chain and is set within a geographical area. This fence would handle goods from neighborhood thieves who are generally located within the same part of town. This fence will also occasionally assist organized crime by moving their hot goods; however, he will never deal with large amounts of cash taken in bank robberies.

The specialist deals in high-quality goods and has a generally select group of customers. Anonymity and service are the hallmarks of his trade. The specialist will move artifacts, gold, diamonds, and cash. This is the individual with whom most professional bank robbers do business, specifically bank robbers who deal in popping safety deposit boxes while robbing the vault. They need to have a place to dispose of the assortment of loot, and this fence is perfect for just that task. A few of these fences operate internationally, so they are very difficult to investigate. Their small, select group of clientele are what adds to the overall security of the transaction. A modest theorem applies to this man's operation: The fewer the number of people who know about the services, the fewer the people who can rat him out.

The outlet fence is a mass-distribution center for large quantities of stolen goods. Many outlet fences are legitimate businesses controlled by organized crime. These people will deal, for the most part, with major break-ins and hijackings. They occasionally deal on an international basis and are difficult to convict due to the multi-layered structure of the enterprise.

Ethnic fences are exactly what the term implies. This individual deals with a small circle of friends and relatives. Illegal weapons are big business in this loosely structured enterprise. Supplying guns to criminals is, for the most part, always handled by an ethnic fence. As opposed to the old days of bank robbery, when the ethnic fence had a very limited role, he is now used by many big-scale professionals as a money launderer. The funds from the robbery are secreted in drug transactions and the money disappears into that vast amount of cash.

What one needs to keep in mind is that there is no such thing as an honest fence. None of the aforementioned fences will take a fall for a major bank robbery, but they could cop to a stolen-goods charge in exchange for the names of the robbers. The professional bank robber will invariably use a fence to exchange his take for safer money, even if he must absorb a discount on his total haul.

For all these reasons, shortly after the robbery or burglary of a bank the first people investigated by police are the known fences in the community. For the robbery to be successful the money needs to be moved out of the area, and this is a job for the fence. Of course the amount of safe money the thief receives back from the fence for his stolen goods is important. A robber can consider himself very lucky if he gets 30 cents on the dollar; most fences operate on 25 cents. By this logic, the theft of old money is a plus. This money cannot be traced and does not need to be fenced. As we will see later, several robberies entailed the theft of used money. Very little has ever been recovered.

One of the differences today, as opposed to the old days of bank robbery, is that today's bandits can lay off their money without using an established fence. Plenty of drug dealers have ways to launder money for a price. Organized crime, still at the helm of the drug business in America, can move huge amounts of cash without discovery. It doesn't matter whether the money happens to be from a bank robbery or from a huge drug deal; the money disappears either way and the robber is on his way with clean funds. The stolen money in question may never surface again. It may, in fact, be in large boxes in a Swiss bank account clear across the world, safely tucked away from any meddling authorities. In such cases, that money is as good as lost.

LAND COMMUNICATIONS

When Alexander Graham Bell invented the telephone in 1877, things got considerably worse for the bank robber. The telephone became instrumental in catching bank robbers on a regular basis in the early twentieth century. It was cutting down the time frame of a robbery and the thieves knew it was something else they had to be aware of when planning a heist. Although the telephone system was not nationwide for a number of years, some communities on the American east coast had service by the late nineteenth century. Up until then the telegraph was the only instant method of getting information from one point to another. Robbers isolated the little town bank they had just robbed with a simple operation; they cut the wires.

Even with the installation of telephone service this procedure was still the best method of slowing down the law. If bandits were not smart enough to think about this, or didn't have time, the cops were but a phone call away. Not only could the banker telephone the police, but police could then call ahead to other law-enforcement agencies. In effect, cops could cut-'em-off-at-the-pass, or at least the next town down the road.

Have you ever wondered why, when you are watching some B-class gangster movie, the bandits cut across country? Wires ran more or less in a straight line from town to town. Robbers figured that if the cops were hot on their trail all they had to do was cut over to the next road that was not in a line from the bank they had just robbed. In the early days, calls had to go through an operator before any connections could be made. The bandits, cutting across country, could buy valuable time while the citizens were trying to locate them; granted, sometimes it worked and sometimes it didn't. It was nevertheless one of the options the bank robber had in those days, and was something to configure into the plan.

Wireless two-way communication, developed in the late 1920s and early 1930s, was to be the next obstacle for bank robbers. With this new technology, cops traveling in cars in the area nearby a robbery could then be dispatched to the scene of the crime. The first radio-controlled police units in the nation were used in New York City in February 1932. Robbers, not to be outdone, got police radios of their own to keep track of the cops. The solution to this dilemma, for the police, was to use multi-band radio transmitters, but even that failed to stop the robbers because they soon learned that scanners would help with that problem. Today every cop on the beat has a two-way, multi-band radio hanging from his belt. Even the neighborhood Meter Maid can call in a holdup in a matter of seconds. All this serves to cut down the time for bandits to rob, and ultimately makes their job just a little bit harder—which is often the best solution law enforcement can hope for.

And as if the bad guys haven't had problems enough getting around alarms, cameras, and radios, in recent years a new device has proliferated over which they have no control at all. The cellular phone—portable, self-powered, and very wireless—has taken the world by storm. How does this affect the bandit? If Average Joe Citizen standing on the corner sees something suspicious at the bank, he can grab his cellular phone and place a free emergency call to the police. If news of a robbery and a description of the getaway car are broadcast on a local radio station, there could be thousands of extra eyes looking for the bandits. Every person with a phone in a purse or a Porsche could be helpful in locating the brigands. This has already happened, dozens of times, all over America. Instead of locals taking up arms against bank robbers, as in the old days, all they need to take up is a cell phone. The results are about the same and there are fewer casualties among the populace.

Within the bank itself the cellular phone is also a nightmare for the robber/burglar. When you add a wireless telephone to a battery powered intrusion alarm system, the robber has a problem. A prerecorded message from the bank to the police can be transmitted even if external power sources are knocked out. A system of this kind is almost impossible for the robbers to detect and is like an invisible bank employee, a phone in hand, watching your every move.

Cellular phones are tied to another boom in technology, the Internet, in terms of its instant communication around the world. The thief must now deal with response and information systems completely beyond his control. In 1996, a bank robber was captured after his picture was included in a list of the FBI's ten most wanted men that appeared on the Internet. The robber had moved to South America, supposedly off the "radar" of authorities, but he made several acquaintances within the American populace of his little community. One saw his picture on a home computer, and shortly thereafter he was turned in and arrested. Ironically, this same bank robber had hooked up the computer system for the person who turned him in. The Internet has been instrumental in the capture of several criminals. Almost no corner of the world is a safe haven for social renegades.

There are now, too, any number of television programs dedicated to the arrest of wanted fugitives. Programs such as "America's Most Wanted" are racking up captures, with assistance from the law-enforcement community, on a monthly basis. Not only are bank robbers included in this kind of programming but so are killers, rapists, child molesters, drug dealers, and your everyday common criminal. This attests to the resolve of the community, now worldwide, to rid itself of lawbreakers. Surely, trash like Bonnie and Clyde would not have lasted as long had the entire American community been aware of their actual crimes.

WEAPONS & TOOLS OF THE TRADE

One of the most troubling factors in today's resurgence of bank robberies is the types of weapon carried by bandits. A century or less ago, it was the pistol, the shotgun, and the occasional Winchester for lawmen to contend with. Today things have changed—to the detriment of the police. With the advent of high-tech weapons, law enforcers have girded themselves in bulletproof body armor. This kind of stuff has been around since the 1920s, but today's version is more efficient. And just when the cops figured that they had the protection they needed, someone invented a bullet to go through it.

Today's high-caliber handguns, loaded with "Black Talon" armor-piercing bullets, have given new meaning to deadly force. Today's well-heeled shooters have updated the old weapons, with the assistance of forward-thinking manufacturers, to become a superior armed force. Military weapons capable of firing automatically with or without some slight modifications are now in the hands of robbers. Back in the twenties, thirties, and forties, the Thompson submachine gun was the weapon of choice. Today the 12-gauge "Streetsweeper" shotgun is more apt to be incorporated into bandits' arsenal. This weapon, with a multi-shot magazine, is a rapid-fire semi-automatic shotgun capable of awesome firepower. Fully automatic M-16s, AK-47s, UZI's, and countless other military issue weapons are now being used by even the most naive amateur in the field. Without a doubt, most police forces are outgunned and often face nearly paralyzing situations because of it. A graphic example of this occurred on the morning of February 28, 1997.

When Emil D. Matasareanu and his partner, Larry E. Phillips Jr., donned their bulletproof vests that February morning, little did they know it was to be their last day on earth. They were also unaware they would be involved in the most massive gun battle ever associated with a bank robbery in American history. Back in 1993 these two men had been arrested on weapons charges in California and sentenced to prison. Thanks to a plea bargain, they served only four months behind bars. The two men were, likewise, the prime suspects in two previous bank robberies which had netted the bandits about $1.5 million. Eyewitnesses to these holdups described the men as "desperate and scary." Several others simply described the ordeal as "the most frightening experience of my life."

At 9:30 A.M., Matasareanu and Phillips entered Bank America's North Hollywood branch, ready for business. It has been established that the men had been assembling an arsenal of weapons during the years after their release from prison. When they were arrested the first time, they were carrying over twenty guns of assorted mechanical attributes and calibers, some of which were fully automatic machine guns. Yet there they were, again, in their flack jackets at the front door to the bank, armed to the teeth. Both men carried modified AK-47s, one with a 100-round drum magazine and the other with several 30-round banana clips taped together. One of them yelled, "All you . . . hit the floor!" By sheer luck, or reflex, one of the tellers hit the panic button when she saw the masked men enter the bank. Unbeknownst to the robbers, the police were on the way.

Everything soon went crazy in the bank and one of the masked men signaled the other to abort the mission. About the time the robbers got back to the door they were confronted by a handful of Los Angeles' finest. Willie Williams, the chief of police, was quoted as saying: "They emptied a 100 round drum before they ever left the door of the building." To the people in the bank, the din was terrifying. To the police, who were instantly engulfed in a gunfight, it was a little more intense than they were used to. Cops and citizens alike were ducking for cover behind anything solid. The robbers shot their way through the lawmen with their fully automatic weapons, impervious to police gunfire. The two bandits were hit dozens of times but their full body armor stopped everything the cops threw at them.

Phillips took cover behind the getaway car, a white sedan, as his partner crept it across the parking lot. The police fire was so intense that this effort never really got going, however. Accidentally Phillips also fired through the windshield of his own car, just missing his cohort. As he walked onto a residential street he fired at the lawmen. Out-gunned, the police dispatched a couple of men to a local gun store. The SWAT Team now arrived and they, too, were forced to take cover.

By now television crews were in the air above the bank. Suddenly this attempted robbery and gun battle was live on television. Phillips crouched between a large truck and a fence as the police closed in. When he stood, the police opened fire; the bandit went down with a leg wound. A second shot hit him in the head. At least this was what was originally reported. There is evidence, now, that this gunman may have stood up in order to kill himself.

The officers returned to the fight when more effective weapons were brought to them from the civilian gun store. The getaway car was then fired on by police and its tires were shot out. Matasareanu attempted to steal a truck, but it wouldn't start. He returned to his own car and unloaded weapons from the trunk, all the while firing at police. Suddenly a patrol car, with machine guns blazing from the windows, pinned the gunman down. SWAT officers took up firing positions behind the car's wheels. The shots coming from the outlaws were steel jacketed, which is a kind of bullet that can penetrate police body armor. So far the gun battle had encompassed a five-block area and had left more than a dozen people wounded, including police officers.

Finally, a helmeted officer shot Matasareanu, who died on the street in handcuffs. Police officers began looking for other robbers because it was believed that four men attempted to rob the bank.

The casualty list had grown by then. Just two outlaws—Matasareanu and Phillips—were responsible for wounding 16 officers and citizens, wrecking several cars, and contributing to two heart attacks. The most miraculous aspect of this encounter was that no civilians were killed.

The search for other robbers continued into the afternoon with no success. The gunfight had taken over 20 minutes, thousands of rounds had been fired, and two bank robbers were dead. Days after the incident, an FBI agent called these two men "the shoot-'em-up bandits." It hadn't taken that long for the public to understand exactly what that gruesome phrase meant; even as it was happening, the gunfight was being rebroadcast in slow motion on televisions around the world. It would be replayed time and again on nightly news broadcasts throughout the nation.

A reporter interviewed a friend of one of the dead bandits who said one of the men had been despondent over an impending divorce. No reason was given for the actions of the other dead desperado. The police returned their borrowed guns to the B&B Gun Shop, thankful to be alive. There had never been a shoot-out between cops and robbers like this one, not even in the Roaring '20s or the heyday of gangsterism in the '30s—and never one that had been photographed and videotaped in the history of the United States.

Prior to this horrifying disaster, Emil Matasareanu and Larry Phillips, Jr. had been successful in only two other heists. But what sets these men apart is that they were willing, and equipped, to go toe-to-

toe with lawmen. They were not worried about an armed assault by police officers; they were more than ready. They had the firepower to suppress any response imaginable by the police, they had the guts to take a bank head-on and they were cool under fire. But the most important element of this confrontation was simple: the cops were under-gunned. No doubt Emil and Larry have become legends in their own time, in some circles. Police, nationwide, already anticipate that this variety of encounter will happen again. Some of the lawmen whom I interviewed seemed surprised that this type of thing had not happened before 1997—given all of the new gun technology appearing every day.

Technology, however, is not limited to guns when it comes to robbing banks. Many criminals never even require an advanced weapon, because their burglary tools are of such sophisticated, state-of-the-art quality. For the professional bank robber to accomplish his task, he needs a wide assortment of highly specialized tools. The average amateur may not even hear of some of these, but the semi-professional bank robber must be familiar with them all, either individually or in combination. These instruments would never all be used on one job—but only because there are just too many to choose from. One must also keep in mind that simple possession of some of these objects is illegal, and they are all well-known to law-enforcement.

The tools of the trade can include: lock picks, Microflame torches, a V.O.M. meter, saws, flashlights, oxygen regulators, explosives, electric drills, jigsaws, sledgehammers, cans of polyurethane and freon in aerosol form (to freeze alarms), masonry bits, a droplight, and wrenches. The list continues with half-volt to seven- and nine-volt batteries, walkie-talkies with altered frequencies, burlap bags to contain an explosion, fans, infrared lenses to see security light beams, crowbars, sheet metal cutters, nitroglycerine, diamond cutting blades, a burning bar, and a core drill. These last two items are very large and heavy, so their use is restricted to areas where they can be operated. If the burglar has a burning bar, he will also need an asbestos fire suit, and if he has a core drill he will need a rubber hose, electric pump and access to a water supply nearby. Naturally, the above are not the kind of equipment that an amateur would know how to use; when authorities find evidence of their use they know what type of criminal they are dealing with right away.

To combat such new weapons as the ones used in the North Hollywood incident and the list above, today's police departments have discovered that they need armored cars in some situations. Armored personnel carriers (APC's) are available should the need arise to protect cops from the firepower of crooks. And there are more than a few major police departments that own tanks. Weapon upgrading has taken place in this nation's law enforcement communities, but more needs to be done. SWAT teams across the country have been armed for years with the latest state-of-the-art weaponry. Laser beam-sighted, long-range rifles are now standard, as is full night-vision equipment. Micro-machine guns are issued to these teams, as are more powerful handguns. Today's rapid-response units (SWAT) are armed more like a military element than a street police squad, simply because that is what is required to fight the new breed of criminal.

Today the chances of civilians being killed or injured is five times greater than it was years ago. The police need to suppress outlaw firepower quickly and with a minimum loss of life; without upgrading their weapons they will continue to be at the mercy of America's gun-toting bandits. This situation is being addressed by the nation's police at a record pace, but until the outlaws realize that their force can be matched by lawmen, there will continue to be dangerous gun fights between the cops and the robbers. The losers will be the American public and police officers killed in the line of duty. If anyone thinks that the Old West or the 1920s and 1930s were bloody, they need only read the newspapers or watch television to see that today is as dangerous a time to live in as any other period in history.

ON LAND, ON SEA, & IN THE AIR

The speed of the getaway has always been crucial to the bank robber's success, but several hindrances have appeared in recent years to make that aspect more difficult. Rapid land communications are only part of the bandit's predicaments. Gone are the days when a bandit could literally outrun the cops. To elude the law, early bank robbers depended on the occasional race horse, as in Jesse James's day, and hot rod cars in later years. If Henry "Bearcat" Starr received his nickname because of a Stutz Bearcat, he made a good choice. The 1912 Bearcat had a four-cylinder engine rated at 60 horsepower. It was one of the all-time classic speedsters. In its day it could outrun most cars on the road. By 1925 the Stutz could reach speeds of over 75 miles per hour. In the 1930s many bank robbers had favorite automobiles. Bonnie and Clyde sent a letter to Henry Ford praising the qualities of his powerful V-8 models. "Handsome Johnny" Dillinger was partial to the Hudson Terraplane and often extolled the virtues of this automobile. It was a car capable of speeds well over one hundred miles an hour. Even in the early days, cops knew that their vehicles would need to be at least as powerful as what crooks were driving.

Today's law-enforcement personnel have top-of-the-line pursuit vehicles. Earlier, these automobiles were tuned by the shade tree mechanic on the police force. He added the carburetors, solid lifters, bored-out engines, and racing suspension needed for chasing the bad guys. Today, more often than not, the cars are built into police interceptor vehicles by the factory.

For over thirty years the Ford Motor Company has provided special engine packages to police departments throughout the country. The Chrysler Corporation has also been in the hot rod police car business for several years, with numerous highway patrols. Most of the cars are set up for extremely rapid acceleration from a standing start. Others are tuned for the high end of a chase capable of exceeding 150 miles per hour. Not only are the cars set up as racers, but so are the drivers. The men and women who drive these pursuit cars have all had special training in high-speed driving. Unusual instructions are given by some of the finest race drivers in the world, many of whom have their own schools to teach professional race-car drivers how to handle their equipment. These police officers are more than a match for the robber who thinks he can outdrive and outmaneuver the cop on his tail. Although most police departments and highway patrol agencies don't wish to engage in high-speed chases they have the equipment and personnel to do it.

Still another anti-crook deterrent has been in use since World War I. Small fixed-wing aircraft have been utilized to locate robbers on the run. In the beginning this was nothing more than attempting to spot the robbers running the rural roads of the state. Once the FBI got into investigating bank robberies, however, its use of aircraft was substantial. This included not only looking for the fleeing felons, but also rapidly deploying their own personnel to the scene of the crime.

It wasn't until the late 1960s and early 1970s that robbers had a new kind of problem in the air. After the war in Vietnam, police agencies began to use helicopters. A number of combat pilots had come back from the war with skills in flying these complex machines in very close quarters, and they brought these skills to law-enforcement. State police, as well as local and federal law-enforcement agencies, found that merely a couple of these whirlybirds could eliminate the guesswork in looking for escaping bandits. Helicopters are armed with powerful searchlights, night-vision equipment, loudspeakers, and thermal-enhancement capabilities. This last piece of equipment can locate a man on the ground by just his body heat alone in total darkness.

When a bank robbery is reported, not only are police cars dispatched to the scene but so are the choppers. Outlaws need to plan their getaway to avoid standing out from the air. Helicopters follow routes high above the roadways and pass their information back to police on the ground. If need be, they hover above the robbers' car or even force it off the road with hair-raising combat-style flying. Nor is it uncommon to see news crews running live television pictures of an escaping bank robber. A bandit can often be seen attempting to elude police officers during a high-speed chase through the streets of some city while being filmed from a "News Copter" at the same time. There is little doubt that this specialized arm of law enforcement deters some bank robbers.

When the FBI fully entered the picture in 1934 the state line limit for local law-enforcement agencies was abolished. The FBI has no restrictions on crossing state lines. For this reason a few bank robbers figured that if they could only get out of the country they would then be safe. This is no longer true, however. Extradition laws have been changed over the years and there are now very few countries where a bank robber can hide. On the off-chance that a bandit should wish to make a run for it out to sea, he may have another problem.

Escape by water has been tried by crooks throughout history, and in the old days a lot of them actually made it. With the influx of drug smuggling, however, the Coast Guard is in an aggressive mode to handle lawbreakers. The twelve-mile limit line of U.S. territorial waters would have to be reached in a very fast boat in order to successfully outrun the launches and aircraft of the Coast Guard. Several bank robbers have been captured off our shores attempting to get past that twelve-mile perimeter. Unlike local law-enforcement aircraft, Coast Guard helicopters and cutters are fully armed. If a bandit should make the mistake of trying to outrun or outshoot them, he can be blown out of the water. Even robbers who make it to their "mothership" are not safe yet. Because of the incursion of drug trafficking in the United States, the Coast Guard can detain ships outside the twelve-mile limit and, if need be, seize them.

Getting away from the police has never been as difficult for a bank robber as it is now. The crook must now consider countless variables before he even gets to the bank, but of course this hasn't stopped some of them from trying.

CONTROLLED ACCESS & BANDIT BARRIERS

In the old days, the armed robber often vaulted over the bank counter to facilitate his crime. Jesse James was known to use this technique from time to time, and it ultimately became so popular that other rogues adopted the practice. The bankers' response to this unnerving occurrence was to place bars and higher barriers across the counter. The bars protected the tellers from a desperado landing in their laps, gun in hand. However, it didn't take long before some of the more athletic bandits figured they could still jump over the counter. John Dillinger was an advocate of such theatrics. There are still banks in the United States that use bars. The only serious drawback is that the robber can still shoot through the bars.

After the failure of many counter barriers, the next logical step in protecting the bank's employees was the bulletproof shield in front of their station. Bulletproof glass has been around since the early 1920s, but it was used primarily in automobiles; Al Capone had a bulletproof car built after someone made an attempt on his life. Bankers felt that this might be the answer, so they installed bulletproof glass and high counter barriers. Bank robbers, not discouraged in the least, found that they could vault over this new system almost as well as the bars. There had to be a better way to foil an athletic bandit from carrying out his task. The options were simple: build a bulletproof shield from the floor to the ceiling of the building. Put doors on it so that the employees could get in and out, and you have successfully protected the help behind the barrier. Other bank personnel were still in the lobby and at risk during a holdup, but the new system was certainly better than the old.

This system is referred to as the "bandit barrier" and it has come into its own within the last decade. In fact, a bandit barrier was in place during the North Hollywood shoot-out. It was defiantly instrumental in giving one of the tellers the time to sound a silent alarm when she saw the armed and masked men enter the lobby. Of course the customers were at the mercy of the holdup men. Problems arose when the robbers discovered that they were not going to get to the money. What ensued was a now-legendary gunfight with Los Angeles cops. It's an accepted fact that most new banks under construction will be utilizing this form of deterrent. Added to this are the retrofit barriers that are being installed on older banks.

Bankers, realizing that the key to preventing armed robberies is to keep guns out of the bank, have added a new twist. The use of weapons detectors has been around ever since airlines decided they didn't want gun-toting passengers. These systems, simple in design, have given the banks an edge when someone has the audacity to walk into their building with a mass of metal. Simply put, a double-door arrangement prohibits the would-be bank robber from coming into the lobby with his or her chunk of iron, thus preventing a situation from arising that would put the bank at risk.

Should the robber attempt to enter the building with a weapon, he is admitted through the first door. At this point a metal detector scans the individual. Should an alarm go off, the door the bandit has just entered will be locked. The second set of doors to the lobby are likewise secured and, in effect, the person is trapped between two bullet-proof doors. To say the least, the crook now has the undivided attention of the bank's guards. The would-be robber must confirm that he is or is not armed. If no weapons are confirmed, the person is admitted to the lobby. However, should this individual be in possession of a weapon, he will be trapped right where he is until police arrive. This system is known as "controlled access" and is finding considerable support within the banking community. The up-side to this security system is that police officers already have their suspect waiting for them when they arrive. There is no need to chase a criminal with a gun in his hand down the street in order to make the arrest.

As with the bandit barrier, controlled access systems are being added to new construction and retrofitted to older buildings. If technology is the answer, then the bankers may be winning. After all, they have the funds to circumvent armed robberies and the occasional burglary. The reality is that most banks don't bother with prevention until some robber/burglar has already figured out how to get around their security. In the game of catch-up most bankers will always lose to the robber. Preemptive precautions against a robber, whom you know is eventually coming, is the only solution open to the banking industry. In a 1998 internal FBI memo, it is stated very simply: "There is no bank which cannot be robbed."

PRISONS

The legendary bank robber Willie Sutton once reflected, "Prison is just the price I may have to pay for my kind of lifestyle."

For the professional bank robber who doesn't plan to use violence in the commission of his crime, prison is not a deterrent. It is, however, a deterrent to using physical violence in the commission of a robbery. There are logical reasons for this.

Assume the robber is arrested according to the law, without mistakes made by the police that would create a complicated trial. After the jury or judge has given the verdict, the judge's first step is to consult the Federal Sentencing Guidelines manual. (The standards here are from the 1998–99 edition by West Publishing.)

The federal sentence for bank robbery is 22 years, but only if it's the criminal's first offense. From then on, sentencing is a little like a smorgasbord for the magistrate. If a firearm was discharged, increase the term by seven years; if a firearm was otherwise aggressively used, add six years; if a firearm was brandished, displayed, or possessed, add five years; if a dangerous weapon other than a gun was used, add four; if a dangerous weapon was implied, although not seen, add three years; if an express threat of death was made, add two years. This weapon business can include guns, knives, bombs, or just about any item which could inflict personal damage to another person or groups of people.

With this assortment, the judge can pick and choose any number of combinations to cover the details of the robbery. What we have so far is the basic 22 years added to the first list of options.

Now we come to the part that can really increase a sentence. To what the judge has already accumulated he can add two more years if the robber commits bodily injury, four years if it is a serious injury, and six years if it is a permanent or life-threatening injury. The judge can adjust these numbers as long as the first list (weapons) and the second list do not exceed eleven years combined. However, sentencing does not end there. If a hostage is taken, add four years; if one is just tied up, add two more years. The possibilities for sentencing, as you can see, are nearly endless.

The violent bank robber knows that the judge can very well force him to spend the rest of his life behind bars. This is especially true if he kills someone during the robbery. A murder committed during the commission of a bank robbery automatically supersedes the robbery charge and becomes the central focus of the prosecution's case. Murder in some states has the mandatory capital sentence of death, which naturally should be considered as a legal option before any conviction on the robbery charges is brought up in court. If the criminal is not given a death sentence, the federal charges for bank robbery would then be added to this murder conviction and he would likely serve the sentences concurrently.

Many robbers think that the amount of money stolen is not a determining factor in their sentencing, but they are wrong. The judge will not add a thing to the sentence if $10,000 or less is stolen. But more than $10,000 adds one year, more than $50,000 adds two years, and more than $250,000 adds three years. The list goes on: more than $800,000 adds four years, more than $1,500,000 adds five years, and more than $2,500,000 adds six. If the robber is lucky enough to grab $5,000,000 but dumb enough to get caught, the judge will add seven years to the sentence.

A first robbery offense may only get the robber the minimum for his sentence, but he also has to be careful about his getaway plan. Using a stolen car during the robbery is a federal offense, and if he is suspected in other, unrelated, crimes, he could be considered an habitual, or career, criminal and get a sentence of life without parole.

The average sentence for bank robbers is between twenty and thirty years; however, due to overcrowding, the typical robber will most likely only serve about a sixth of his time. Criminals may not spend nearly as much time behind bars as the huge sentence headlines in the newspaper would lead the public to believe, but neither do they receive the kind of rehabilitation that might mold them into productive citizens. This is not for lack of trying on the part of social scientists to come up with a formula to turn black sheep into white ones. To make matters worse, a large percentage of criminals have no intention of changing anyway. The estimates for recidivism, or going back to a life of crime, are as high as 90 percent among ex-cons who served for a serious crime, and over 50 percent for all ex-cons. The best guess today is that there are at least 1,000,000 convicted felons on the streets of America, either on parole or in some pre-release program.

Is going to prison for bank robbery a deterrent? Sutton said it was the price of doing business. Ninety-nine percent of all professional, nonviolent bank robbers do not consider prison a deterrent. For the nonviolent professional, prison provides no more deterrent than does a rather complex alarm system that needs to be defeated. On the other hand, the violent bank robber should have cause for reconsidering his line of work. Incarceration would be a setback for any bank robber. Depending on the savagery of the crime, it could mean the difference between losing ten years of his life or staying free. The bottom line is: Just how far is the robber prepared to go in the quest for easy money?

Judges have all the tools they need to keep robbers behind bars. It's the prison system which is in trouble. If bank robbers know they will never serve their entire sentence behind bars, there is no reason not to rob banks. Mandatory sentencing is a goal many state and federal courts would like to have in place, but so far it's only an illusion.

This chapter has hopefully established just how much is going against the average bank robber, while also relating how robbers through the years have devised methods to get around every new system to keep them out of banks. As authorities and bankers developed newer methods for protecting themselves and society from thieves, the thieves got smarter. Had Jesse James looked up and seen a television camera watching him, or a helicopter tracking him and his horse, or heard police radios setting up roadblocks, would it have made a difference? The most likely answer is probably not. A small percentage of bank robbers still make their plans so well that almost no mistakes are made during the robbery and they escape immediate capture.

So, after taking into consideration all of the alarms and surveillance systems, why would anyone want to rob a bank? Vast sums of money have always been the motivation for bank heists and this will not change. Today, unlike in the days of old, bank robberies are more a game of numbers. For the professional to succeed he must consider all the variables a bank has to offer, then plan accordingly. The amateur is walking a tightwire; with today's technology, he doesn't really have a chance in the long run. He may seize a few thousand dollars in a snatch-and-grab style of robbery, but his days are numbered.

The true professional is the robber whom we will examine next. As innovations during the twentieth century created both greater dangers and rewards, an expert breed of criminal was destined to appear. The careers of such men continue to inspire thousands of would-be criminals. Through their exploits—successes and failures alike—we will see the evolution of a criminal aware of his past while still keenly attentive to the possibilities of the present.

Chapter 4

The Thinkers

"Obviously crime pays. Otherwise, there'd be no crime."
—G. Gordon Liddy

An unemployed shoe salesman walked into a midwestern bank and gave the clerk a note demanding all his tens, twenties, and thirties. He was arrested 15 minutes later. In Los Angeles, two robbers armed with shotguns made everyone lie on the floor. But because there was no third robber to gather up the money and put it into the sack, the two fled in panic. A gang of three took on a midtown bank one afternoon in 1982. Everything was going as smoothly as could be expected for a spur-of-the-moment robbery; they had the money, but when they exited the building their unattended getaway car was hanging from the back of a city towtruck heading down the street. The scofflaws had left their vehicle in a no parking zone! During a Utah holdup a robber walked up to the bank cage and asked the teller to hand over the money. As she was getting the money together for the bandit, he fainted. Then there was the would-be-robber who wrote his "This is a stickup" note on the back of his own gas bill.

The average robber today does not have a plan when he enters the bank, but makes it up as he goes along. Accounts such as these have been passed on by law-enforcement personnel with increasing frequency in recent years. Although somewhat humorous, they also describe the inferior ability of the current crop of holdup men. The FBI's profile of today's bank robber is a man in his mid-20s, unemployed, with a large collection of personal debt. In many cases on the

East Coast, this man is unarmed and passes a note to the teller along with verbal abuse and threats.

As we already know, most robbers are apprehended shortly after their holdup. In recent years the FBI has been getting out of the bank robbery business. It has turned investigation of these crimes over to the local authorities because they are so easy to solve, and has focused its extensive investigative resources instead toward organized crime and other federal offenses.

A few of the many criminals who attempt to rob banks each year do have a plan or a method of robbing that will allow them to stay free for at least a while. For instance, there is the story of an elderly gentleman who innocuously entered a series of banks. He approached the tellers, and was very polite in his assertion that this was, indeed, a holdup and that he didn't expect any trouble. All of his robberies occurred during the lunch hour, and always in downtown banks. When he had the satchel of money he simply walked out the door into the noontime throng and disappeared. By the time the police had arrived, he was long gone. Ultimately the man was captured but not until he had committed a number of productive heists. He had some marginal success because he recognized his advantage as an elderly person and knew that people would have a hard time recognizing him or believing that he would rob them in the first place. His was not the most brilliant plan ever devised, but it did work for a time.

Other robbers have used appearances to their advantage and achieved short-lived success. One male criminal pulled at least a half dozen notable bank robberies dressed as a woman. Sure, some of the female tellers later said he was a guy, but even they weren't all that positive. The day after his capture there were two more bank robberies and both of them were apparently accomplished by women. Again, the tellers didn't know for sure whether the crook was really a woman, and he was never captured. Then there was a rather heavy-set woman who robbed three banks before she was caught. After her first robbery she was described by the media as a male bandit.

The confusion that these people created during their holdups allowed them some time to get away, so one could say it was their "plan" that worked. They were not as successful as they may have hoped, but some of them certainly fared better than the majority of would-be bank robbers, only because they had a *plan*.

The truly professional bank robber is aware that someone could identify him and therefore has an excellent motivation for disguises. But for the veteran bank robber identification is, surprisingly, not all that important; most authorities know who pulled the job shortly after it's been done. His modus operandi is his calling card. The actual robbery or burglary is only the anticlimax to all the stealth and planning it takes to pull off a perfect robbery. For this reason the professional creates his strategy and then sticks to it; there are no spur-of-the-moment deviations such as killing someone on the way out the door. Of course, the best laid plans can and often do go awry, but the experienced bank robber usually doesn't consider murder a solution to poor planning.

Planning is the key determining factor for any professional bank robber. The men we will now examine recognized this one crucial element of the "business" and made relatively successful careers of it. Certainly, they have served as examples for up-and-coming criminals for how to commit robbery successfully, just as they have caused innumerable headaches for bankers and law-enforcement officials alike.

WILLIE "THE ACTOR" SUTTON

William "Willie" Francis Sutton Jr. was born to a hard-working Irish family on June 30, 1901, in Brooklyn, New York. He was one of four children and he informed his pals when he was 14 years old that he wanted to be a criminal lawyer when he grew up. His ambition was eventually fulfilled, but in a very unusual way.

Sutton, who would become one of the most famous bank robbers of the twentieth century, began his life of crime at the age of 10. He and a friend broke into a department store and took the money out of the cash register. As a teenager, his idols were dockside gangsters who ran the pier areas of New York. When Willie was about 15, he secured a job in a land title company, which handled legal paperwork for land purchases. This business had its own banking section and a large safe whose inner workings fascinated Sutton. His favorite observation was that anything with a hole in it could be picked.

Safe manufacturers were changing their products almost monthly in an effort to circumvent burglars. Sutton, not to be outsmarted, would order the instruction booklets and statistics on a particular type of safe and the manufacturers actually sent these to him. By the time Sutton was 21, he was already an accomplished safecracker. He had also learned the basics of alarm systems while engaged as a part-time small appliance repair man. About this same time, because he had several show-business connections he acquired a curiosity for actors and their makeup. This, too, was to play a part in what was to become Willie Sutton's criminal life.

Sutton's first major robbery took place in the office of his girl-friend's father, from whom they stole $16,000 in cash. He and the girl left town the same night and headed for Albany, New York, but were caught. The detention, pressed by the girl's father, was for burglary, grand larceny, and abduction. He went before the judge and received a suspended sentence if he promised never to see the girl again and get a job.

The employment Sutton now landed was that of a "burner," cutting steel plates with an acetylene torch in a New York shipyard. By his own account this job gave him daydreams of cutting into bank vaults. What's more, he became so adept at using a cutting torch, he was able to invent a miniature version of the equipment that could be used in close quarters. Looking at Sutton's life now, it is easy to see what direction it was going. Willie enjoyed the challenge of robbing banks and he had geared his early life in that direction. If there ever was a young man with a life's goal, Willie Sutton was that man.

His first bank job was not successful. He and his ambitious partners had to leave before they could get into the vault. Sutton was arrested for this crime and sentenced to Sing Sing prison for 5 to 10 years, in April 1926. This first of several incarcerations for Sutton began when he was only 25 years old. After three months at Sing Sing, he was transferred to the New York State Prison at Dannemora, about 20 miles south of the Canadian border. Sutton spent three years at this facility and was released in 1929. He had passed his time in prison doing some reading in psychology, particularly in how to control other people's responses in stressful situations, and corresponding with a girl he married after his release.

Considering that the onslaught of the Great Depression and the crash of the stock market took place at about the same time as his marriage, Sutton and his wife were about as well off as they were going to be for some time to come. The nation was ripe for bank robberies, and there were a lot of them; this was the heyday of the bank-robbing period, a time when gangsters were at their most active. Willie Sutton was in the right place, with the right kind of knowledge, at the right time in history to become successful. And, although Sutton knew some bigtime gangsters, he would ultimately be his own boss.

Several trademarks distinguished the Willie Sutton approach to a bank heist. He always carried a gun but was vehemently opposed to violence. This is something he learned early in his career, and he never fired a gun during a robbery. The second feature of "The Sutton Method" was that he and his associates took control of the establishment as soon as they entered the building. They accomplished this with very polite, yet firm, orders. Bank employees and customers were placed in chairs, out of the line of sight of passersby, and were either tied or handcuffed to the chairs. He was never abusive to these people and sometimes even joked with them. Then he would ask the bank manager or president, always by first and last name, to please open the vault; they always did. This aspect of his strategy was doubtless a result of the psychology reading he had done, as well as his extensive research of the bank he was going to rob.

Another facet of Willie's skill was his use of deception. He enjoyed using disguises; throughout his career, he used police officers' uniforms, Western Union uniforms, postal workers uniforms, and myriad of others, along with facial makeup and hair coloring. His theory was that he should wear some kind of uniform that would convince the guard to let him in. To hear Sutton tell it, this worked almost without exception, and the result was that no one could describe what he looked like. For this reason William Francis Sutton became known as "Willie the Actor" and so the legend began.

His freedom from prison after his release in 1929, however, lasted only 22 months. During this time he committed dozens of bank robberies, several jewelry store heists, and a few small business robberies. His partner, a man named Lester, turned on him when he was arrested, and Sutton was sent back to Sing Sing in June 1931. Technically he was still on parole, so he had a mandatory 30-year sentence hanging over his head. This trip to prison was not for his paramount crime against society—bank robbery—but for the robbery of a jewelry store.

In Sutton's career he was to spend a total of 36 years in the prison system, but Sutton always considered prison a good time to learn.

After serving a little over two years Sutton escaped from Sing Sing. His skills as a bank robber facilitated his gaining freedom, and lock picking and steel cutting were some of the talents he brought to bear in his escape. Needless to say, the escape of one of the most well-known bank robbers in the nation caused quite a stir in the newspapers. Sutton's base of operation now became Philadelphia at the same time as his banking endeavors took place back in New York.

His new crime spree lasted only 14 months and he was again in the hands of cops. During this time frame, however, it is said that "Willie the Actor" robbed over four dozen banks. He now endured another trial and another sentence; this time 25 to 50 years under the usual bank charges. This sentence was to be satisfied at Eastern State Penitentiary in the very heart of Philadelphia, one of the oldest prisons in the nation. Willie Sutton was a known escape risk—to wit, his escape from Sing Sing—folks in Pennsylvania weren't about to take any chances. He was placed in isolation on escape watch for the first 18 months of his time.

Although Sutton was avidly planning an escape, he didn't get a chance until he'd been in the prison over 10 years. With several inmate colleagues Sutton got out under the wall and into the community of Philadelphia. He was captured almost immediately and returned to prison; the aftermath of a quick trial was an additional 10 years added to his sentence. After a short hunger strike Willie Sutton and four of his fellow escapees were transferred to one of the other prisons in the state system at Holmesburg, Pennsylvania. It only took Sutton a year and half to break out along with the same four associates with whom he had been transferred. Two of them were picked up shortly after the escape, but one of the others and Willie Sutton got away. Sutton went back to New York and reacquainted himself with some of his old buddies, free again after 12 years behind bars.

If nothing else, Sutton was a man with a mission; he really liked to rob banks. It was a challenge for him to outsmart not only alarm systems and the bank itself, but he loved to bedevil the police. He not only held up banks disguised and with polite manners, but he was also a master burglar. Sutton was one of only a handful of bank robbers in this nation's history who could do it both ways. This, of course, made him a double threat to the banking establishment. His research for a burglary job was just as extensive as it was for an armed holdup. Nothing was left to chance and his modus operandi was well known to the authorities. Although not overtly, for the next five years Sutton was back in the bank business. Sutton laid low for the first two and a half years after his escape from Holmesburg, pulling fewer than a dozen robberies. Then he got a nose job and for the next two and a half years went on a bank-robbing binge, hitting bank after bank—thereby becoming a regular on the FBI's Ten Most Wanted List. FBI circulars carried information about a $50,000 standing cash reward for Sutton, with the highest amount being $70,000 at one time. It would go without saying that Sutton was a one-man crime wave in some of the bigger communities on the East Coast. Of course, like Jesse James, he was accused of far more robberies than he ever committed. The number is obscure, but the estimate has been as high as 60 banks during this two-and-a-half-year period; the robberies were holdups as well as burglaries. Finally, he was apprehended five years and one week after his escape from the Pennsylvania corrections institution at Holmesburg.

When he was arrested in New York in 1952, New York City Police Commissioner George Monahan declared: "Sutton was the most sought after criminal in the United States. We've caught the Babe Ruth of bank robbers." Even though he was armed when he was captured, the cops knew he wasn't the kind of man to use a gun. He was 51 years old at the time of this arrest. By then Willie Sutton had become a folk hero, but a quotation from his own book says it all, "Hell, I was a professional thief. I wasn't trying to make the world better for anybody except myself."

Sutton's minimum sentence could have been as little as 132 years, but in all likelihood he was going to have to serve the maximum of 3 life sentences plus 109 years. His three escapes from prison and dozens of bank jobs had finally caught up to him. The authorities tacked on a weapons charge, with consecutive sentences, and the time just added up. This legend was then incarcerated in the New York institution known as Attica. Believe it or not, Sutton was not down in the mouth about this turn of events. "This is the price you have to pay if you want to do the kinds of things I like to do," he stated. He began, almost immediately, planning to get out. On this occasion, though, he went about gaining his freedom just a little differently from the way he had in the past.

Several years went by and Sutton had his run-ins with prison authorities. He was locked in the isolation section and not allowed to mix with the general prison population. During this time he became interested in the legal aspects of the American corrections system and in its complex adjudication maneuvers, and Willie Sutton, bank robber and escape artist, became a jailhouse lawyer, thereby realizing his boyhood dream.

Sutton felt that the fastest way out of Attica for him was to prove his convictions had been erroneous from the beginning. He claimed he didn't deserve all the time he had been given for his offenses and even claimed that some segments of his convictions were illegal. Sutton became a well-known character within Attica's walls. He gained some successes for a few inmates, but his own case took a little longer.

By the latter part of 1969, Willie Sutton and his lawyers had finally laid all the groundwork necessary for his cases to be heard. Some of his problems were with the Philadelphia convictions in the early 1950s and his subsequent jailbreaks. There had also been difficulties about the jurisdictions in force between the cities of New York and Philadelphia. By the time Sutton was 68 years old he was in bad physical shape, however. He had been operated on once for a blocked artery, and by the time he went to court for the last time he was in danger of losing his leg. The whole idea of his parole reassessment was that he should be released because of ill health, and that he had already done enough time.

Thus Willie Sutton was released back into society on Christmas Eve 1969. Up until the last minute there was question whether this was going to take place. There is still skepticism as to whether he actually proved his case or if the authorities just felt sorry for him. With the help of author Edward Linn, Sutton co-authored a book on his life in 1979 titled *Where the Money Was*. This book glorified Sutton and his exploits almost to the point of declaring him the patron saint of bank robbers. A point one needs to consider is that for all his professionalism in the field of banking, he spent a great many years in prison. The hundred or more bank robberies attributed to Sutton, netting him an estimated $2 million, had a very high price tag. Nevertheless, he became a superstar in his own lifetime—and all without use of violence. This alone would set Sutton apart from the run-of-the-mill robbers of his time and unquestionably from today's batch of outlaws.

Willie Sutton, the consummate reprobate, never in his lifetime demonstrated remorse for his crimes. He was proud of his work and felt that his time in custody was payment, in full, for his endeavors. Sure, he had gotten away with a couple of million dollars, but he had also spent over half his life behind bars. He was never considered a Robin Hood but the word "rogue" would surely apply. In his later years he embarked on a limited career of public appearances commenting on how a life of crime doesn't pay, unless you write a book. He even became a consultant on matters concerning bank security. Willie Sutton died on November 2, 1980, in Spring Hill, Florida, where he had retired.

Without a doubt his decision not to use violence in the commission of his crimes kept Willie alive as long as it did. He was never compared to Jesse James, and for good reason. Sutton was a gentleman robber who not only believed that people would do what you want them to do by using forcefulness masked by kindness, but also lived by this credo. Willie Sutton, despite his years in prison, had been a very successful bank robber.

BRINK'S ARMORED CAR COMPANY

There is another side to bank robbing that should be explored here. The smart thief learned early on that the money in banks had to come from somewhere, which meant that someone or some company was transporting it. This task, at least in the middle of the twentieth century, was primarily handled by the Brink's Armored Car Company.

The Brink's company has, since its inception, been involved with the banking business. It specializes in transporting money from one location to another—a point which has not gone unnoticed by bank robbers and holdup men. At one time or another everyone has envisioned the big bag full of money falling off the back of a Brink's truck. Often this money is completely untraceable; it's either new money going to a bank or old money going to a federal reserve depository to be destroyed. One can safely assume that wherever there is a Brink's armored car on the move, money is inside. I have used Brink's only as an example. Today there are hundreds of armored car companies all over the nation.

The first Brink's robbery took place in Boston on January 17, 1950. The crime, pulled off by minor miscreants, netted the robbers $2.7 million in cash and securities. Although these robbers should have fallen into the amateur classification, they did case this job very well. They even went so far as to gain entrance to the Brink's building by accessing the security company's office, and taking a close look at the system which protected the fortified building.

On January 17, the thieves entered the Brink's business dressed in Halloween masks, imitation Brink's uniforms, and rubber-soled shoes. They relieved employees in the counting room of $1,218,311 in cash. The balance of the loot was in negotiable securities and bearer bonds. Total time, from the moment the robbers drove up to the building until they drove away, has been estimated at about 18 minutes. There were no shots fired; nor were any people injured. It had all the trappings of a military exercise with split-second timing and no wasted movements.

The robbers were to lay low for at least six years, the statute of limitations on armed robbery, although a couple of the bandits did not do this. It cost the FBI over $25 million to investigate this robbery. Most of this money was used for reward money and payoffs to underworld snitches.

Eight men were finally convicted of the crime and given life sentences. The three surviving members of the gang were released from prison in 1980. This holdup was referred to as the Great Brink's Robbery for years. In 1980 a movie of this event called *The Brink's Job* hit on some of the lighter aspects of this case. In fact, the old convicts cleared up a few points for the film's producer—points that had eluded the FBI at the time of the incident.

This 1950 event was a wake-up call for both Brink's and the FBI. How had petty crooks gotten around all of the company's formidable security? Probably the single most important factor was that a Brink's facility, or any other armored car company, had never been hit before. Just like Jesse James's first armed bank robbery, the novelty of the crime was integral to its success. The summation would be that these men did their homework and had the guts to go for it, regardless of the odds—the same motivation required for almost any major holdup. This first Brink's job was not the last, despite heightened security within the company. Fifteen years later, on Sunday, October 25, 1965, four petty (until then) thieves again took on the Brink's Armored Car Company. The Syracuse, New York office was relieved of $430,000, but this robbery had a different twist. In order for the bandits to gain access to the vault area of the building after the alarms had been defeated, they employed a 20mm Finnish (Lahti) anti-tank cannon. It was the first documented occasion where a cannon had been used to commit a robbery. Authorities estimated it took 33 rounds from this gun to make a hole big enough for one of the perpetrators to enter the vault. Unfortunately, the gunfire damaged thousands of dollars in currency and coins because of the explosions of the armor-piercing shells. They either burnt up the cash or melted the coins.

Unbelievably, this robbery was committed during a heavy thunderstorm, something which had not been planned. People living and working in the general area didn't hear a thing during the event. None of the money or any other clue was ever recovered except for the gun. A snitch revealed that it had been dropped off a bridge, sunk in about 30 feet of water. The robbers were likewise "recovered" and sent to prison—indubitably to ponder just where they went wrong in this innovative approach to burglary. However, the second Brink's job was a success from a robbery perspective; it was another case in which being amateurs may have had its good side. The thieves had a viable idea and made it work. These artillery robbers are out of prison now, maybe somewhat wiser.

Other attempts at robbing armored car companies have been made, but none have been nearly as captivating as these two first ones ever attempted. Now we will look at one of the most successful bank robbers of all time, a man who understood the rules and risks of the profession and who profited immensely from this knowledge.

GEORGE LEMAY

The crime that George Lemay would be most remembered for was committed during a Canadian holiday, Dominion Day, July 1, 1961, at the downtown branch of the Bank of Nova Scotia. This burglary/bank robbery netted Lemay and his associates an estimated $2 to $4 million. There was $400,000 in cash, $165,000 in jewelry, and more than $60,000 in stocks, bonds, traveler's checks, rare stamps, and gold pieces. Most investigators agreed that a number between $2 and $4 million was only a guess. A lot of people who had been robbed either didn't know or didn't want to share with the police exactly what was stolen when the 377 safe-deposit boxes were hit.

The overwhelming opinion at the time was that George Lemay had masterminded this break-in. The robbers gained access through a 12-by-18-inch hole blasted through the two-foot thick concrete floor of the vault. But there was more to Lemay than his skill in setting up one of the biggest Canadian bank heists of all time. He was also the first bank robber in history ever to be captured by using a satellite.

Lemay was born in Montreal and in his early years worked for his mother's real estate business as an agent. Well built, good-looking Lemay was considered the man-about-town of Montreal's high-rolling set. As a child he had given thought to becoming a priest but gave up this idea shortly after leaving parochial school. When he was 26 years old, his first wife, Huguette, disappeared from their fishing boat off the Florida coast. This tragedy was the first of several contacts Lemay would have with authorities in Florida. His wife's body was never found, and to this day it remains an open case. Most of the investigators felt there was a strong likelihood that she had met with violence, but they could never prove Lemay's involvement.

Lemay returned to his self-built cottage on an island in the Laurentian Mountains in Canada. He would spend several years living like a hermit in this cabin. When he did venture forth his journeys always took him back to South Florida. His contacts with the underworld of both the United States and Canada were a fringe relationship; he wasn't a gangster or mobster, but he knew many of them. He had, however, been questioned any number of times concerning crimes in both countries. In early 1962, five of his accomplices were arrested for their part in the 1961 Canadian robbery. They were tried and convicted, but Lemay got away.

Frustrated, a team of investigators from the Royal Canadian Mounted Police, Scotland Yard, and the FBI added Lemay's picture to their lists of wanted men. These lists, containing photographs, were then transmitted to the Early Bird Satellite in orbit around the earth. The photos, along with descriptions in several languages, were then ricocheted into the homes of millions of television viewers around the world. It didn't take long; Lemay was arrested on board his ship in Fort Lauderdale, Florida. He boasted after his arrest for the Halifax, Nova Scotia crime, "It took a satellite to catch me!"

Lemay was taken to the "escape-proof" Dade County Jail in Miami. While there, he married the only witness against him in his pending case. Of course, the only proper thing for him and his new bride to do was to go on a honeymoon. By tying a wire to a radiator and going through the only window in his jail cell without bars, George Lemay escaped. He was to remain at-large for 11 months, but was finally captured by two FBI agents in the Golden Nugget Casino in Las Vegas, in August of 1966. Tried in Canada, he was sentenced to eight years on January 17, 1969. He was 42 years old at the time.

Lemay didn't request a parole in 1973, though he was eligible for it under Canadian law. He is out of prison now, possibly living the life he has always enjoyed. In 1988, Lemay was seen living a retired life on board a 45-foot "day sailor" motor launch. But today, George and the boat are both gone. As of this writing there is no telling where George Lemay is, but if he's still alive he must be quite comfortable— the $2 to $4 million in loot was never recovered.

THE BOSTON "COPS" ROBBERY

Law-enforcement officers are as human as any bank robber, and therefore can sometimes succumb to those same feelings of greed that drive many criminals. When cops team up with lifetime criminals to pursue their goals, the results can often be disastrous for everyone.

Over the Memorial Day weekend of 1980 the little community of Medford, Massachusetts, had a robbery. The Depositor's Trust Bank was relieved of an estimated $20 million in cash and jewelry. When the six robbers—three cops and three mobsters—got around to counting the take, they found about $1.5 million in cash and the rest in jewelry. The robbery received a lot of press because police officers were involved, something the public wasn't ready to accept. The crime, described quite well in the book *The Cops Are Robbers*, by Gerald W.

Clemente (one of the thieves), is an atypical account of what can go wrong during a bank burglary.

Even though most of the robbers' names were known shortly after the event, this burglary/robbery was a success. Because authorities were dealing with corrupt police officers who otherwise had solid alibis, there was difficulty in placing the men at the crime scene. Furthermore, all participants had laid their plans well and made no major mistakes during the heist.

The robbery spanned three days. The six men gained access to the bank through a business located next door. The alarm system had been bypassed by one of the men, an experienced bank robber who had served time in prison for just this kind of venture. Using concrete bits mounted in high-powered drills, they entered the upper section of the bank, over the vault. Once they had cut holes through the ceiling of the bank, they discovered that they couldn't simply punch a hole; they had to use explosives.

Sand bags and explosives were brought into play. The blast occurred while one of the cops was standing watch outside the bank to keep other cops and the general public away from the action. When the group finally entered the vault and peeled the doors off the main safe, they discovered only $60,000 in cash, far less than anticipated. However, the bank also had several hundred safety deposit boxes. Once the thieves began to knock the hinges off these boxes they learned where the real loot was located.

Cash by the handfuls, loose diamonds, antique jewelry, and heirlooms by the bag were taken. Security bearer bonds were left in a pile on the floor. The first night of this burglary netted the men hundreds of thousands in cash and goods from the vault. Plans were made for a return trip the second night of the long Memorial Day weekend. Again the lock boxes were the target and this time the men got with it, extracting about two times as much as the first night. The physical bulk of stolen goods filled two military-style duffel bags. It was about all the men could carry or drag to their getaway van.

The third night, they worked as long as they could without running out of their predetermined time limit, and they had to leave about 500 boxes untouched. The estimate of the take given in Clemente's account was $20 to $25 million dollars. The amount was never confirmed, because very little of the loot was recovered. Some officials feel

Clemente's figure may be about $10 million dollars high, but there never was a complete list of goods taken. As we have seen before, a number of victims who were robbed were unable or unwilling to supply a list of stolen items. It was suggested at the time that there could have been mob money in some of the plundered safety deposit boxes. And then, too, patrons of the bank who lost items and funds didn't know the true value.

Each member of the gang took a share except for the jewelry; this was handled by just one man. In fact, jewelry was the preponderance of the net worth in the robbery. True, each man had a wad of cash to hide, but only one had access to the real treasure: the gold and jewelry. That man was the loose connection in the whole plot and he disappeared about a year and a half after the robbery. Because the man was never arrested for the heist, Clemente never used his real name in the book. Hence the gold, jewelry, and loose gems were never divided among the other thieves.

Where this stash is today is anybody's guess. The man with the jewelry was not a cop; he was a gangster, employed only for the job. Most of the cash was untraceable, and with old, untraceable money it is impossible for investigators to follow a paper trail.

From the beginning of the investigation there were a lot of problems. All of the culprits had solid alibis for their actions during this holiday weekend. Also, the fact that half of the suspected thieves were police officers made the entire investigation explosive. Although suspicious of the lawmen, investigators were reluctant to process this case swiftly. With time running out on a state statute of limitations on bank robbery, things were working for the robbers. In fact, the thieves were so confident that they were going to get away with the first robbery, they actually started planning a second. This scheme was ultimately scrubbed, however. A couple of the robbers soon began throwing money around and two of the police officers even got into the drug business as dealers. Money problems and big deals in the drug trade created bitter feelings. The mistrust among the robbers, heightened by drug use, came to a head three years after the robbery. While high on cocaine, one of the outlaw cops shot one of the ex-cons and almost killed him. When the officer was arrested for the shooting, he rolled over on the others.

With a domino effect the whole group went down. After the trials were over, four men were found guilty out of the original six who had committed the crime and received a combined maximum total of 87 years behind bars. The statute of limitations on bank robbery in Massachusetts was six years. These men were five and a half years into the time limit when they were finally convicted of the crime. In other words, had they kept their mouths shut and not bickered among each other they could have pulled it off. Over the years a number of criminals have found that the statute of limitations could work to their advantage, and many crimes have gone unprosecuted because of it.

The cop who ratted on the others got immunity and was placed in a witness protection program. Clemente, the author of the book *The Cops Are Robbers,* received a maximum sentence for a first-time offense of 30 to 40 years in Walpole Prison. Clemente, though not eligible for parole until 1996, was released from Walpole in January 1995, but was taken into custody by federal authorities. After serving a remaining concurrent federal sentence he was released to the Masschusetts Parole Board in 1999. He is currently still on parole in that state. However, somewhere in the world the man with $17 or $18 million in gold and jewelry is undoubtedly living a very comfortable life.

THE BOYS

The spirit of teamwork has always had a prominent role in bank robberies, and few have pulled bank jobs as a team better than "The Boys." David Grandstaff, Bruce Fennimore, and Doug Brown were given this name after a series of successful heists that left the authorities baffled and the public intrigued. For the most part their jobs were the high yield kind—they hit big targets. All three men were from the Des Moines area of Iowa and were well known to authorities when they were active.

David Grandstaff grew up in the lower-income area of Des Moines known as The Bottoms—a disadvantaged, mostly German, community. Cousins and kin were all part of a very large extended family structure. In his youth Grandstaff engaged in petty theft, and along with a host of other youngsters, got in trouble with the law. Most of the crimes were minor but set up "the boys" for bigger things to come.

For now they were a bunch of "ducktailed," leather-jacketed punks with a lust for crime. Grandstaff was incarcerated in the Training School for Boys at Eldora for stealing a car when he was 14 years old.

In and out of reformatories as a kid, he then had a stretch at a real prison when he was 17, for armed robbery. Grandstaff's real education began while he was serving a 10-year hitch in the state prison at Fort Madison, Iowa; later, he was transferred to Anamosa, then was paroled after only two years. However, due to his ongoing criminal behavior he was recommitted, then released from prison in 1966.

Soon after his release a crime spree seemed to spring up in Des Moines. Small stores, gas stations, and little businesses everywhere were being held up. The robberies were committed by the same group of men. There was always the same modus operandi but never the same kind of car, and the thieves always disappeared—almost right in front of police. The lawmen were dumbfounded; they knew who was doing the heists but couldn't catch them. Finally, the crime wave got so bad that the city fathers warned the police department that heads would roll if this thing wasn't cleared up.

But then the gang decided to stop taking all these chances for such a small amount of money and to go after bigger fish. Their first big bank job was a burglary in the little town of Minas, Iowa. With considerable effort they took the safety deposit boxes and the vault—not a whole lot of money but a beginning nonetheless. The Boys were now full-fledged bank robbers.

Their second bank heist, on February 14, 1967, was not a glorious success either, but they did pluck $15,000 out of the little bank of Kellogg, Iowa. This was also the first occasion when a bank president and his family were held hostage by bank robbers in the United States so the robbery attracted the particular attention of the FBI. One bandit, an occasional partner-in-crime to The Boys named George Weir, was captured in California but David Grandstaff remained free. FBI agents searched his mother's house, but neither he nor any of the money was found. Grandstaff had fled to Las Vegas.

Facing seemingly insurmountable odds, Grandstaff eventually came back to Iowa and turned himself in. He plead guilty on one count of bank robbery and was sentenced to 20 years in Leavenworth. His partner, George Weir, got the same amount of time at Terre Haute, Indiana. The overriding factor in Grandstaff's makeup was that he didn't care for violence. He was one of those outlaws who carried guns during robberies but didn't use them except to frighten. Without a doubt this characteristic assisted him in getting a lighter sentence. Grandstaff was transferred to the federal prison in Atlanta and was released in August 1975. This last hitch in prison was to be his graduate course in armed robbery; he got plenty of instructions while in stir.

By 1977, the three original members of The Boys were getting restless for something to do. Their first of a new series of robberies occurred in October. This was the robbery of a Lewis System's armored car while it was making a delivery to the Central National Bank of Des Moines. Although an exact figure on how much they took has never been released, it was considered to be in excess of a quarter million dollars. In December 1978 they robbed another armored car outside a Des Moines Coca-Cola plant; $500,000 was the amount reported stolen, but the total take was actually more like $300,000.

On February 28, 1980, The Boys robbed the Davidson and Licht Jewelers in Walnut Creek, California; the take was a half million in jewels. Another jewelry store fell to them on May 22 in Phoenix, Arizona. This holdup netted the gang $1.5 million in jewels. The Mid-States Bank of Denver, Colorado, was hit for $100,000 in February 1981. Jewelry stores and banks were their favorite targets, but when things got tight they went after grocery stores. By best estimate, the number of heists during this four- to five-year spread was about 30.

On April 22, 1981, their target was the First National Bank-Cash Depository in Tucson, Arizona. Planning had always been the hallmark of Grandstaff's work. He made sure timing was accurate and that movements of employees in and around the depository were predictable enough to make a timetable. This system had worked for them for years in this business, and there was no reason to think it wouldn't work again. Once inside the building, they would take charge of whoever was there—not unlike Willie Sutton's technique. Fear played a big part of this strategy, and for The Boys it had always come off like clockwork. In Tucson they secured a cleanup man and two officers of the bank, without violence and very quickly. This, of course, after the vault had been opened by an employee. The holdup took less than 20 minutes, and the thieves left over a half million dollars on the floor because the denominations of the bills were too small. The stack of stolen bills totaling $3.3 million was four feet high, five feet long, three feet wide, and weighed approximately 350 pounds. Afterward, their van was abandoned and the cash transferred to automobiles for their escape from Arizona. The local newspaper called it the biggest single robbery of a standing bank in U.S. history.

Within 24 hours the FBI had a good idea who was responsible, but they were having a hard time getting positive identifications from witnesses. The Boys, in the meantime, purchased another car and then split up, all going in different directions. Within 72 hours their pictures were seen in newspapers all over the nation. The FBI's collective nose was out of joint; they wanted these guys. Even the Banker's Association posted a $25,000 reward.

The agent in charge of this investigation was willing to stretch the rules a little to catch these bandits. The stretching started out small; only four photographs were used in the spread they offered to the possible witnesses. Not a big deal, but against all police techniques for a photo lineup. The FBI knew that Grandstaff's men were the ones and there seemed to be no reason to confuse witnesses with extra pictures. If this had been the only shortcut the FBI took, it would have been bad enough. But this was not the case. The Bureau's own records showed other breaks with standard procedure: everything from manufactured evidence to lying by agents in their field reports.

Thirty days after the holdup one of the robbers, Bruce Fennimore, was arrested back in Des Moines. This thief had made several mistakes, only one of which was driving a brand-new $30,000 Corvette around a town where he was known. An informant notified the authorities. In September 1981, the last two desperadoes wanted for the Arizona heist were arrested in Denver without incident. Even though Doug Brown and David Grandstaff had weapons, they made no attempt to go for them. They knew that the wrong time to get physical was when the cops had the drop on you.

When Brown and Grandstaff were arrested the FBI searched their possessions and vehicles, finding $177,000 of the "untraceable" money. Another $20,000 stashed in Brown's car somehow disappeared during the FBI probe. The FBI denies any knowledge of the lost loot.

Over three years passed before an indictment was handed down against The Boys for the Tucson bank job. Brown and Grandstaff had been held on charges stemming from the Phoenix jewelry store heist and bond jumping. Grandstaff hired a well known lawyer and Brown got a court-appointed attorney. Both of these legal eagles set up an air-tight defense, like witness identifications, snap answers by prosecution witnesses, and the FBI's poor approach to gathering evidence. Add to this a paid snitch for the state and you get an idea of what the defense lawyers had to work with. They just kept hammering one witness after the other, discrediting the prosecution's case.

The jury only took an hour and a half to acquit. Jurors hated one of the witnesses, didn't care for the FBI's handling of the case and didn't like the bankers at all. To top it off, they thought it had been a setup from the beginning. The Tucson Police Department, however, was cleared of any wrongdoing in the collection of evidence.

David Grandstaff and Doug Brown were paroled, only months apart, in 1989 after serving eight years for their involvement in the Phoenix jewelry store robbery. For all intents and purposes they have given up the life of crime and are living quietly in different parts of the country. Only about a quarter million was ever recovered from the $3.3 million. This kind of money could give almost anyone a very low profile for a while. The fact remains that if there hadn't been paid informants on FBI ledgers, these guys would probably still be running loose. All of their family members, and friends, were well cared for while they were active in this business. The FBI believes that the gang stole at least $10 million in their bank robberies, and most of this money has never been found. The Boys will be remembered as very successful bank robbers who demonstrated how to plan and execute such a crime to perfection—which is the mark of any true professional thief.

THE GHOST GANG OF DAVIS COUNTY

The Boys were not the only group of thieves who succeeded through precision teamwork, and probably could not even be considered the best. A sure candidate for that distinction would be the men we will examine now. Due to a continuing investigation into their activities, I will not identify the state where their series of holdups took place. Suffice it to say, it was within the southern Sunbelt, and all within the same county. These bandits and the loot have never been located, although investigators have a pretty good idea who was responsible. Their total take in three years of robberies has been estimated at between $3 and $4 million. Later, I will go into the reasons why this gang was so successful. For now, let's see what a series of perfectly executed crimes looks like.

Davis County was an affluent community that attracted well-to-do elderly people, mostly because of its comfortable climate. The median age of homeowners in the county was about 70. The income for these people consisted mostly of investments, pensions, and Social Security. Davis County boasted two fair-sized areas within its borders, the largest with a population of approximately 200,000, the smallest with 125,000. There are six golf courses in Davis County and hundreds of tennis courts to help keep the older folks in good shape. The one thing that this monied county also seemed to have in abundance was banks. There were almost more banks in Davis County than fast food chains—something that had not gone unnoticed by a very skillful and determined group of robbers.

We'll give these outlaws some assumed names. Jack was the leader and brains of the gang, and had never been arrested for anything. His brother Bob was the second in command, and brought electronics wizardry to the group. Like his brother, he had never been in trouble with the law—not even so much as a parking ticket. Bubba was the man with the torch; he knew how to cut a vault. Bubba had been arrested when very young, but in his adult life he had no police record. These three men made up the core of the gang, and all had been close since they were children. The little cluster of friends had pulled off several robberies over the years but had never even been suspects in the crimes. None of these jobs had been committed in their home state; on the contrary, these heists were executed all over the nation, with not one shred of evidence left behind.

Two others were associated with this group of thieves, but they were not part of the originals. Ted was the mechanics expert and was the most skilled driver of the tandem. He drove the getaway cars, assisted in the strong-armed part of any holdup, and had nerves of steel in tight situations. Berry, the fifth and last member of the gang, had connections to fences, which would be important once they got the hot money. Berry and Ted both had criminal records in their youths but, like the rest of the gang, were clean as adults.

The gang had one trademark which is uncommon in this business of robbing banks: they could do it both ways. They were exceptional burglars but they also had the guts to take a bank head-on in an armed holdup. Over a six-year period this gang removed an estimated $12 million from assorted banks throughout the county. Another interesting fact about the group was that they never hit anything but banks. Unlike most bank robbers—who tend to branch out into robberies of grocery stores or armored cars—the Davis County boys stuck to what they knew best and probably profited greatly because of it.

The Davis County series of robberies begin late in 1975 with the First City Bank & Trust. The bank itself had been built in the late thirties as a free-standing building. Over the years other businesses had built up along both sides of the bank and, in essence, created a little strip of shops. Customer parking was in back of the mini-mall and along the curb in front. It was in an older section of town, but there were no residential dwellings in the immediate area. Like a lot of small businesses in the Sunbelt, all of the establishments closed by 6 P.M. in the evening and didn't reopen until the following morning. There were no all-night businesses within those five blocks.

This first heist was by textbook entry through the roof sometime between 1 A.M. and 3 A.M. on a Sunday. A small charge of explosives, muffled with sand bags, opened up the roof. There was a cross hatch of steel bars spaced about six inches apart embedded in concrete, but this was no problem. Bob had dismantled the alarms and, between Bubba and Berry, their entrance into the bank only took 20 minutes. The vault, a 1945 Mosler model, took two small charges of nitroglyc-erine before opening. As the lookout, Ted remained on the roof with a walkie talkie. Jack and Bob were the only men in the vault and didn't take long to finish their work. This burglary netted the bandits $297,000 in cash and another $102,000 in negotiable securities.

Duffel bags were filled with the cash and securities and the gang was out of the building in a little over an hour and a half. They removed all their tools, dropped to the ground via a rope, and entered a 1969 Ford station wagon. This car headed south into the industrial area of town, about a mile away. The car pulled into a large warehouse and the building's doors were closed. One duffel bag went into a light blue Chevrolet Tudor sedan and the other went into a brown four-door Ford. The station wagon was wiped down and its license plate was removed and thrown into the trunk of one of the other cars.

All three vehicles pulled out of the warehouse six minutes after they arrived. The Ford wagon and the Ford sedan drove off together to a junkyard about three blocks away. The wagon was replaced from where it had been taken the night before. The extra driver got into the other Ford and away they went. Each group had rented rooms in the immediate area of the industrial district. They all went to their respective lodgings and took naps. The cars were known by the residents of the neighborhoods so parking them on the street was normal.

When the authorities arrived at the scene of the crime, they found a very expertly robbed bank. Later in the morning three of our robbers hitched up a fishing boat and headed for the shore. This was something the three of them had been doing for a few months, about every other day. Ted and Berry took the Ford and went to their regular jobs just like every other day for the last four months.

There was not a clue as to who had committed the crime. There were footprints in the dust that the blast had created, but these prints could have matched at least 80,000 people in the community who wore deck shoes. The police, the highway patrol, and the FBI secured all the roads in and out of town, checking every vehicle for suspects in the robbery. Never mind that they had no idea of what, or who, they were looking for. And, in fact, this dragnet was not implemented until a full five hours after the actual robbery. Of course, by this time the duffel bags had been moved to a safe place. The usual suspects all over town had been picked up and were in the process of producing alibis. Snitches were pumped but didn't know a thing. Every investigative agency was coming up with exactly the same thing: absolutely nothing. Days turned into weeks and then months, without ever producing a single break.

Within 10 days of the heist the loot had been split up and what cash didn't need to be laundered was stashed. The money that needed to go through a fence, and the securities, were removed from the city through the post office. For the most part our gang never left the city at any time during the four to five months after the robbery. The authorities blamed the caper on outside robbers who managed to elude their extensive dragnet. Known bank robbers as far away as two thousand miles were given unofficial credit for the burglary.

The authorities were beginning to believe that this was a professional job committed by a gang of well-organized thieves from back east or out west. Then again it could have been a bunch from up north or even South American terrorists who had by now left the country. Of course there were certain FBI agents who believed this was the work of organized crime. Things had just started to settle down in Davis County when our band of robbers struck again. This time they changed their modus operandi.

Almost six months had elapsed since the first robbery, and the gang had prepared for part two of their assault on Davis County. The rainy season had set in and afternoon showers were as predictable as the sun coming up in the morning. On a Thursday afternoon during a rather heavy thunderstorm, four men walked into a branch of Davis County Exchange, one of the state's major banking chains.

Ted was outside, sitting behind the wheel of a hopped-up Dodge station wagon at the curb, slightly away from the front door of the building. Jack, carrying a sawed-off shotgun, entered the bank first. All the men were wearing nylon stocking masks and all were armed. Bob had a 9mm automatic; Bubba, like Jack, carried a shotgun; Berry had a .44 caliber revolver. There were only three employees in the bank at the time and two customers. The robbers entered and closed the distance between the door and the counters so fast that the employees didn't even have time to hit an alarm. Bob and Bubba herded all the extra people to a little office off the lobby. Berry, Jack, and the vice president headed for the vault.

Jack made it clear to the bank officer as he stuck the shotgun in his ear: "Open the vault, walk in—don't give me any shit—and I won't blow your goddam head off!" As one can imagine, the bank employee was more than helpful. It was the first of the month and the cash was almost overwhelming. The bank, anticipating cashing a lot of checks that week, had over a quarter million dollars in the vault. Bubba did the honors and placed the $251,000 in two duffel bags. All the customers and the bank employees were then herded into the vault and the big wheel was given a spin. The men removed their stocking masks, concealed their guns under their raincoats, and headed for the street.

It was pouring rain when the foursome left the building and tossed the bags in through the lowered rear window of the station wagon. All four men entered the car and Ted nosed it into traffic. He made two left turns on the almost deserted streets and entered the garage of a ranch house eight blocks from the bank.

There was nothing unusual about this wagon coming up the street about this same time of day and going straight into the garage with a bunch of men in it. This group of men had been doing the same thing, at the same time of day, for the last three months. The neighbors also knew that two of the men would enter a white pickup truck and the other gentlemen would leave in the light blue Chevrolet. As far as the snoopy neighbors were concerned, this was a bunch of construction workers who carpooled. The people on the block got so used to seeing this same event, day in day out, that they paid little attention. What the neighbors didn't notice this time was that the men leaving in the truck both had duffel bags.

Police arrived at the bank shortly after the vice president sounded the alarm from inside the vault, but this had been almost 10 minutes after the heist. By that time four of the bandits had already left the ranch house. The showers had let up, the sun was out, and Jack had already pulled his black Honda road bike out of the garage. With his black helmet on, he waved at a couple standing in their yard as he tooled down the street. It would be the last time anyone would see him in that neighborhood. It would take three weeks before the authorities located the house, a very clean stolen getaway car, and not much else.

The robbers had again disappeared. Not even the neighbors could come up with an accurate description of what these men looked like. What made it even more frustrating for the investigators was that the bank's own surveillance pictures were no help. They still didn't know who these robbers were. In fact, they hadn't even considered that they may be the same gang that had committed the burglary months before. This was a new group of outlaws as far as the cops were concerned. Once more, all the known suspects were rounded up. Once more, all this research into the lives of the local known criminals ended the same way as with the first robbery: a dead end.

Our gang of thieves hadn't left Davis County though, they had just moved across it. The other community, which was about half as big as the first, was to be their new base of operations. All the cars and the motorbike had been disposed of and new vehicles were in the stable. The stolen money had been transported out of town, compliments of the U.S. Postal Service. This time all the men lived separately and never associated with each other in public. Of course in private they had been very busy. Almost a year after the first robbery, and six months after the second, they struck again. This heist, of two banks over two nights, was the one that was going to put the unknown outlaws on the Most Wanted list.

The first bank, located in the heart of the little community, was another textbook burglary. Our bandits got away with $650,000 in only over three and half hours' work. Again it was a roof entry and it wasn't discovered until Monday morning. The second bank, robbed on Sunday, was only a little different. Located in a suburb about eight miles from the first, it, too, was not discovered until Monday. The second bank was entered through a back door that was all but hidden from view. Alarms had been defeated and the gang only took 1 hour and 45 minutes to pull the job.

A large stolen about-town truck backed up to the door just long enough to give the burglars time to get into the bank. Ted then drove the truck into a line of identical trucks parked 200 feet away. When the inside boys were done, they radioed Ted and he backed up the truck to the door and the robbers were off. The truck was driven, with all the bandits inside, to a garage about four blocks away. The loot was transferred to two other cars and the about-town truck was returned to where it had been stolen: just 200 feet from the bank. The second haul was estimated at $460,000. In two nights, and about six hours of work, this gang had netted $1.1 million dollars. Again, by Monday morning the men were gone.

All the gang members maintained regular jobs within Davis County, so they laid low by doing their jobs. They didn't spend their loot in the typical fashion, but they did manage to get all of it out of town, again through the postal system and package delivery companies. These last two robberies, like the earlier two, were attributed to the Ghost Gang of Davis County.

The group of bandits took the rest of the year off, but there was one more heist on the planning board. This holdup was to be their last job in Davis County and they intended it to be their crowning achievement. It would also mark the termination of their careers in this enterprise; afterward they planned to retire after a fruitful career. Up to this point, every holdup they'd committed had been planned almost two years in advance. The only detail about their robberies which was in question was the amount of money that would be in the banks they were planning to rob. So far, everything had come off better than expected. In the money department they were ahead by about $1 million dollars. In the time department they were right on schedule.

For the last couple of years Davis County had been preparing for its centennial. The county had organized parades, parties, and speeches by state and federal dignitaries—all the trappings of a full-fledged celebration. This third weekend in August was expected to draw crowds in the tens of thousands. People were coming from all over the tri-state area to celebrate 100 years of contented living in Davis County. This was the setting for what was to baffle law-enforcement personnel for the next 10 years. And, like the rest of the gang's holdups, the crime would never be solved.

The largest bank in the county had six branch banks scattered all over the area. The centennial celebration began on Friday and would run through Sunday. The robbers believed that this main bank would have somewhere between two and five million dollars in its vault by Monday morning. These proceeds, deposited by the branch banks into the main bank, would be from the weekend jubilee. Their target was therefore the main bank on Monday afternoon.

At 3:45 P.M. on Monday, three masked men walked into the lobby of the bank. Six people were in the building at the time and all of them were forced to move to the far side of the lobby. The door was locked and the bank president, J. C. Todd, was escorted to the vault. Jack used his favorite threat so the man was very cooperative. The president was then handcuffed between his legs and set on the floor in the corner of the vault. Bob had secured the other patrons and employees with a length of rope in a little alcove off the lobby. Jack and Bubba now began to fill the duffel bags. Ted and Berry drove the panel truck up to the rear door of the building when they received the radio message to do so from Jack. On the side of the truck was a logo advertising a carpet cleaning business. At precisely 3:55, Jack, Bubba, and Bob threw three duffel bags into the rear of the truck and followed them in. In these bags was a total of $2,194,600 in cash, 99 percent of which was used (old) money.

The bandits had been in the bank 10 minutes. There had been no shots fired and no one injured. After they were in the truck, Ted drove it down the main street of town for four blocks. He turned into an alley and proceeded about one more block. There he pulled the vehicle into a parking lot with about 30 other trucks; all were identical. The five men moved the three bags full of money into a station wagon and left the area. Nobody had made a big deal out of it, all five men were wearing shirts belonging to the carpet cleaning company, shirts they hadn't even donned until after they had left the bank. Not one bank employee had seen the getaway truck or what was written on its side. The carpet cleaning company didn't know a thing either.

Officially the alarm was sounded at 4:07 P.M. Our thieves were safely inside the garage of a rented house two miles from the bank by 4:15 P.M. They would remain inside this house for the next two days. On Wednesday one large package and five smaller packages were picked up by a parcel shipping company with a destination of Dallas, Texas. On Thursday, five separate, nondescript automobiles left Davis County. Jack's car was the only one of the five that was stopped. Jack told the authorities whom he worked for, which they confirmed, and presented his travel plans. He was on a scheduled vacation from work and was released without question. All five men went in different directions, but within a month all were together again, in Texas.

There was now a split of the cash and securities that had been stockpiled in Dallas from all their jobs. The men had taken a total of $3,954,600 from five banks in Davis County within a period of a little over two years and nine months. After a rather subdued party, the men split up again.

None of these thieves have been located, charged, or convicted of these crimes, nor has any of the stolen money ever been recovered. The biggest single factor in their lack of an arrest is that no one can identify these men. The robbers continue to remain the Ghost Gang, if only for a lack of any better way to describe them. No fingerprints were ever found, let alone matched to known prints of the robbers. They made no attempt to leave the area after committing the robberies. Last of all, they were good at what they did. The fact remains that five banks were robbed and the robbers were never captured. Because of the expiration of the statute of limitations on the robberies, there is no longer any chance at this time to even charge these men.

This is the *official* version of what happened, but there is a bit more to our story. Jack, Bob, and Bubba are reportedly living in a South American country under the guise of an import-export company. Their business is a huge success and the three are respected. The bulk of their stolen money is in a Swiss bank account along with proceeds from their business. Ted and Berry have gone their separate ways and, as far as I know, have never been involved in any other criminal activity. For safety's sake these men do not keep in touch with each other. They do, however, know where to find one another, if the need to communicate should arise, and so far there has been no need. When something worked as well as this series of robberies did, the best thing to do was to just keep doing what you have been doing.

Herman "the Baron" Lamm would have been proud of this group of thieves; they had done their homework very well. If these were not perfect crimes, they were close. This group of bandits was, without a doubt, the exception in this business of robbing banks. Of course, law-enforcement still treats those robberies as open cases. If, for some reason, the men working this case should come across pertinent information, it will be entered into the file dedicated to these robberies.

But when the statute of limitations runs out, so does a lot of the interest. Nonetheless I have it on good authority that at least one retired FBI agent is still attempting to solve this string of heists. The perfection of these crimes, and the growing legend of how the Davis County boys managed to pull off such incredible heists, will ensure that some investigators will continue to search regardless of the odds. Perhaps some day we will know more about these men. Until then, we are left with only their crimes and the price of recovering what was lost.

JIMMY "THE GENT" BURKE

While the Davis County Gang certainly included some of the most skillful bank robbers ever, there are still other types of robberies that should be described in order to get a full picture of this type of high-stakes crime. A modern cross between highway robbery and bank robbing was the famous Lufthansa Heist of 1978.

On December 11, 1978, seven men robbed the Lufthansa Air Cargo Terminal at Kennedy International Airport of an estimated $8 million in cash, gold, unmounted jewels, and foreign currency. These fellows loaded seventy-two 15-pound cartons and boxes into their van and escaped without a trace. Forty cartons had U.S. Customs Department American banking seals attached. This was the largest heist in the history of the United States. Not counting foreign money or jewels and gold, the American cash was estimated at $5 million, of which $4 million was untraceable old money. This currency was being shipped from German banks back to the United States for exchange. Thus, even though this crime can fall under the heading of a hijacking, it would also qualify as a bank robbery. It was a common practice at Kennedy International for any number of banks to use foreign airlines to act as the transportation vehicles for their banking concerns, making the airlines an extension of the banks' operations.

Due to glitches in Lufthansa's normally extraordinary security procedures, there were a lot more valuables on hand than the crooks ever imagined. The fact that there had to have been someone on the inside was established almost immediately by the FBI. Although the FBI became the primary investigative agency, six other police organizations were hunting for the robbers. A proverbial Chinese Fire Drill would be a good description of the police jurisdictions committed to the solution of this crime. Not only were there overlapping agencies, but also overlapping investigative teams; naturally the whole investigation got out of hand rather quickly. Problems such as these are what assist bank robbers in the short run.

Three months after the robbery the FBI was at a standstill with the case. Two employees of the Lufthansa Cargo Terminal were suspects from the beginning, while the possible mastermind was thought to be Jimmy Burke, a local hoodlum who had unofficial connections to the New York Gambino family. But this was about all the authorities had to go on. It was thought that Burke was the key to breaking the investigation wide open. He had a ragtag assortment of associates in his corral and several were suspects in the holdup. A half million dollars' reward was up for grabs to anybody who could shed some light on the case, including possible suspects. However, the money was unsuccessful in tempting anyone to snitch.

Jimmy Burke had a reputation for dealing harshly with people who crossed him. Even with the reward, no one would have wanted to anger Burke. The case finally broke for authorities when one of the inside men suspected by the FBI attempted to leave the country. He was taken into custody and it didn't take long for him to give up the other insider. The FBI felt it had the framework for a solid conviction when the two insiders were questioned, but this wasn't to be.

At one time the Bureau had 125 agents on the street chasing leads in New York and around the world. Suspects' cars were bugged and beepers were attached so the FBI could keep track of the cars and conversations. A small break came when the Department of Justice apprehended one more of the suspects. Just when the FBI and local police thought they were going to get a handle on this case, the rules changed. Over a period of months witnesses critical to this investigation started turning up—dead. One merely disappeared. Another was found dead by questionable means; two others were found shot to death in the front seat of a Buick. Another was most likely compressed into mush in a car-compacting operation. A man and his wife in their pink Cadillac were disposed of in similar fashion. One witness took an involuntary free fall from a light plane over the Atlantic. A woman, somewhat disconnected from the robbery but not from the other victims, was found in a steamer trunk washed up on a New Jersey beach.

Six months after the robbery the FBI was stuck again. They still had nothing to go on and witnesses kept ending up deceased. There was little doubt in the minds of authorities working the case that Jimmy Burke was literally cutting his odds down to size. The tried-and-true methods of the underworld were being vigorously employed. Only two remaining people even had a chance of assisting the court in taking Mr. Burke down on this robbery; these two men, minor burglars, were literally all the FBI had left. They were kept under surveillance by federal agents in the hope that Burke would not be able to get to them.

Then, from an unexpected source, came a break. A low-life, drug-addicted, drug-peddling sexual deviant named Henry Hill made arrangements with authorities to get Burke. Prosecutors were hopeful that Hill would be the key in getting an indictment on Burke, but again there were difficulties. Hill could not really tell the investigators all that much about the robbery. At best, Hill was a fringe associate, and he had not been included in the planning or execution of the robbery. However, Hill and Burke had done business in trafficking drugs. Burke had financed some of Hill's lucrative adventures in the drug business, and the government felt it could at least make a case against Burke for that.

Hill was an ex-con and so was Burke, who was still on parole for an infraction earlier in his career. In 1980 James Burke was arrested for parole violation and drug commerce, a serious offense in New York State. His business dealings with Hill were enough to revoke his parole, simply for associating with known felons. Burke was on ice—for the time being.

A couple more bodies now turned up. These men had not been associated in the Lufthansa robbery, but it was believed they died because they had crossed Burke in a business deal in Florida. Even with their remains, the cops couldn't pin it on Burke. More time passed while agents attempted to make their case. Authorities slowly realized that Henry Hill might still be their ace in the hole. One afternoon, after a long FBI session with him, Hill dropped a bombshell. He casually mentioned that he and Burke had attempted to shave a few points in Boston College basketball games by bribing some of the players. There it was—interstate racketeering! This is a federal offense and there seemed to be proof enough to make the case.

Maybe they couldn't get a conviction on Burke for the robbery and murders, but they could make this latest allegation work. Of course Hill, ever the self-promoter, sold the same information to *Sports Illustrated* shortly after he had given it to the FBI in secret. This almost sank the case before it ever began, but the prosecutors were able to work around it. Burke's trial came to order on October 1981 in the packed federal courtroom in Brooklyn, New York. He was to be tried for fixing basketball games, with Hill as the star witness against him. However, Hill's testimony was a disaster from a prosecution standpoint; even Burke's lawyers didn't feel threatened by it. Fortunately for law and order, a Boston College basketball player did much better.

Burke was convicted on January 23, 1982, and sentenced to 20 years for his betting offenses. But Burke's convictions were not over yet—his past was just starting to catch up to him. Henry Hill came up with more information for the government about Burke's activities. He remembered details of a boast Jimmy "The Gent" had made about one of the last two murder victims attributed to him. When the evidence checked out, Burke was brought to trial on state charges for second-degree murder. He was convicted and, in December 1984, was sentenced to 25 years to life in prison.

The last remaining suspect in the air cargo heist, unable to make a living without Burke's help, took to robbing drug dealers. He made one mistake by robbing a connected dealer and was taken care of according to the rules of that game. Even his sleeping girlfriend had a silenced pistol placed in her mouth and was dispatched to the hereafter. As far as the government was concerned, the case was now complete.

Burke, who will spend the rest of his natural life behind bars in Lewisburg, Pennsylvania, still feels no guilt. At least 13 people died as a result of the Lufthansa robbery. As with the Brink's holdups, this was not a bank robbery in the strictest sense, but several New York banks took the loss. Due to the volume of funds transferred, none of it was marked. The million or so dollars that could have been identified was laundered through the local mobs of New York and New Jersey so it was dispersed rather quickly. The stolen jewelry was never recovered. None of the other murders connected to this case were ever solved. Burke was a rogue who deserved exactly what he got for his crimes. He still has a long reach, however, so Henry Hill will be looking over his shoulder for the remainder of his life.

AMIL ALFRED DINSIO

A skillful thief with a steadily successful modus operandi was linked to at least a dozen bank burglaries during the 1960s and '70s, with a total take estimated at over $30 million. In his home region of northeastern Ohio, this man had no peers. The average, "everyman"-looking Amil Alfred Dinsio would have never been picked out of a crowd as a bank robber. However, his reputation as a criminal of the highest caliber preceded him, which we will come to see.

Perhaps the most important part of Amil Dinsio's modus operandi was that he never worked with strangers. His brother James was a cohort, as was another brother. Ronald and Harry Barber, his nephews, and Charles Mulligan, Dinsio's brother-in-law, were all part of the team. In what was to be their last robbery, in 1972, they included one other man not related by blood, Phillip Christopher, but generally they just stuck with family. A fantastic career led up to this last robbery, which is the one we will review in order to describe Amil Dinsio. Their last set of burglaries was to be a two-bank caper, beginning in the little community of Laguna Niguel, California. The two robberies, 45 days apart, would net the gang between $5 and $8 million dollars and secure for them 20 years in prison.

It all started in February 1972, when Amil Dinsio and his wife made a trip to Los Angeles from Cleveland. Charles Mulligan was the third member of the group on this journey. It was to be strictly a reconnaissance venture to "case" the target. The United California Branch Bank of Laguna Niguel, in Orange County, was selected.

Located within the Monarch Bay Shopping Plaza overlooking the Pacific Coast Highway, the bank locale was perfect. Because of California architecture this bank was ideal for rooftop entry. Further, there was cover around the building itself and the roof was concealed because of the building's false front.

Our conspirators purchased a 1962 gold-colored Oldsmobile and then assembled the mountain of tools needed for the job. Mulligan, using an old friend from Ohio as a patsy, managed to store the car and tools inside his garage. By March everything was ready and the gang went back to Ohio, where, driving this time, Dinsio and his gang laid all the final plans they needed. Some of their advance intelligence gave them a rough idea about how much money would be on hand. About a week later a band of at least six men all left Cleveland and flew to Los Angeles. The burglary was set for March 24, 25, and 26, a holiday weekend. This time frame, not unlike those of thousands of other bank heists, gave the gang the maximum amount of time to pull the job.

About five days before the robbery, Dinsio and Mulligan made a test run on the bank. After converting a 220-volt power source, located on the roof by an air-conditioning unit, to 110 household, they cut a hole in the roof. Dinsio entered the building to survey the site for the robbery. When he was satisfied that the job was plausible, they sealed up their entry opening with roofing tar. They added a small piece of mirror, which could be spotted from a distance with binoculars. From the safety of the Laguna Hills area they could tell if their entry had been discovered; it wasn't.

These precautionary procedures were not spur-of-the-moment ideas. Amil Dinsio was a professional. He had liberated millions from dozens of banks by making sure everything was right before he embarked on any job. His theory, tested with over 10 years of experience, was a combination of not being surprised when he got inside the bank and having the right tools for the task. Dinsio knew that once he started in on the vault it was too late to discover he didn't have the right kind of equipment to finish.

On Friday, March 24, 1972, at least six, and maybe eight, men began their assault on the California bank. Because of the massive amount of equipment needed for this job, at least two cars were used. The entry hole was reopened and the band of thieves dropped into the building. The vault was constructed with approximately 18-inch-thick slabs of concrete so holes were bored. Explosive charges were packed into these holes and, with the help of dirt-filled burlap feed sacks, the charge was set off. No one in the immediate area was aware of the enormous explosion, which blew a two-foot hole through the top of the vault. All that remained was a 12 by 12-inch crosshatch of steel-reinforced bars. All the alarms had been taken care of, so their operation had gone unnoticed. This was as far as the gang was going to go that first night.

When they returned Saturday night and moved lights and implements into the vault, they were startled by the number of safety deposit boxes. There were 500 bright and shiny boxes of all shapes and sizes. These deposit boxes were no match for a chisel-faced heavy hammer. It only took seconds to knock the hinges off and open these mini-strongboxes. It all started out systematically enough, but by the end of Saturday night the entire vault area was littered with empty boxes. The treasure was placed in burlap bags, and what could not be fenced or spent outright was added to the pile on the floor. On Sunday morning the robbers left with some of their booty and a lot of unneeded tools. This hardware was placed in a false bottom in the trunk of the Oldsmobile along with three gold coins. None of the gang has ever given a reason why these coins were added.

On Sunday night, the gang finished up what was thought to be the last aspects of an estimated $5 to $8 million robbery. Out of 500 boxes in the vault the gang opened and rifled 458. The take included cash, stock certificates, treasury notes, coins, travelers checks, bonds, and diamonds. As we have seen previously, however, such numbers are subject to wide discrepancies, and of all the materials stolen, few things could be traced. One customer did record the serial numbers of a bunch of bills that had meant something to her. There were a few descriptions of some mounted jewelry, but the pieces were not all that unique and could have been fenced anywhere.

Come Monday morning the bank officers could not open the vault. Dinsio had seen to it that the door to the vault was jammed, which afforded the robbers several hours head start on the authorities. It took until late in the afternoon before anyone discovered that there had been a robbery. The pile of safety deposit boxes and other discarded material in the vault was a sight to behold. There was little doubt that this had, indeed, been a major haul. The FBI was notified immediately, but by that time our gang of thieves had left town and were heading back to Ohio.

Six weeks after the California heist, the Second National Bank of Warren, Ohio, was hit for $430,000. The thing that gave the investigators reason for thought was that the modus operandi was identical to the Leguna Niguel job. The theory became simple: break the Ohio robbery and you will also have the West Coast bandits. FBI agents dove into this case, checking every conceivable lead. There were five basic mistakes made by this band of thieves, and these errors were their undoing.

When airline reservations were checked between Ohio and L.A., several known robbers' names were included. The crooks' first mistake was using their real names to travel to California. Their second mistake was using their real names at the motel they stayed at during their visit prior to the robbery. The third error was that telephone records from the motel implicated a local man in the plot. This was the guy who unknowingly had stored the gold Oldsmobile. The fourth blunder was that one of the gang members used his own name when he rented a townhouse in the Laguna Niguel area. Dirty dishes left behind in this townhouse revealed a few of the gang members' fingerprints. But the last, and most important flaw in the overall plot, was due to Amil Dinsio himself. Not only were the gold coins found in the car with the tools, but so were his fingerprints. The gang had taken great care to wipe down all the tools and they were, indeed, clean. But when investigators opened one of the flashlights discovered with the tools, Dinsio's prints were found on the batteries.

The serial numbers recorded by a depositor in the bank matched some of the bills found on one of the robbers. Five of the eight gang members were rounded up. The total loot recovered from the California heist amounted to a little less then $4 million. The five bandits, including Amil Dinsio, were found guilty and sentenced to 20 years each.

When you look at the superstars in this occupation, Amil Dinsio, would have to be included. An estimated career take of over 30 million dollars would rank right up there with some of the all-time highs. He may have been as plain as a brown paper bag, but there is little question he knew his trade. His mistakes were simple errors in an otherwise brilliant scheme. As we have seen in past chapters, it's usually elementary things that catch crooks. Most of the high-tech stuff the investigators have to work with will never really outdo good old-fashioned police work.

JAKE "LEFT-HANDED" SMITH

When Jake Smith hit the ground for the last time, he was dead at 40 years old. His bank robbing career had spanned better than 15 years and by all accounts he was one of the most successful armed robbers in American history.

Jake Smith was like Amil Dinsio in many ways, in that he was simply an incredible bank robber and strategist. Smith was born in 1940 near the community of Hot Springs, Arkansas, to an upper-middle class family. Jake was a poor student only because school was boring to him. He had been given intelligence tests and always scored very high, but his grades were dismal. He was arrested for petty burglary at 14, when he and two others broke into a liquor store. The judge sentenced young Jake to reform school for two years, and he was released on good behavior 14 months later. But Jake was a mischievous kid and it wasn't six months before he was in trouble again, this time for stealing a car and taking a joyride to New Orleans. Jake was reinstated in the reform school for two more years, and was almost 18 years old when he was again released into society.

For three years Jake Smith stayed out of trouble. Then a series of armed robberies hit Little Rock. These holdups, all committed by a single individual, baffled police. All had the same modus operandi, but the police could never follow the trail long enough to catch the perpetrator. A lone bandit, armed with a small handgun, would walk into the establishment, state his business, take the money, and leave. There were no definite descriptions of the masked man, but the person robbed would often conjecture that it was an older individual. And there were no verbal threats, only the gun in the face and the demands. Jewelry stores, small grocery stores, and the occasional liquor store all fell to the "Left-Handed Bandit."

Smith was questioned by police for several of these robberies, but he always produced a solid alibi. His first bank robbery is believed to have been committed in Hot Springs, Arkansas, when he was about 24 years old. The First Arkansas Bank & Trust was held up by a masked, left-handed bandit and relieved of $71,000 in old money. The employees of the bank were both tied to chairs while the tills and vault were rifled. No one was injured, and by all accounts the robber was polite. Again the witnesses stated that without a doubt the robber was about 40 or 50 years old and very calm. There was also little question that the bandit specifically went after old money; he knew what he wanted. No alarm had been sounded and his escape was effected with few witnesses. By the time police were called, about 45 minutes later, Smith was well on his way out of town. Even had he been stopped by lawmen, they would not have found the used money or the gun on him; it had already been disposed of by Smith at another location.

Ten days later, the "Left-Handed Bandit" struck again, this time in Little Rock. A small neighborhood bank was hit for $124,700 in mostly old money. This robbery, like the first, entailed no violence and left all three employees tied to chairs when the robber departed 30 minutes later. The employees described the bandit as an older man, in his forties or fifties, and very cool. In fact his departing remarks to the people were, "Thank you very much for your cooperation and it's been a pleasure doing business with you!" This "elderly" robber then walked out of the bank and made his escape without notice from passersby. The employees were freed about half an hour after the heist.

The FBI, along with local law-enforcement personnel, didn't have a clue as to who the robber was. Other than the obvious similarities the only real lead was the time of the robberies. They both occurred at 10:30 in the morning. Jake Smith was not a suspect and, in fact, after he secreted the stolen money he went to his regular job and there was nothing unusual about his activities. Cops mounted a local search for all known left-handed bank robbers between the ages of 35 and 60 years of age.

For the next three years at least 20 banks throughout Arkansas, Missouri, Oklahoma, Texas, Louisiana, and Mississippi were hit by the "Left-Handed Bandit." Always with the same modus operandi and always with the same results: old money, tied-up employees, no mistakes. The robber had been captured on video surveillance cameras but to little avail. He always wore a mask, was very polite, and was described as an older gentleman. Needless to say, he made the FBI's Most Wanted List after his sixth bank job, and his total take from twenty-some robberies has been estimated at about $4,500,000.

On a routine criminal sweep of Little Rock, Smith was hauled in to the police station. The sweep cops were looking for the left-handed robber. Jake had several things going for him during questioning. He wasn't old enough, he was right-handed, and not one witness could pick him out of a lineup. Even his voice was different than the supposed bandit's. His house had been searched and nothing was found which could tie him to the holdups. His alibis were checked and there were no discrepancies. Smith was not a viable suspect for the robberies and was released.

For the next couple of years no more bank robberies could be linked to Smith's well established modus operandi. Then Springfield, Missouri became the target of Smith's attention, and there he again attracted the attention of authorities. Supposedly, when he was on vacation in the Springfield area, he was detained for questioning by an observant FBI agent. This man had seen the same suspicious individual in front of the same bank three days in a row. There was no evidence to tie Jake to an impending bank heist so he was again released. It was pointed out to him, however, that he was now being watched by the FBI as well as by local authorities. In reality even the FBI did not think he was a suspect, but giving him a good scare couldn't hurt.

Smith's name was routinely added to a possible list of suspects in the "Left-Handed Bandit" open file. A week after his encounter with the FBI in Springfield another bank in Little Rock fell victim to a holdup by this same well-known bank robber. Smith got rid of the hot money, $92,000, but was picked up the next day for questioning. Along with several other gentlemen Smith was considered one of the best suspects. Once again in a search of his house no gun, money, mask, or anything else connecting him to the crime was discovered. Begrudgingly, he was again released.

In the minds of the investigators Jake Smith was looking more and more like the bandit, but there was no proof. The authorities decided to put a tail on him and see if anything developed; unfortunately, it didn't. In fact, Smith gave the tail a hard way to go several times; he drove a hopped-up four-wheel-drive pickup truck and it wasn't uncommon for him to turn suddenly off the paved road and head across country.

Smith went about his usual business for the next year and a half without drawing the interest of the authorities. A 55-year-old left-handed bank robber had been captured and the cops thought they had their man. But a little leg-work proved that this crook was not the one sought. To make matters worse, shortly after this suspect was released Smith hit again. His take in this small town robbery was sparse but it made his point. Once again he was hauled in, again he was questioned, and again he was turned loose.

By the time Jake Smith turned 38 he had single-handedly robbed over 40 banks with a calculated total take of over $10 million. By this same time he was the prime suspect in several major heists. What the investigators didn't know was how he was getting rid of the money. He had once been stopped within 20 minutes of a bank robbery and nothing was found—no money, no gun, no mask. His movements were checked and any number of locations were searched to no avail; there was no way to tie him to any of the stolen money. Smith now stayed out of the bank robbing business for two years. His last robbery was committed shortly after he turned 40.

There may be a couple of ways to look at what happened to Jake Smith in his last holdup. It could be that his luck just ran out or that he made a mistake. He had done his homework; he knew what he was up against. An older midtown bank building with six teller's stations was his target. About a dozen employees could be a problem, but he had dealt with this many people before. There was only one bank guard, an older man, who would not be an obstacle. Smith had changed the day of the hit from Tuesday to Thursday only because the armored car company didn't come for the used bills until late on Thursdays. The largest accumulation of old money would be in the bank by noon on Thursday.

Jake "Left-Handed" Smith rolled down his ski mask just before he pulled open the door to the bank. A female employee spotted the masked man about halfway across the lobby and sounded a silent alarm. Smith's order for all tellers to step back from their cages and come around to the front of the counter was obeyed immediately. They and five customers were herded into a side office. Smith went about his business with the vice president as he had done so many times before, unaware of the absence of the guard. He had just filled his sack with about $90,000 in used currency and was moving toward the door when a single shot rang out in the lobby of the building. The hostages screamed in terror as the deafening noise echoed off the internal stone walls of the structure.

The .38 caliber bullet, fired from a long-barreled Smith & Wesson, struck Smith in the middle of his back between the shoulder blades, severing his spine. Fragments also entered both lungs and a small piece of shrapnel entered his heart. He staggered for five or six feet and collapsed dead in front of the doorway.

Because of the silent alarm lawmen arrived before the smoke had even cleared the lobby. When the mask was removed, there lay Jake Smith, the man suspected of over 40 unsolved bank robberies. "The Left-Handed Bandit" had been stopped once and for all. The guard was hailed as a hero, the cops congratulated one another, and the true identity of the robber was now known. This should have been the end to this account—but it's not.

Other than the $90,000 recovered in Smith's last holdup, not one dollar of the other robberies attributed to him has ever been located. The $10 million supposedly stolen by this man has never been found. Somewhere there is a cache of untraceable old money taken from countless bank robberies by Jake Smith, and without that money there is no legitimate way to tie Jake Smith to these other heists. Sure, the authorities brag to each other and the press that this was indeed the "Left-Handed Bandit," but to this day there is no real proof.

Jake was not married. He had lived in a comfortable house but had nothing to indicate the kind of money that must have passed through his hands. There were no secret hideaways that authorities could find in any other state. He didn't have a motor home or a large boat, not even a safety deposit box in any bank which could be found. He owned no vacant property that could have been used as a burying ground for the loot. None of his relatives were living high on the hog. Likewise, he never used a partner nor did he have any close friends. So what happened to the money?

There is little doubt that Jack Smith was a successful bank robber. The fact that the money has never been found, nor is it likely to be, only attests to his skill. He never spent a day in jail for robbing banks, which also confirms Smith's expertise in this occupation. Aside from questioning Smith several times, police came up against a stone wall with this robber; he did not divulge a thing to them that would help. Rumors spread that he gave it all to the poor, like a modern Robin Hood, but these have never been proved. Only one man would have known where all the money was, and he is buried in the All Souls Cemetery outside Little Rock. And in the interest of efficient police procedure, all the bank robberies attributed to Jake Smith, the "Left-Handed Bandit," have been closed.

The foregoing are some of the best bank robbers who have ever lived. These men used their intelligence to beat every possible system of defense that banks ever constructed, and they were successful because they were able to think of options that authorities probably had not considered. Fortunately for the banks and police, these characters are also exceptions to the rule. The group of thieves we will look at next illustrate the more common image of what the bank robber is today: crude, uneducated, and in desperate need of money any way he or she can get it. Their mistakes are often humorous but also frightening in a way; they are men and women who will do absolutely anything for some free cash, regardless of the risk to themselves or others.

Jesse James at age 17, while fighting for the Confederacy in the Civil War. Sneak-thief burglars would no longer be the primary threat to financial institutions once the James Gang began to bring military tactics to the profession of robbing banks.

The self-styled "Wild Bunch," or "The Hole in the Wall" Gang, as they were also known. From left: Henry Longabaugh (The Sundance Kid), Bill Carver, Ben Kirkpatrick (The Tall Texan), Harvey Logan (Kid Curry), and Robert LeRoy Parker (Butch Cassidy). The gang had this photo taken after robbing a Nevada bank and mailed it to the institution along with a thank-you note. (AP Photo/ Swann Galleries, John Swartz)

The Dalton Gang after their last (unsuccessful) bank job, at Coffeeville, Kansas. From left: Bill Powers, Bob Dalton, Grat Dalton, and Dick Broadwell. Four civilians also died in the gunfire. Emmett Dalton, badly wounded, was sentenced to life in prison, and served 15 years. (Dalton Museum, Coffeeville, KS)

Jesse James, in a photo taken during his years defying the law. Though his image today is well known, law enforcement in the late 1800s was hampered because they were not certain what he looked like. (Jesse James Museum, Kearney, MO)

Frank James was a far better marksman than his younger brother, but due to a cooler temperament no murders were attributed to him. Jesse, on the other hand, is credited with at least a dozen killings. (Jesse James Museum, Kearney, MO)

Henry "Bearcat" Starr bridged the desperado days of the Wild West with the modern era of bank robbing. Reputedly the nephew of "bandit queen" Belle Starr, Henry was the first bank robber to use an automobile in a hold-up—a Stutz Bearcat, hence his nickname. (Western History Collections, University of Oklahoma Libraries)

John Ashley, right, with an unidentified companion. On one
occasion Ashley phoned a bank so that tellers could put out the
money in advance of his arrival. His Everglades Gang met a violent end after they attempted to wrest control of the Florida
bootlegging industry from northern mobsters.
(Fort Lauderdale Historical Society)

In 1934, President Roosevelt created the Federal Deposit Insurance
Corporation, which made bank robbing a federal government concern.
Ardent crimestopper J. Edgar Hoover, head of the FBI, tackled the
problem with zeal.

Charles "Pretty Boy" Floyd was a professional criminal who robbed at least 60 banks. Random violence never occurred while he was committing a heist, but it did sometimes erupt when he was leaving. Floyd was inspired by the "Robin Hood" aspect of Jesse James's legend and would sometimes destroy banks' mortgage records during his hold-ups. (FBI Photo)

When Floyd was discovered hiding in the Ohio countryside, FBI agent Melvin Purvis was dispatched to find him, not necessarily to bring him back alive. Witnesses reported that after the ensuing shoot-out, Purvis ordered a posse member to finish off the wounded Floyd. The agent refused, so Purvis drew his own .38 caliber revolver and finished the job. (FBI Photo)

Harvey "Old Harve" Bailey was known during his 20-year bank robbing career as "The King of the Heist Men." He wielded a Tommy gun in the Union Station massacre, in which four lawmen were killed, and was later arrested after teaming up with Ma Barker's gang. "The old woman couldn't plan breakfast," he later opined. (FBI Photo)

J. Edgar Hoover, right, with his "sword-arm" Melvin Purvis, striding purposefully in one of many photos the FBI released to inspire public confidence. An elite, nationwide police force, the FBI, it was said, "always got its man." (FBI Photo)

Bonnie Parker is perceived by some as a frail victim of the Depression and
her own hopeless romanticism, but by others as a crazed psychopath.
(Western History Collections, University of Oklahoma Libraries)

Clyde Barrow

Bonnie's partner in crime, Clyde Barrow, did not rob banks professionally
as much as he used them to fund a nihilistic murder spree.
(Western History Collections, University of Oklahoma Libraries)

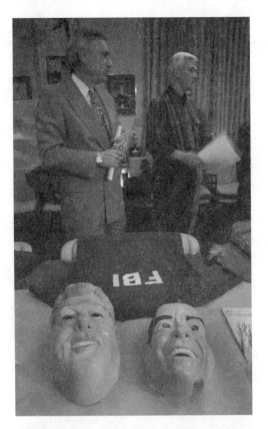

The "Midwestern Bank Bandits" were caught by the FBI in January 1996 after committing 18 robberies. At left, FBI agents David Tubbs and Max Geiman talk to reporters after raiding a house in Shawnee, Kansas, where they found some of the robbers' tools. (AP Photo/ Cliff Schiappa)

That same day the FBI's Ted Jackson, below left, held a press conference in Columbus, Ohio, where he displayed some of the bandits' guns and pipe bombs. Bank robber Peter Langan had been arrested after a shoot-out the previous day and his partner, Richard Lee Guthrie, had been picked up in Cincinnati. (AP Photo/Chris Kasson)

James "Jimmy the Gent" Burke, suspected mastermind of the 1978 Lufthansa airport heist, is led off in handcuffs in April 1979. The record take of at least $6 million was largely cash being exchanged between German and New York banks. (AP Photo)

Jimmy the Gent left a trail of bodies in his wake as he tried to evade the law; however, the FBI was able to identify six of the gang members, below. One was arrested, two were found dead, and the others are still being sought. (© Bettmann/CORBIS)

Willie "The Actor" Sutton, in 1952. A consummate professional who eschewed violence, Sutton became famous not only for his countless robberies but for escaping from high-security prisons. It was Sutton, after being asked why he robbed banks, who provided the famous rationale: "Because that's where the money is." (AP Photo)

Craig Pritchert, shown here while playing for the University of Arizona Sun Devils in 1983. At age 36, Pritchert abandoned his three children and became a bank robber, along with his 25-year-old pierced and tattooed girlfriend, Nova Guthrie. The duo pulled off at least 12 successful heists in the West. (AP Photo/The *Tribune*)

Patty Hearst, renamed Tanya by the Symbionese Liberation Army (SLA) that kidnapped her, was caught on bank surveillance cameras while participating in the SLA's hold up of a San Francisco bank in April 1974. (AP Photo)

A scene from the spectacular North Hollywood heist in 1997 when two bank robbers, wearing body armor and armed with modified AK-47s, were surprised by police. As SWAT teams converged, regular police ran to a gun store to procure heavier weapons. By the time the carnage ended, both brigands had been killed, after shooting 16 people and prompting two heart attacks. (AP Photo/*Los Angeles Daily News*)

Chapter 5

The Dunces

"Society produces the rogue so that it may punish him."
—Unknown

The people we have looked at in preceding chapters were bank robbers. Some also took on jewelry stores, grocery stores, and the occasional small business, but for the most part they struck only banks. To attain the status of a well-known bank robber, at least in the twisted view of fellow criminals, is an accomplishment. Banks, after all, comprise the richest targets and are also far more heavily defended against predators. The petty crook who robs a bank—maybe as an afterthought to another crime—is not a bank robber in the truest definition of the term. Usually such people rob liquor stores, gas stations, homeowners, convenience stores, little old ladies, Girl Scout troops, or other easy prey, and only end up pulling bank jobs by mistake.

The real bank robbers do not want to be associated with these nickel-and-dime, small-time thugs, so there is a class distinction. However, the nation's prisons are full of men and women who would love to refer to themselves as bank robbers even if they are not. What they are is a collection of armed robbers who just happened to get up enough nerve to attempt a bank robbery. Be they the actual gun-wielding desperado or the flunky who drove the car, they'll only refer to themselves as bank robbers until the prison doors slam shut behind them. Then their only audience will be inmates who know the difference between a bank robber and a punk.

In this chapter we will study some of these want-to-be bank robbers. Penitentiaries are well stocked with folks like them, so finding suitable subject matter is not a problem. The difficulty is space to fit them in, because failed practitioners of the fine art of bank robbing far outnumber those who have enjoyed success.

Curiously enough, the state of Texas figures prominently in the history of bank robbing in every era, including our own. On a recent hot summer's day a modern desperado strode into a small-town Texas bank that was within shouting distance of an army base. The robber approached the teller's cage, .45-caliber automatic in hand, ski mask on his face, and with a brusque attitude. It was payday, not only for the military but for the local community. Yet this man only got $9,000 from the tellers, and was captured within 15 minutes.

This robber made a few mistakes in his plan of operations. Our bandit was a military man; this would have explained the fatigues. It would not explain why he was wearing his own fatigues, the ones with his name and unit patch on them. Local law enforcement along with military police simply went to this man's unit and arrested him. Of course, the robber was dumbfounded that the police had caught him after his brilliant scheme. But he is now doing a stretch in a federal correctional facility in another state. His trial and conviction took just about as long as his holdup. Most other inmates refer to him as "The Fool of C-Block." He'll have several years to think about where he went wrong.

Then we have the fellow who saw the police drive up to the bank while his robbery was still in progress. He already had the money; the employees were on the floor. The police informed him through a bull horn that the bank was surrounded and he had no way out. With his vast inexperience in robbing banks he made the only self-protective choice he could think of—he locked himself in the vault! Have you ever seen a house cat who thought she was hiding from you with her tail sticking out from the hiding place? It took only minutes to extract this chap from the vault. It also took a jury only minutes to give this bank robber a little time to think in a midwestern prison. Pathetic as this story is, he's not the only convict who has pulled this maneuver.

Another midwestern bandit held up banks with a small-caliber handgun and a note. He committed several of these robberies before the authorities could establish his modus operandi. What was so different about this robber was his method of escape. He was finally captured after over a dozen successful holdups, and his escape vehicle was impounded. Witnesses had no problem identifying the robber and his 10-speed touring bike at the trial.

We also have desperadoes who accidentally shot *themselves* as they were committing the crime. Or we could examine the holdup experts who crashed their getaway cars and were captured; but, again, there are just so many of them. There is a case, however, where children committed several holdups. In the short run, these children from dysfunctional households got away with their crimes—the youngsters were eventually captured, and their parents went to prison.

We also have the lone bandit attempting to act like Jesse James by vaulting over the counter. His only problem with this maneuver was that he caught his foot in the teller's cage and crashed on the other side. He broke his arm and shoulder and threw his hip out. He wasn't all that difficult to catch as he limped along the sidewalk like the Hunchback of Notre Dame.

Another time a lone bandit entered the bank, pistol in hand, and everyone noticed him. He was the only other person in the building other than the employees. One hit the panic button immediately. It was a silent alarm, so the robber had no idea this had already happened. When he finally got into his act, employees thought he was a nut so they gave him the money—bags and bags full of it. So much, in fact, he had to use a dolly to get it all to the door. His car was only a few feet away but there were by then a platoon of cops between him and the automobile. Naturally, shooting it out with his realistic-looking BB gun was not a high priority on our robber's list of options. He chose to sit down against the building and cry. He was escorted to a waiting patrol car, muttering incoherencies to himself. Someday, he'll be able to tell his grandchildren all about what might have been—but only after he finishes his prison term.

Regrettably, a few robbers using real guns and confronted with similar situations took their own lives. Sometimes getting caught is just a whole lot better for everyone concerned. In the same vein, there have been several bandits who held on to their toy guns just a little too long and died at the hands of well-trained police officers.

Toy guns and disguises to mask the losers who perform most bank robberies are a staple of the trade. Understanding the logic behind wearing a Santa Claus outfit during a robbery—which has been done more than a few times—may be a little hard to do. However, even recently bank robbers have attempted this form of disguise, fortunately with little success. A man dressed in the red suit and shiny black shoes typical of any Saint Nick strolled into a bank in mid-December a few years ago, holding a small nickel-plated revolver in his hand. After committing his crime, the fool then had to engage in a foot race with a patrolman, all while trying to juggle the outrageous costume. Over the course of a block and a half, Santa lost his pillow, beard, hat, and whatever money he managed to get during the robbery. His real downfall were those shiny shoes, however, for the boots that covered his sneakers tore apart and tripped him up. He was captured without a struggle by the pursuing policeman, and will have plenty of time to think about just where he went wrong in his devious holiday plans.

Several other peculiar disguises have been used across the nation from time to time, often in many of the robberies chronicled here. There have been masks of Batman, Spiderman, Superman—and a whole host of presidents. There have also been monsters, skulls, clowns, pirates, gypsies, and even a gang that dressed up as the Seven Dwarfs. Of course, along with that old standby, the ski mask, a woman's stocking over the head has never completely gone out of style.

The more sordid aspect to these individuals is that a lot of them are also the killer kind of robber. Far too many holdup men today feel they need to kill the witness in order to ensure a successful heist. In the bank-robbing business this has never been the case. Most banks inform their people to hand over the money at once and not give the bandit any excuse to start shooting. Time after time we have seen armed robbers who didn't use violence get away with huge amounts of money. Why on earth do today's robbers feel they need to blow someone away? It's only the low-life thug, new to the business of sudden unauthorized banking withdrawals, who needs to use his gun. Not only is this a coward's way out of a tough situation, but it was probably part of his sorry little plan from the start.

We will look now at some of the more complicated, but no less inane, acts of dunce robbers over the years. Their stories can be amusing at times, but one can't forget that they are tragic too. They are signs of people living on the fringe of society with few options and fewer brain cells. Naturally, they constitute a recipe for disaster.

IN THE SHADOW OF BONNIE & CLYDE?

Chris has tattoos all over his body, most of them of the jailhouse variety. He has served time for entirely too many crimes to still be walking the streets, but thanks to the parole system he is out again. His experiences run the gambit, from reform school through county work farms to the Big House. Just to look at this man, most people would assume he had no self-respect. In today's parlance he looks like a bum; but then again, he would have looked like a bum in any day and age, for he is constantly dirty, with long hair, scruffy clothes and an overpowering body odor. Chris looks, and acts, like the loser he is.

Not to be outdone, Madge is also a piece of work. A regular drug user, like her boyfriend and lover, she has the same peculiar appearance. For the average man she would not be someone to take home to meet mother. Foul-mouthed, with a half dozen tattoos on her arms, legs, and chest, she has about the same odor problem as Chris. The two of them were made for each other. Not that Madge hadn't started out in life with all the comforts; she had. But over the years the drug culture she so admired had teamed her with a large number of unsavory types. Chris was merely the last in an interminable succession of derelicts she had fallen in love with.

Chris's forté has been petty theft. Most of his robberies and burglaries have been minor and were rooted in his drug dependence. Madge has been arrested a few dozen times for trafficking in drugs and for prostitution. She has even pulled several 30-day hitches in the county farm for her criminal behavior. She, too, is on parole; not that it matters much. When she needs a fix or more money to buy drugs on the open market, she simply turns to prostitution to feed her habit. What has happened to Chris and Madge was inevitable, in a way; they were both living a life of crime, and the only suspense was waiting for it all to catch up with them.

Even for Chris and Madge, the small-time robberies were only producing small-time profits. After the fences got their share, simply not enough money was left for the kind of drugs the couple needed. Of course they thought they were big-time, but this was part of the drug-induced psychoses exhibited by most addicts. Madge came up with an idea for a robbery, and Chris gave it deep thought. This whole accessory. Chris got five years for his efforts in a plea-bargain agreement for turning in his prime drug supplier; he only served a year and a half. Madge, whose family had some high-powered connections, got off with a one-year sentence and five years probation. They're back on the streets, but there have been changes. Madge had a baby in prison, and the court system let her keep it. She's still into drugs, but now lives with her family. She still engages in a little prostitution, but only when needing money for the baby. Madge qualified for state welfare and to all outward appearances, seems to want to get her life back together.

Chris, on the other hand, is back to his old lifestyle. Madge's baby is Chris' child, but he wants no part of family life. This man, just like thousands of others, is walking the streets of America killing time until he makes his next big mistake. If drugs don't kill him, or if some business owner doesn't blow him away during a robbery, Chris will remain an unlit fuse. He'll probably end up in prison someday, trying to convince someone how he used to be a bank robber. He would, no doubt, be better off getting a job in a car wash.

THE QUINCY BROTHERS

When the Dalton Gang came to their humiliating finale in Coffeeville, Kansas, one of the factors in their failure was that most of the town knew who they were. In fact, the man who sounded the alarm knew all the men, and knew that they were up to no good. One would think that few other bank robbers would ever attempt a robbery in a community where they were well known; however, stupidity has not died out since those times. There have been at least one hundred cases where the bandits were known by the personnel of the bank being robbed. Most of these cases entailed local robbers and small-town banks, but not all. Without going into a lot of detail, it's safe to say that all these robberies were solved quickly.

Of course, there's something comforting about going into a place where one knows how things are done, where there is a predictable routine one can count on. All of these robbers assumed that everyone would go along with their wishes; after all, everybody knew them or their reputation. A few of these attempted stickups ended in tragedy when the outlaw was gunned down. Many ended with the robber not getting the money because the teller thought it was a joke. And, yes, there are cases in which the thief shot an innocent bystander. Simple logic should tell the would-be holdup man that robbing their own neighborhood bank is foolish, but it still happens.

Take for instance the Quincy brothers. Three young men, all with experience in strong-armed holdups and petty burglary, decided to rob their hometown bank. The only reason this financial institution had been chosen was convenience. In a town with a population of less than twenty-five thousand the community had only one bank. Everybody in town knew the Quincy brothers since they had been children. Now in their twenties, with several assorted prison sentences under their belts, they were ready to move on to the big time. When their highly visible truck pulled up to the curb in front of the bank, and two of the brothers went in with masks on, a store owner called the sheriff.

The guns were as real as the demands of the two brothers. The teller, who had gone to school with both men, handed over everything in her drawer, about $16,000. Shouted threats about more money did nothing but confuse the bank employees. Two shots were fired into the ceiling; nothing changed. The two bandits settled on what they had and headed for the door. The third brother, still in the car, knew something was wrong when he heard the shooting. The two outlaws in the bank came out the door at about the time the sheriff and three highway patrol officers arrived. By now the third brother had a gun in his hand. The brief shoot-out only lasted about a minute. No words had been exchanged and the three brothers lay dead on the ground.

The Quincy family buried all three boys on the same day after a quick service at the local Baptist Church. All were spoken of in quiet tones, about how they had endured a troubled life. Their elderly parents could offer no reasons for the actions of their children. As far as the community was concerned, the matter was never discussed again publicly. Unfortunately, there are shades of Coffeeville all over this country.

"LITTLE JOHN" LITTLE

I'm going to refer to this man as John Little, not his real name, only because he is still doing time in a federal prison for his last bank robbery. Little was born in 1936 and grew up on a small truck farm outside Cheyenne, Wyoming. When he was seven years old, his father was killed in a train accident, and shortly after this his mother remarried. Little's new stepfather was a real "piece of work" when it came to being a good example for his stepson. He was a small-time burglar and car thief who had done time in state as well as federal prisons on three separate occasions. John's mother did her best to raise him, but he was a sickly child and a poor student.

Every time there was a small break-in or a car stolen in the general area, Little's stepfather was taken in for questioning. Soon Little himself fell in with a bad crowd and it wasn't long before he was arrested for a burglary. His mother pleaded for him and a kindly local judge placed him on probation for his first offense. By the time Little was a teenager, however, in the early 1950s, stealing cars and committing the occasional robbery was a way of life for him.

By then Little was under the felonious tutelage of his stepfather, his education including defeating the simple alarms in use at the time on most businesses. Cracking a safe was learned on the job with his stepdad. During one of these break-ins, the two of them were arrested. Little was sent to reform school and his stepfather went to prison for life as an habitual criminal. John Little was only 17 years old, and he spent just a little over a year in the institution until again, with a lot of begging from his mother, he was freed.

For the first year or so after his release, Little led an exemplary life. He got a job with a construction company as a heavy machinery operator and part time welder; he even had a steady girlfriend. On the surface everything looked normal. He kept in touch with his probation officer and the local police forgot about John Little.

About a year and a half after Little's stint in reform school he hooked up with two ex-roommates from that institution. While he had been incarcerated he had learned a lot more about burglaries and robberies than his stepfather could ever have taught him. John Little's first bank robbery took place two weeks before his twentieth birthday. The three reform school buddies took on a small-town bank in central Wyoming, gaining access by punching a hole through the wall. That first robbery netted the trio about $19,600 in cash and another $8,000 in negotiable securities.

The threesome got away clean and embarked on a somewhat elaborate spending spree. Little bought a new car and proposed to his girl-friend. The other two members of the gang purchased new cars and high-powered stereo equipment. For some reason the small community outside Cheyenne paid very little attention to Little's newfound wealth. After all, he did have a good job and seemed now to be a model citizen. That summer, he married and settled down to a work-a-day lifestyle.

Regrettably the other two felons didn't do so well. One of them was captured attempting to cash a bearer bond stolen in the heist, and then he wasted no time turning in the other two to reduce his sentence. Little and his partner were arrested and indicted for bank robbery. After a rather short trial the two were sentenced to 10 to 15 years. The third member, the rat, received a five-year suspended sentence for breaking and entering. Little began doing his time at Leavenworth in 1955.

In 1966, Little was released after serving 11 years of his sentence and he promptly returned to Wyoming. While he'd been in prison his wife had divorced him and wanted nothing to do with him. His mother had died during this time, so he really didn't have much to come home to, and being an ex-con didn't increase his chances of landing a good job. He did manage to find some part-time work but his life was miserable. The few minor burglaries he committed gave him only enough money to eat. Meanwhile, the local police were keeping an eye on him, much the same way they did his stepfather, and it didn't take Little long to discover that a life of crime was about all he had going for himself. He relocated to the Denver area and began forming a gang. His strategy, formulated while in prison, was to rob banks.

On Monday, June 19, 1967, John Little and two accomplices, all masked, walked into a branch bank in downtown Denver, Colorado. This wasn't a burglary but a full-fledged armed holdup of a federally insured bank. One of the bandits moved all the customers to one side of the room and Little, with his other partner, ordered the bank manager to open the vault, which he did. About the time the big door swung open, the bank guard pulled his .38 caliber revolver and fired a shot at the trio. The shot from the guard's gun hit the bank manager in the middle of the back and killed him instantly. Little turned and fired three shots at the guard with his .45 caliber semi-automatic. The guard slumped to the floor and died within minutes.

The outlaw who was watching all the customers attempted to keep order, but it was no use. The small crowd of people bolted for the bank door; two of them were wounded. Little and his associate scooped up as much money as they could. Now, because alarms had already been pressed, the sounds of approaching police sirens were unmistakable. A police car pulled into the rear parking area about the time the three bandits cleared the building. After a brief shoot-out with the lawmen in which one of the robbers was killed and two cops were wounded, Little and the other man escaped. The two bandits split somewhere between $123,000 and $98,000, depending on whom you believe, and headed out in separate directions. The next day John Little discovered the details of his heist: three men killed and two lawmen wounded. Little was in trouble, and he knew it.

Law-enforcement had no clues to go on in regard to this holdup. The dead bandit was identified as Thomas Thorne but the trail seemed to stop there. He had no known associates in the bank-robbing business and authorities could not trace his movements prior to the holdup. The spent shell casings from Little's automatic were no help, but an observation by a witness was interesting: one of the robbers, the one who seemed to be in charge, was very short.

John Little, true to his name, stood only five-foot-one in his socks. It didn't take the feds all that long to get a pretty good idea of who the ringleader of the gang might be. But again, nobody knew where John Little was; he had disappeared from Wyoming and there was some question as to whether he was even alive. An unconfirmed report came in that John Little had been killed in a gunfight with other robbers over a loot dispute.

A month later another Colorado bank was hit, almost an exact duplicate of the first. This time it came off without a hitch, however, and no one got hurt. The robbers carried off over $135,000 in cash. There were surveillance camera photos of the crime, but the three outlaws all wore ski masks, so the pictures were not all that helpful. The one glaring clue was the little guy standing in the middle of the trio. No doubt the same diminutive chap who was involved in the first robbery had struck again. The gang split up, Little going "on the lamb" in Omaha, Nebraska, and the entire group stayed out of sight for over a year.

Although the FBI had absolutely no proof of John Little's involvement except that he was a short bank robber, the Bureau attributed the two Colorado holdups to him. He was placed on the FBI's Most Wanted List shortly after the second heist.

Little now changed his appearance; he added elevator shoes, died his blond hair black, and grew a mustache which he also colored black. He took to wearing glasses, which he didn't need, and got a part-time job in an auto-body repair shop. By and large John Little, wanted fugitive, disappeared into the wilds of downtown Omaha. His picture was meanwhile published in several newspapers, and somewhere along the way a considerate reporter tacked on the handle "Little John" to his official description. There he was, right up there with the likes of "Pretty Boy," "Bugs," and "Killer."

In late 1969 one of the Denver robbers was apprehended committing a minor break-in of a liquor store in South Dakota. The man, a convicted armed robber, had done two hitches in the past and was looking to cut a deal. He was not, however, even a suspect in the Denver holdups. To save himself from a conviction as a career criminal and a life sentence, he copped to the Colorado robberies and started naming names, confirming the FBI's suspicions that John Little was, indeed, the mastermind of the robberies and murders in the Colorado holdup.

An all-out manhunt for Little resulted in his arrest in Omaha in March 1970. While he was being taken from Omaha to Denver to stand trial he managed to escape from the two deputies assigned to the transfer, and thanks to a series of mixed signals by lawmen, Little remained at large. He was eventually sighted in the Boulder, Colorado area in mid-July 1971. The community of Boulder was blanketed by over a hundred lawmen to no avail; John Little appeared to have escaped again.

By August 1971, Little was going to attempt what would be his last bank robbery. As a wanted man he really had no friends he could trust. He also knew that if he were captured he would spend the rest of his life behind bars or be executed. He'd committed a few minor burglaries within the last year by himself and had gotten away with them. He only wanted one more score and then he would leave the country. He thought if he could just pull off another bank job—by himself—all his troubles would be over. He could live a comfortable life in a foreign country and give up this life of crime.

The bank Little chose for this final heist was on the outskirts of Colorado Springs. It was a flat-roofed affair with a false western front extending up past the roof line which would give him cover while he was working to gain access through the roof and into the vault. He cased the target, found that it would be a moderately big score, and planned to begin on Saturday night and be gone by very early Sunday morning.

There was little traffic through the area during the weekend, so he figured he wouldn't be bothered. By 10 P.M., he had already taken out the alarm system. At two in the morning nobody heard the muffled explosion that ripped a three-and-a-half-foot hole in the roof of the bank. Below lay the vault, and Little's cutting torch made short work of opening up an orifice big enough for his small body. The two-by-two steel plate crashed to the floor of the vault. Little dropped in the three burlap bags and his pry bar; even his little sack lunch made the trip. Everything looked like a go, so Little himself plunged into the center of the vault.

It only took about a minute for "Little John" Little to understand his only mistake in this, the last of his robberies. It would be hard to tell what gave him his first clue; maybe it was the twisting of his ankle when he hit the floor. Or it could have been when he began to look around the vault and noticed that all the money was along the walls, in shelves. Most likely it was that sickening feeling in the pit of his stomach when he realized he had forgotten his rope. The ceiling of the old vault loomed eight and a half feet above the floor, somewhat out of reach for the five-foot-one-inch burglar. Worse, there was absolutely nothing in the vault which could be moved into place for him to stand on.

Not to be dissuaded, Little thought if he just stacked up the money, about $145,000, he could at least reach the hole in the ceiling and maybe his rope. But that was another problem. He had thought there was about half a million dollars in this bank, but he found quite a bit less than that. The paltry pile of money would only get Little about two and a half feet off the floor, and he would still be about eight inches short of the hole. Of course he couldn't jump up, off a stack of used bills, and reach the ceiling. He tried it and the money kept falling down, as did Little on his twisted ankle. He knew he must resign himself to his fate.

Little passed the rest of what was left of Sunday dreaming about what could have been. He didn't have a gun, so he knew he was going to have to come up with something really unique when the bank opened on Monday morning. He planned to hide, just out of sight of the open vault door, and surprise whoever unlocked it. He planned to put his hand in his sack lunch bag and pretend he had a gun. Maybe they would buy it.

What Little failed to consider was the effect his blast had had when he blew the hole in the ceiling. Although it had not been a huge blast, it had knocked ceiling tiles to the floor and left a fine coating of dust all over the bank lobby, which was noticed as soon as the vice president of the bank entered the building. At that moment, Little didn't know there was anybody in the bank, but he was ready. When the door of the vault swung open, out jumped Little into the waiting gunsights of over two dozen cops. "Little John" Little's only comment, as he slowly raised his hands above his head was, "I guess I screwed up!"

Little was tried and convicted of three Colorado bank robberies and the second-degree murders of three people: one bank officer, one guard, and one of his accomplices. Little was 63 years old in 1999, and he will be eligible for parole sometime in the late 2030s.

THE COLUMBIA, MISSOURI, ROBBERY

While some parts of the John Little story may be amusing, the next story—about an unfunny and brutal holdup in May 1994 in a small town just outside Columbia, Missouri—demonstrates just how terrible the crime of bank robbing can be. Because of an ongoing investigation, and pending litigation concerning this robbery, there are a few details which I cannot go into.

A man and a woman entered the bank at about 10 A.M. The gentleman was holding a shotgun and the woman carried a semi-automatic pistol. There was no question as to what their intentions were in the bank, and an employee responded accordingly, hitting the alarm button. It was a silent alarm, so no signal was ever heard by the robbers. Because the police station was almost across the street, the cops got there about the time the robbers were declaring that this was, indeed, a holdup.

The officers opted to stay outside the bank. The robbers, seeing them there, were left with only a few choices. They scooped up the tellers' cash and grabbed one of the bank employees to use as a hostage and shield. The local police decided not to confront the robbers, and allowed them to exit the bank and enter their getaway car. The local constabulary notified the State Highway Patrol and the county sheriff's office.

Up to this point all that was known was that two armed bank robbers with a hostage were heading out of town on a major highway. When the bandits reached the highway they stopped the car. None of the police officers heard the shot or even saw what happened, but suddenly the door of the getaway car opened and out fell the body of the bank employee. The robbers then roared on down the highway.

The bank employee had been killed with a single shotgun blast to the head. By now the sheriff's office had dispatched two cars, as had the Highway Patrol. Within six minutes of the robbery the state police had their helicopter dispatched to the area. Within a few more minutes this aircraft was over the getaway car and the police in the helicopter saw the body on the side of the road. By radio they were informed that now they were not only dealing with bank robbers but also cold-blooded killers.

The chase lasted about 20 minutes with the outlaws and lawmen exchanging gunfire. As the chopper made a low pass over the bandit's car, it received a hit from the shotgun-wielding killer. The pilot was wounded and forced to land. Other lawmen now forced the driver of the getaway car, the woman, onto a side road. When the car screeched to a halt, the cops surrounded the bandits. Bullhorns were used to convince the robbers to surrender, but this wasn't to be.

Seasoned lawmen, hardened to their chosen profession, stood aghast as the female bandit got out of the car. She turned, pointed her weapon at her companion and fired at the precise second when her male counterpart fired his shotgun. She staggered a few feet and collapsed on the side of the road; the man came out the other car door and died just outside of it. The woman died from a blast to the chest; the man from a gaping head wound. Kansas City and St. Louis television stations dispatched their own helicopters so they had a view of the dead suspects.

The two robbers had decided to kill each other rather than take process only took a couple of hours and the robbery of their first bank was on for the next day. They both honestly believed it was going to be their big score—the ticket to the major leagues of crime.

Chris had to get a gun and even the guy who sold it warned him it might blow up. Well, for $10 it didn't have to work, it just had to look as if it would. The linchpin of their strategy was to borrow a get-away car, and they got one from a friend without telling him it was to be used in a bank robbery. That evening there was lovemaking, lots of beer, and great dope. Both of them knew that tomorrow was going to be the biggest day in their lives. Hell, by tomorrow night they were going to be rich. Madge suggested that they move to Europe and live "the good life" after the robbery. Chris was more inclined to Mexico. Either way, everything was looking good the night before the heist.

Chris sauntered into the bank at about 11 A.M.; Madge was parked at the curb with the motor running. Chris didn't even see the guard walking up behind him as he was trying to get his gun out of his waistband. "Big Tim" McQuire, an off-duty metro police officer, was without a doubt the wrong man for Chris to mess with. The cop out-weighed the emaciated bandit by 60 pounds and was built like a weightlifter. As officer McQuire stuck his 9mm automatic into the back of Chris's head his comments were short: "Drop the gun, punk, or your brains will decorate most of this lobby."

Chris was stupid but he wasn't suicidal; he managed to do two things at once on the officer's command. He dropped the gun and wet his pants. Then, suddenly Chris was on the floor. In fact, it happened so fast and hard it knocked the wind out of him. He wasn't even aware of being handcuffed by the big cop. Officer McQuire then reached for his belt radio. "OK, dip-shit, who's sitting in the car out front?" Chris was glad to give the policeman a very detailed description. He even went so far as to describe what Madge was wearing, her hair color, and her name. Officer McQuire passed this information on to his dispatcher by radio. Madge never had a chance; she was dragged out of the car and spread-eagled on the sidewalk. The four plain-clothed detectives who accomplished this also noticed a pungent odor of urine about her.

When the trial came up, Chris was charged with attempted bank robbery, although he had never uttered a word in the bank that he was making a holdup. Madge was charged along the same lines as an their chances in a shoot-out with the cops. When the outlaws' bodies were examined it was established that no police bullets had caused their deaths. The robbers had died at their own hands. This fact was never carried on the local radio or television stations, but the Bonnie and Clyde aspect was played for all it was worth. The murdered bank employee, a father of two, received only a casual comment. The robbers' haul was less than $10,000.

In contrast to the days of Bonnie and Clyde, many rural American communities do have plans and systems in place to deal with possible bank robberies. And not only are most of the highways patrolled today by the state police, but the local county sheriffs have a strategy. No longer can bandits make a run like they used to. In the old days little banks in towns like Columbia, Missouri, were isolated; those days are over. The roads and even the air can be covered on short notice, the bandits caught like flies in a web.

There is the occasional holdup today where the bandits get away, but this couple was not so fortunate. When the robbers were confronted by the overwhelming response of law enforcement they took the quickest way out. If they had chosen to shoot it out with the lawmen their fates would have been equally sealed.

THE BOMB SQUAD

A little west of the Columbia tragedy, two men armed with a bomb robbed another bank the same day in Kansas City, Missouri. These outlaws made a threat about blowing up the building if they didn't get what they wanted—which did not make all that much sense but was taken seriously by the lawmen nonetheless.

This time the bank employees handed over the funds and the robbers left a little souvenir as a thank you. It took the city's metro bomb squad about a half hour to disarm the thing while the two robbers got away. The two crooks continued to pull jobs, using the same exact modus operandi, for over a year. Eventually, it was discovered that the two men responsible for this robbery had been wanted in connection with over a dozen similar robberies all across the nation. It was believed that there were more than two men using this same modus operandi. In early 1996, some of their bomb-making equipment was discovered in a storage facility in Johnson County, Kansas, by federal investigators.

An arrest was made in connection to at least three bank robberies in the Kansas City area that tied back to other robberies in other parts of the country. Two men were taken into custody and charged in the entire string of holdups. One of the bandits rolled over and named two other men as accomplices. This gang of men had been tied to at least a dozen and a half holdups which used the same bomb ruse. The bombs, however, were not fake. They were the real thing, and the damage one of these contraptions could have caused was significant. These robbers were not only prepared to use explosive devices, but they also showed a total disregard for the employees, or police bomb squad technicians, who might come in contact with the bombs. Richard Lee Guthrie Jr., was one of the men captured for this string of robberies. Guthrie hanged himself in his cell in Covington, Kentucky, in July 1996, rather than face conviction on 19 counts of bank robbery. Others charged were Peter K. Langan, Scott Anthony Stedeford, and Kevin McCarthy. These men will be indicted for federal explosives offenses as well as for bank robbery.

THE ROOKIE

I'll refer to this man as Kenny only because he'll be incarcerated for the next seven years and releasing his actual name would not be helpful for his life after prison. Kenny walked into a bank confident that he had covered all the bases needed to pull off a robbery. He gave the teller his note and waited for her to comply with his wishes. His bag was filled with approximately $10,000—an awesome amount for a first-time robbery, Kenny thought as he left the building.

Not unlike several thousand bank robbers before him, Kenny went on a spending spree almost immediately. He paid off a few bills and bought a few baubles for himself and his girlfriend. *This bank robbery business is really an easy way to get money*, he must have thought, as he planned another. Sadly, he didn't get the chance to put his second foolproof plan into motion; he was arrested by the FBI two days after his first robbery.

Kenny had only made one mistake. After he left the bank, the teller he had given the note to noticed a pad lying on the counter. When she picked it up, it appeared to be a checkbook, complete with address, phone, and account number—Kenny's checkbook. The only reason he hadn't been arrested the same day as the robbery was that he hadn't gone home yet. Kenny was pounced upon by FBI agents as soon as he arrived at his residence. Seven years was a charitable sentence for Kenny. At least he won't have to explain his first and last robbery too often.

PAT O'KEEF

Some people, like Kenny, try to rob banks without any sense of the expert knowledge it takes to commit such a crime. Others, such as Pat O'Keef, make crime their life and explore all the avenues of the lifestyle before robbing banks. In the end, of course, men like O'Keef often end up meeting the same fate as poor, misguided Kenny.

When Pat O'Keef walked into a room, people noticed. He was well over six foot, six inches tall, and weighed at least 300 pounds. Raised in a good Catholic home, he had even been an altar boy. There's no way to tell what happened to Pat, but somewhere along the way he turned mean. Even in grade school he was the school bully, and as he got older he just got vicious. If there was only one fight after school for the entire week, you could bet that Pat O'Keef was either in it or starting it. By the time he finished grade school he had already been arrested for biting off the ear of another kid. He'd also been taken before a juvenile judge for killing small animals half a dozen times. His mother and father had been warned that their boy was heading for trouble.

High school just made matters worse. O'Keef didn't like high school so he spent very little time there. Fighting was again a problem, but now he was over six feet tall and weighed about 200 pounds. O'Keef would not take any guff from anyone, and this included his parents. Teachers were deathly afraid of him, as were most of the other kids in school. Girls only went out with him once, and considered themselves very lucky if they weren't raped. By this time O'Keef was beginning to have little run-ins with the cops. He had stolen a car for a joyride and was arrested after he wrecked it. The judge gave him probation and again warned his mother and father, "You had better do something with that boy or he's going to kill somebody someday." When O'Keef was 17 years old, a man who had been drinking staggered into him as he came out of a bar. The drunk—who was almost as big as O'Keef—made some comments about O'Keef's relationship with his mother and the fight was on. But the drunk was no match for Pat O'Keef. Bystanders attempted to break it up but O'Keef just wouldn't leave it alone. It could have been over in a matter of seconds but O'Keef wouldn't finish the man off. He hit him hard enough and often enough to break three ribs, his jaw bone, and three smaller bones in his face, causing blood to flow everywhere. O'Keef was giving this man a real beating, and no one wanted to step in between the two for fear of O'Keef's turning on them. Finally the drunk slumped to the sidewalk. An ambulance was called but the medics on the scene knew the man was dead when they drove off with his body. The police arrived and took statements from everyone, but no one was willing to tell the truth about what had happened. It was simply a fight between an abusive drunk and a teenager. Officially the man died because of a massive head injury in a fistfight. Everyone else knew that Pat O'Keef had beaten the man to death and gotten away with it.

Seventeen years old or not, his mother and father had seen enough; O'Keef was asked to move out of the house. They said they didn't really care where he went, but he wasn't welcome anymore. Young O'Keef moved in with a group of bikers who had a flophouse a few miles out of town. Now he could do what he wanted to do: drink beer all day long, smoke a little dope when he had it, and he didn't have to go to school.

O'Keef blended in with the rest of the trash living in the house. And, because of his reputation and size, the other men didn't mess with him. Petty break-ins were now how he got his money—something the rest of the flophouse taught him how to do. But the nickel-and-dime robberies couldn't produce the kind of money O'Keef wanted. Over the next three years the young man evolved into a long-haired, leather-clad, motorcycle gang member. His new circle of friends had graduated to armed robberies and O'Keef was a natural. Because of his size he really didn't need a gun for a strong-armed holdup; in fact, he pulled off a few stickups with only a tire iron. Along with several others of this group he was arrested a number of times for the investigation of robberies, but he was never convicted because the victims, or the eyewitnesses, refused to identify him.

The afternoon of January, 23, 1981, Pat O'Keef and two other men walked into a midtown bank. The bank guard made a mistake by stepping in front of O'Keef in an effort to block their passage, and O'Keef hit him in the head with the butt of a sawed-off shotgun—a blow which assigned the man to a coma.

The two other bandits approached the tellers' cages and demanded all the cash. In a matter of 10 minutes it was over. The three robbers ran around the corner and jumped on their bikes to roar out of town. Two and a half hours later, the FBI and local authorities had surrounded the flophouse. O'Keef attempted to convince his associates to take their chances in a shoot-out with the cops, but was talked out of this by wiser heads. The three bank robbers were arrested along with a host of others. A search of the house revealed that there was enough dope there to start a drugstore. DEA (Drug Enforcement Administration) officers and state police were summoned. Stolen goods by the truckload were removed for evidence. By all outward appearances the lawmen had hit the jackpot. The stolen money from the bank robbery, $28,000, was recovered.

Pat O'Keef and his two associates were sentenced to 26 years each for their part in the bank robbery. The other cases for the possession of dope and stolen goods didn't fair as well, however. Most of them were thrown out because the search warrants had not been correct, but the bank robbery conviction stood. O'Keef was going to do his time in a federal prison.

There O'Keef fell in with members of the Aryan Nation and passed his time without a lot of hassle from other inmates. Seven and a half years later he was released because of overcrowding. Although his prison time was a little inconvenient for O'Keef, prison also gave him an education he couldn't have paid for anywhere else. In this short time O'Keef learned everything he needed to know about robbing banks—or so he thought. And he got the chance to put all this new information to good use in a very short time. Back with his biker buddies, they planned another bank job. This time Pat O'Keef was going to be the leader and there weren't going to be any mistakes.

At 10 A.M. on the morning of July 15, 1991, four men burst through the double doors of the First Metropolitan Bank of Carrol

County, a small community on the outskirts of Minneapolis. Pat was in the lead when they approached the tellers' cages. Though unknown to them, the alarms had already been sounded when O'Keef ordered the vice president of the bank to open the vault; two of the other robbers, meanwhile, cleaned out the tellers' drawers.

Up to this point everything seemed to be running like clockwork. Three bags of money were filled up and the robbers were heading through the door when all hell broke loose. The robbers saw the cops at about the same time the cops opened fire. Two of the leather-covered outlaws were killed instantly in a hail of gunfire. O'Keef and the other robber, although both were slightly wounded, ducked back into the bank building. This show of police force was no accident, nor was it a standard response to a bank robbery. O'Keef and his biker buddies had been under surveillance by local as well as state lawmen for several months following his release from prison, and they were ready to deal with the criminals at the first chance they got.

Bank patrons and employees started screaming when the bandits reentered the lobby. There was now no way out the front door and the back door was also covered by lawmen. The only thing the robbers had going for themselves was the hostages. In about an hour the FBI took charge of the situation, showing up with several agents, a hostage negotiator, and a SWAT team. When the phone rang in the bank and the mediator wanted to speak to the man in charge, O'Keef took the call.

It was so simple even O'Keef could understand it: "You release the hostages and come out of the bank, unarmed, or we're coming in after you!" A little dumbfounded, O'Keef asked if there were any other options. The FBI agent on the other end of the line, although friendly, was very firm: "We don't deal with kidnappers or bank robbers. You have 15 minutes to make up your mind." Of course, one thing O'Keef didn't know was that the federal SWAT team had slipped into position overlooking the bank entrances.

O'Keef told the FBI agent that he had hostages and that he and his friends were prepared to shoot them if need be. The agent told him, "Go ahead, but we'll be in the lobby with you in about six minutes." O'Keef said he had to think, and he would call him back. The agent called O'Keef three minutes later. Again the terms were to come out the front door, unarmed, and nothing would happen to them.

The two outlaws, figuring the agents wouldn't shoot helpless female hostages, grabbed two women and headed for the door. Both men had guns in their hands when they came out of the building. The agent in charge now gave both men one more command to drop their weapons and turn the women loose. His request was answered by a shotgun blast from O'Keef's 12-gauge. Only two more shots were fired that day—FBI sharpshooters hit both men, simultaneously, in the center of the forehead.

The bank-robbing career of Pat O'Keef had ended in a pile of blood-soaked leather on a city street in a midwestern town. O'Keef had always gotten his way because he was big and brutal. He figured the lawmen were going to back down; after all, everyone he had ever faced in his entire life had done just that. This could explain the ridiculous look on the bully's face when the bullet hit him. It has been described to me as a look of total disbelief.

WALLY, THE CAR-WASH AMATEUR

Tragedy such as Pat O'Keef's is not as uncommon as lawmen would like it to be. Take, for example, the story of Wally. This young man was only 17 when he attempted to pull off his first bank robbery. The bank teller slapped his hand as he was reaching for a stack of bills inadvertently left unattended by the teller. Wally got no more than a good ass-chewing for his efforts and a short sermon on the meaning of "Thou shalt not steal." Wally, however, didn't seem phased by such admonishments. A few years later he was arrested for shoplifting, then was arrested for car theft. He would spend two years in prison for the car heist, and Wally's stint in the penitentiary put him in contact with several known bank robbers, none of whom were very good at their chosen profession. Nonetheless, those who can't do teach, and Wally was an eager student.

When Wally was released he went straight for about two years, getting a job in a car wash. But the bank across the street from the car wash attracted his keen interest. He could set his watch by the time the armored car arrived each day. Friday seemed like the best day of the week; on those afternoons the bank took in a flat cart obviously filled with sacks of money. "Someday I'm going to rob that bank on a

Friday," Wally told his fellow employees. Most of them ignored him because he was known to exaggerate from time to time. Wally, however, was serious.

Wally, who lived alone, began to plan his first and, hopefully, his last bank robbery. There was just so much money in that bank on a Friday that he wouldn't have to rob anything else for the rest of his life. At least this is what he thought. All he had to do was get away. He bought a gun; he already had a car, and he set the following Friday as the date for his big bank heist. All week long Wally watched the armored car drive up to, and away from, the door of the bank, all the while dreaming of the riches he would have in just a few short days.

On Friday, Wally excused himself from the line in the car wash and headed for the men's room. Five minutes later he was following the flat cart full of money through the double doors of the bank. His automobile was parked in the alley next to the building. All he had to do was get the money and run to his car 20 yards away. When the armored car guards reached the lobby of the bank, Wally pulled his pistol. "This is a stick up! Everybody put up your hands!" There were about 125 people in the bank. Wally never saw where the shots came from.

Two off duty police officers fired at almost the same instant. Two bank guards fired a split second later. One of the armored car guards fired two shots. Wally went to his knees, his gun still in his hand. Of course Wally would never know exactly what those nine bullets did to his body—he was dead before he hit the ground.

All of his car-washing buddies would see Wally taken out of the bank on a stretcher. They would see him loaded into the coroner's van and driven downtown. The comments among his co-workers were all about the same: "We thought he was kidding!" Wally met the same fate that befalls at least one holdup man or bank robber about 10 times a month in the United States. The armed robber is shot to death by well-trained law-enforcement people.

The instructions Wally had received from his prison mates didn't include contingencies such as what to when a bank lobby is full of people, or how to react to heavy gunfire from a bank's employees. It didn't help that the young man himself was a fool, and paid the ultimate price for his stupidity. But, as sure as God makes little green apples, another Wally will walk into a bank with robbery on his mind.

This Wally, Bud, or Bubba will also most likely end his career in robbing banks on a stretcher headed for the coroner's office.

ROBERT GRIMES

Robert Grimes had been born in a rundown section of New Orleans and his father took off when he was just a child. People who knew him well eventually called him "Snuffy" because of his cocaine habit. "Snuffy" was a product not only of a broken home but of the streets as well. He turned to petty crime before he was 10 years old. Breaking and entering was his crime of choice when he was a child, but when he was 13 years old he stole a car and was sentenced to a year and a half in a reformatory. Grimes's social peers all had similar criminal records, so he didn't stick out all that much. His older sister, Angela, had gone into a life of crime, so to speak, when she became a 15-year-old hooker.

Grimes was a coke addict by the time he was in his twenties and supported the habit with countless minor robberies and burglaries. Taking on a bank seemed a logical solution to "Snuffy's" problems. It took so much hot merchandise to get so little money from the local fence, why not go after a bank and get lots of money at one time? After all, he had used a gun in a couple of his holdups; how could a bank be that much different?

The local cops knew he was a burglar and small-time holdup man, although he had never done serious time. They never suspected he would try to rob a bank—it simply did not fit his profile. Grimes's two associates for his bank heist were so similar to him that they could have passed for brothers. They, too, were minor thieves and junkies. They had also been in trouble with the law since they were kids. This little gang of three was going to show the world, and their friends, that they had what it took to pull off a bank job. After a night of smoking crack, the three robbers were prepared to go.

At 10:15 A.M., on July 5, 1995, Grimes and an accomplice entered the downtown lobby of one of Oklahoma City's biggest state banks. Both men had sawed-off shotguns. The third man, behind the wheel of the getaway car, had a pistol. The two inside men were wearing the obligatory ski masks. "Snuffy" and his partner rushed the tellers' cages brandishing their weapons, and notified the 30 people inside that this was a stickup. A junior bank officer hit a silent alarm button on her desk and then went along with the other hostages to the far side of the lobby. The bandits cleaned out all the drawers, scoring about $21,000, and stuffed the money into two pillow cases.

Grimes and his partner headed for the door and their getaway car. About the time they got into the stolen Buick, a police car came screeching to a halt in front of them. A second, then a third, and finally a fourth came in from the rear and blocked the robbers' exit. "Snuffy" and the driver jumped out of the car and fired at the lawmen. Grimes was hit in the leg and shoulder and went down immediately. Grimes's partner, attempting to get out of the backseat while still firing his gun, was hit in the head and killed instantly. He crumpled half in and half out of the car, what was left of his head lying on the street. The driver took two police bullets, one in the chest and one in the back; he would die within an hour.

The police officers rolled Grimes and the barely alive wheel man over on their stomachs and cuffed them. Our desperadoes' "moment of glory" lasted about 13 minutes from the time they had entered the bank. The shoot-out with police took only a minute and a half. Less than 10 shots had been fired by the lawmen. No one had been wounded by the bandits, although a few passing cars sustained minor bullet damage from the outlaws' weapons. The crowd gathered around the fallen outlaws and stared with amazement at the carnage.

Robert "Snuffy" Grimes was charged with bank robbery and two counts of second-degree murder. The stolen car and assorted weapons charges were added on for good measure, and Grimes received 38 years for his first bank job. He will spend the rest of this decade, and a good deal of the next, trying to decide whether his 13 minutes of fame were really worth it.

One of the overriding facts contributing to today's rash of killings during holdups is the epidemic of drug abuse in our nation. A thief, high on something or needing a fix, is more likely to kill than his straight counterparts, who, though they may be equally nefarious, are at least not subject to a chemical imbalance. The drug user's bank robbery, thought out during a euphoric high or within the depression of withdrawal, is usually doomed from the start. An old adage still holds true, "Never get between an addict and his habit; someone will always get hurt." Prisons are bursting with young drug-addicted bank robbers who only wanted to score another big drug deal.

JAMES KIMBALL

This next story about a career criminal is also tragic in a way— another person lost to a life of crime. James Kimball is a bank robber, of sorts, who escaped from his last job with $165,000 in stolen cash. It took investigators from the FBI three months to capture him after this last robbery, and he is currently behind bars. He should be doing the biggest part of a four year sentence for bank robbery—that is, if he doesn't die first.

Kimball's first conviction came after he stole a truck when he was just 15 years old. He got three years in a detention center for that crime and was later convicted for writing bad checks, committing forgery, fraud, and stealing. Kimball has been in and out of jail for most of his adult life. He was married twice, and both times was divorced while behind bars. He has been convicted and sentenced on federal and state charges nine times in four different states.

The last bank robbery of Kimball's career was committed in the First National Bank of Hutchison, Kansas, around noon on June 28, 1994. Kimball walked into the bank and requested an audience with one of the bank's officers. About halfway through a very superficial conversation, he handed the woman a note telling her that this was a holdup. He was holding a box, which he said contained a bomb, and he would use it if she didn't fill up another box with $100, $50, and $20 bills. The "bomb" was an empty Chlorox detergent box, but the bank officer didn't know that. The banker filled the robber's order with $165,000 in assorted denominations. She later said that Kimball was very charming and polite during their encounter and she had a hard time believing he would really blow up the bank. Nevertheless, she smartly followed his instructions to avoid any problems.

When Kimball left the bank he proceeded to Wichita by bus, where he spent some of the stolen money on a whole new wardrobe. This included Western shirts, boots, a hat, a belt, and new pants; he had no problem living it up on some of what he'd taken. Kimball then chartered a private plane to Albuquerque, New Mexico, where he remained for only one day before moving on to the Denver area; there he stayed in a downtown motel that cost him $250 a night. During the day he would rent a limousine and take day trips to mountain gambling resorts.

His next stop was Los Angeles and a $90 per night downtown hotel. He had a few bad teeth taken care of and struck up a relationship with a once wealthy woman in Beverly Hills. They spent their time playing gin rummy and seeing the sights. Kimball never attempted to hide after his bank robbery. He did, however, use another name while he was basking in the California sunshine. And he only made one serious mistake: he returned to Denver and attempted to use the same limo driver he had employed on his first visit. Of course the FBI hadn't been sitting on their hands all this time; they had already talked to the driver. Kimball was arrested in Denver without a struggle.

James Kimball had been in poor health for several years; he had even had one lung removed because of cancer. Everyone who met the man had the same thing to say about him: he was a class act, a gentleman, one of a kind. Even the Beverly Hills socialite was shocked to hear of his arrest for bank robbery; she couldn't believe that her friend was a holdup man. Kimball's own words describe his feelings about his spending spree: "No matter what they do to me, no matter how long they keep me in jail or even if I die here, they can't take away those few months I had."

There are a few final things I should mention about Mr. Kimball. He had just been released from Leavenworth four days before his $165,000 dollar bank robbery. He had been paroled after serving four years on a five-year sentence for forgery and theft. True, he was dying of cancer; even the judge who sentenced him for the robbery said, "If I thought you'd live longer than this sentence, I'd make the sentence longer." If anyone was cognizant of the odds against him, James Kimball was. After all, when Kimball was arrested in 1994 for his bank robbery, he was 71 years old.

BETTY OLDHAM

Another example of a sadly misguided person led into a business that was over her head is Betty Oldham. Her career in robbing banks was short-lived; she really only robbed one. In fact, even to call her a bank robber is an injustice to others in the trade. She held up her first bank when she was 21 years old while high on pot. The only reason she got away with it was that it was so unusual for a woman to walk into a downtown bank with robbery on her mind. The employees went along with her wishes and filled up her little sack because she was holding a very big gun. She was so nervous, and obviously high on something, they didn't want to take any chances of making her mad. Her first armed robbery succeeded in that she did get away with it and no one knew who she was. For the benefit of the cameras she had worn a wig and big sunglasses.

Women in the bank robbing profession are rare. There are perhaps more robberies committed by women than are reported in the news, but they don't happen often. In most cases women accompany a male associate in the commission of the crime; for them to act alone is rare. This in itself made Oldham's little $4,400 holdup something the authorities wanted to look into further.

If we were to look into Oldham's background I doubt we would find much pointing her toward robbing banks for a living. She was a normal little girl with a very bad temper. Raised with two brothers in the South, at a young age she knew how to stand up for herself. Even the other little boys didn't mess with Oldham. She'd knock a kid on his butt in a heartbeat. She had a predictable adolescence and dated several different boys in high school; Oldham had a reputation for being nice, but you didn't get fresh with her.

After high school, in the early sixties, Oldham started running with a fast crowd. She was swept into the anti-Vietnam War frenzy and became immersed, as well, in the hippy lifestyle of psychedelic drugs, tie-dyed clothes, and unburdened romances. Oldham developed a taste for marijuana and LSD, and it wasn't uncommon to find her in a dream world of her own throughout her early twenties. Living in one flophouse after another with one grungy boyfriend after another and no visible means of support seemed to be her lot in life. She was part of the decade's lost generation. Of course, the reason for her first bank heist was to get money for more drugs. After the holdup she was unsure where the money had come from. She had no accomplices; she had acted alone, using a stolen gun. Her second bank job was thought out a little better.

In 1971, Southern California became the scene for this woman's last cognizant act. Oldham walked into this second bank like she meant business. Her commands were met by all employees and no buttons were pushed. That big .44 Magnum she was carrying had a tendency to govern everyone's actions. She walked to the counter, laid the bag in front of the first teller, and from then on everything went wrong. Two employees bolted for a door and Oldham took a shot at them. She missed, but by then she had lost control of the situation. Two more shots were fired and a general panic erupted in the lobby of the bank. People ran for the doors, leaving no one to fill up her bag. By then, she didn't know what to do; she simply backed herself into a little office when the cops took over the lobby. They were shouting things at her but she didn't understand what they were saying. Oldham had taken a hit of LSD just before she entered the bank and now the stuff had kicked in. She was losing it and she knew it. A sense of panic overwhelmed her and she began to cry.

Two officers, one on each side of the office door, told her to throw out her weapon and come out with her hands up. Dozens of people were looking at her. This crowd was in total disbelief and amazement when Oldham placed the massive handgun under her chin and fired a single shot. I would like to report that when Oldham came to everything was going to be all right, but this isn't the case; she was taken to a hospital in very critical condition. The bullet had gone through her mouth, through her sinus cavities, severed the optic nerve, then passed through her brain and out of the top of her head.

Oldham's body healed as well as could be expected. She was alive, but that was about all. She can't speak, she is all but totally blind and her brain will never function normally again. She has very little control over most of her bodily functions. After several months she could walk, but only if she could feel what was around her and had help. She likes to be seated by a window with the sunshine on her face, and she tends to play with her fingers, tracing the sill. Oldham had been a very pretty young lady, and even now is still attractive. Her right eyelid droops a little, and the only visible signs of the shooting are the scars on the underside of her face and top of her head. Her family visits once in a while, but she doesn't know who they are. She will spend the rest of her life in a state hospital for the criminally insane as a ward of the state, and will remain so until she dies. Today she is 50 years old and has already been in this same institution for 12 years. She still doesn't know her own name or where she is.

Was Betty Oldham a bank robber? The answer would have to be yes and no. She pulled off one successful heist and was never indicted or convicted of robbing a bank. When it was determined what shape she would remain in, all charges were dropped. At first there was belief that she might recover from her wounds, but this never came about. In essence, Betty Oldham received a life sentence for her one productive bank robbery. For all practical purposes, Betty's life ended when she was about 21 years old.

OTHER DUNCES

There are so many tales of idiocy among bank robbers that I think a few more should be included here. Some are tragic, some are violent, and some are so ridiculous that it's difficult not to laugh at how people can be so incredibly dumb. It is easy to see today why the FBI has lost a lot of its interest in bank robbers: there are simply not enough good ones left in the business.

Take, for instance, a 26-six-year-old man named Jerod Class. He walked into a Norfolk, Virginia, bank on December 10, 1994, high on PCP, and demanded money at gunpoint. His wishes were met immediately, but as he turned to leave a guard went for a sidearm. Class fired and killed the guard instantly; when he exited the bank he was met by three armed city police officers. Firing his 9mm semi-automatic assault pistol, he charged the lawmen. One officer was hit, but his vest protected him from death. Class was hit three times by the lawmen's bullets but the PCP kept him coming. In fact, he was shot four more times but still didn't go down. His gun empty, Class attempted to reload, but at this time one of the police officers blew off the biggest part of his head with a shotgun blast. Only then did the bandit succumb to his wounds. Not counting the shotgun blast, he had been shot seven times to very little effect.

Jerod Class had been successful at dealing drugs, but this was his first attempt at robbing banks. Most notable drug dealers do not imbibe their own product, but Class was an exception. While high on

PCP his actions were unpredictable. The reason he was so hard to stop outside the bank was the power of the drug. In effect his body was unaware it had been wounded; the fact just didn't register in his mind. Local citizens who knew Class were conscious of his drug habit and were not surprised at the tragic results of his failed bank robbery.

On average, an incident such as this will occur once a month somewhere within the continental United States. There are also hundreds of men just like Class doing time. The only reason they are in prison is that the cops weren't forced to use their weapons as they'd been with Class.

A somewhat different case occurred when three men who could not speak English walked into a Minnesota Bank and Trust. The three were illegal Mexican aliens who had been in the United States for four days at the time of their holdup.

Poor communications was the root of the overall confusion during this heist. The tellers, although willing to do anything to accommodate the robbers, had no idea what they were talking about. The robbers, frustrated at not being able to communicate their wishes, became violent. One of the tellers was struck over the head with the barrel of a sawed-off shotgun and fell to the floor unconscious. Another woman was struck in the face with a fist by the leader of the gang, and was knocked to the floor. Several people, customers of the bank, bolted for the door, and shots were fired by the bandits, but luckily no one was hit.

A police officer passing by the bank at the time of the robbery now called in to his dispatcher. Within two minutes 18 lawmen were outside the bank building. The Mexicans had obtained a bag of money and were heading out the door when they encountered the police. Again, communications broke down during the effort to stop the fleeing outlaws. Shots were exchanged and all three robbers were wounded. These men will hopefully learn to understand English while they serve out their time in a federal prison.

During their trial it was discovered that the three were wanted for bank robbery in Mexico but had escaped the law. Their career south of the border had been moderately successful, but in the United States they were failures. This was a case in which they were pretty good at what they did, but they chose the wrong place to do it. They might have been more successful pulling a bank job in Southern California or Texas, where more of the population understands Spanish. These three men will have the next 20 to 25 years to reflect on the importance of communication skills while committing a crime. However, once they finish their sentence in the U.S., they will be transported back to their homeland, where they doubtless face additional bank robbery charges.

The unusual events that take place in the bank robbing business never cease to amaze an observer. Take, for instance, Judge John White's foray into a life of crime. Yes, I said *Judge* John White, an ex-judge from Leavenworth, Kansas. While a lawyer White had access to other people's money, and he promptly took advantage of his financial windfall. Over a period of several years he personally "misdirected" much of his clients' funds into his own bank account. When some of White's benefactors discovered that the good judge was robbing them, they confronted him. He, of course, had no valid explanation for his actions. Charges were brought against him for his wrongdoing and a trial date was set.

In February 1997, Judge John White pulled up to the drive-through window at a branch of Bank Midwest in Kansas City, Missouri. When asked by the teller if she could help him, he informed her that it was a bank robbery. She thought he may have been kidding, so she asked again if she could help him. Judge White stated again that it was a bank robbery, even though he flaunted no weapons. The young lady, while standing behind three-inch bulletproof glass, excused herself from White, informing him that she would be right back. She immediately called the police.

To give the cops time, excuses were given for the delay in filling White's order at the window. Judge John White was still sitting in his car waiting for the money when the police arrived. Did this man actually believe that his approach to bank robbing—no doubt the laziest on record—would work? Well, all the data is not yet in, but as far as the Jackson County's prosecutor's office is concerned, they have enough to try him for bank robbery.

If Judge John White is convicted—and the odds are against him—he will be 90 when he is eligible for parole. The clients he stole from will never get their money back, but the Judge will have more than enough time to think over his mistakes. You can bet that real bank robbers he'll encounter while incarcerated will be helpful in pointing out flaws in his technique. And they will, no doubt, refrain from taking him to their collective bosom as a kindred spirit.

Another fellow—let's call him Andy—knew a little more about robbing banks than the Judge did, mostly because his idol since he was a child had been the legendary Jesse James. He took to wearing cowboy clothes and boots; he bought a six-shooter and a hand-tooled western holster, and he even had a cowboy hat. This getup alone would not have singled this man out unless Andy lived in New York City, which, unfortunately for him, he did. Aside from the six-gun and holster he became a common sight on the streets of the Big Apple. To most people who encountered him he was another harmless "nut case" and they left him alone. That was until the day in 1955 when Andy walked into the bank, this time with his "iron" on.

The tellers and customers were taken aback at the sight of a Western outlaw pointing a gun at them. The guard was even a little hesitant, thinking this was some sort of stunt. When the robber demanded the money, everything suddenly came into focus for the onlookers—this was a real holdup and that was a real gun. Normally Andy was almost totally unaware of what was going on around him. His full-time job was unloading trucks of produce at the market, not robbing banks.

It was not surprising, then, that when the guard pulled his weapon and commanded the "outlaw" to drop his, somewhere within the reaches of Andy's vivid imagination stood Jesse James, face-to-face with the sheriff. Outlaw Andy did not seem to comprehend what was taking place. The witnesses said he didn't respond to the guard's instructions to drop the gun and only one shot was fired that day. "Jesse James" would never rob another bank in New York; he was pronounced dead at the scene.

It was later discovered that Andy had been suffering from a mental condition since childhood; but not even his own family thought he would do something like this. His co-workers were all shocked that their friend had even attempted a bank robbery. To them Andy seemed a little odd, but harmless. It was known, however, that he spent much of his spare time watching old Western movies. In his own mind he was Jesse James and what he did was normal. His delusions ended in a failed bank robbery and his own death.

Not all failed bank robberies end in death, as some of these stories may be giving the impression. Some robbers have been simply too dumb to even get to that stage. In Baltimore in the late 1990s, police responded to a robbery at the Signet Bank and found Jefferie Thomas not far away from the bank, counting his money. Bank employees quickly identified him as the robber, whereupon his counting was interrupted by the police. Mr. Thomas was arrested; he will stand trial for bank robbery.

In Kansas City, the midtown branch of the Central Bank was robbed for the fourth time in a little over a month in 1999. The disguised desperado doing the deed entered the establishment, ordered his bag filled with money, and quickly exited. The fourth robbery itself was not all that memorable in terms of how much money was taken, but the robber is worth mentioning. Several witnesses were able to direct police officers in the general direction of his escape, thus facilitating the capture. Why was this "bank robber" so easy to apprehend within minutes of the holdup? In this case the problem was a too-conspicuous disguise. After all, a youthful African-American male with a long blond wig and hot-pink lipstick would have been hard to ignore. This gentleman will be charged with federal bank robbery and will undoubtedly have quite a bit to tell other, more adept, bank robbers about his brief career.

Twenty-two-year-old Steven Richard King was arrested in Merced, California, in 1998 for trying to rob a branch office of Bank America. Witnesses stated that he approached the teller pointing his finger like a kid playing cops and robbers. As he aimed his "gun" he demanded the money. The unflappable teller told King to wait and walked away. King, somewhat impatient, became tired of waiting and left the building. He then walked across the street toward another bank. Once inside this second bank, Mr. King vaulted over the counter and attempted to grab the keys to a cash drawer. A bank employee beat King to the keys and told him, "Get out of here!" Police found this bank robber with the wonderful imagination hiding in some bushes outside the building. He was arrested and will have to explain his actions in a court of law.

Then there was Vernon "Bud" Tolmie, who was being questioned by police in Murfreesboro, Tennessee about his involvement in a recent bank robbery. When the questioning became intense Mr. Tolmie took a plastic wastebasket liner and placed it over his head in an apparent suicide attempt. This effort was thwarted by lawmen and Bud Tolmie will stand trial for bank robbery.

If there's such a thing as a totally dumb person, then Clarence Payne of Syracuse, New York may be it. This man attempted to rob a bank in that community, but left empty-handed when a teller turned on a security camera. He was caught and sentenced for two to four years in 1992 for his efforts. Then, in January 1997 he went back to the same bank and handed the teller a holdup note. Fleeing with all of $63 in marked bills, he was arrested about an hour later. In both of these robberies the tellers were able to identify Payne because he regularly cashed checks at the bank.

A bank robber being chased on foot by two city police officers in Dallas made the mistake of pointing his gun at the pursuing lawmen. The bandit was hit in the leg and arm by police bullets and taken into custody. It was discovered, shortly after his arrest, that his weapon was a plastic toy gun. The loot was recovered, the outlaw was tried and convicted of bank robbery, and he is now serving time for that offense.

When a man walked into the First Union Branch Bank of Lakeland, Florida, everything seemed to go wrong. The teller couldn't read his holdup note because of his illegible handwriting and told him so. The would-be robber became frustrated, snatched back his note, and ran out of the bank without any money. It's a simple premise that any third grade teacher would be happy to explain: Good penmanship is important if you plan to be successful.

David Hindmarsh strolled into a Fort Lauderdale bank and handed the teller a note. He threatened to set off a pipe bomb if his demands were not met. The teller asked Hindmarsh to wait. He waited and waited; in fact he waited over 20 minutes. During this time the teller had of course talked with her supervisor, who in turn called the police. The teller handed Mr. Hindmarsh a bag containing $1,500 and he left the building. But knew when he cleared the door that he may have made a mistake. He was met by armed police who immediately took him into custody. The pipe bomb turned out to be a cardboard toilet paper tube. It's doubtful he will be telling anyone in prison that he used to be a bank robber.

Two sixteen-year-old neophyte bank robbers walked into a west Texas Bank with ill-gotten riches on their minds. Since this was their first bank robbery they couldn't have expected what was going to take place. Five of the eight customers in the bank were off-duty Highway Patrol officers cashing their paychecks. Two of the three remaining customers were the county sheriff and his deputy, doing the same thing. The other customer was a bar owner, also armed, depositing his proceeds from his previous night's business. All the customers looked up when the two young larcenists stepped inside the door and loudly announced, "This is a stick-up!" The boys had hardly finished their sentence when they found themselves staring down the barrels of eight handguns. The two dropped their weapon (one gun between them) and surrendered without incident. They will be spending the next four years in a state reformatory.

An elderly gentleman walked into a New Hampshire bank and handed the teller his holdup note. She read it, opened the drawer, and filled his bag. He thanked her, politely, then dropped dead of a massive heart attack before taking more than a step with his money.

As a profession that frequently involves violent death, it's not surprising that bank robbing will occasionally touch on the paranormal. The following tale was related to me by a retired, and previously convicted, bank robber. Its authenticity cannot be proved, but the man who told me was dead serious about his account. Sometime during the early 1940s two bank robbers were killed during a holdup in a Southern bank. Both men were dispatched by alert guards in the lobby of the building, which had been built in 1911. The structure itself was a two-story affair with a second floor dedicated to office space. It wasn't until the 1950s that unusual events began to spook nighttime cleaning crews.

The people who maintained the building began hearing strange sounds coming from the second floor of the bank. When these noises were investigated by the crew they couldn't see anything. But they heard voices and low talking coming from the president's office, located at the head of a flight of stairs. Several of these incidents were reported to bank personnel but, for the most part, the noises were attributed to overactive imaginations. Finally, after numerous complaints by the janitorial staff, a junior bank officer was assigned to spend the night in the bank. He heard nothing.

This same bank was burglarized in 1962 by one of the more proficient bank box men in the business. While he was attempting to gain entrance to the vault he suffered a slight stroke. Unable to continue his project due to physical infirmity, he remained in the building throughout the night. When the burglar was gathered up the next morning by the police, he related a story about the ghosts he had encountered during his night in the bank. The fact that most of his hair had turned gray during his overnight experience was not lost on his family members. He was, of course, arrested for attempted bank robbery and went to prison. However, it didn't take long before the news spread that the bank was haunted.

So persistent were the reports about ghosts that other would-be holdup men and burglars bypassed this bank. The voices, which had been heard by multiple people, were thought to be the two robbers who had been killed in the 1940s. The burglar who had spent the night in the bank with the spirits went totally mad six months after his arrest. At least this is what was reported to me by his cellmate. He was transferred to an insane asylum, where he remains today at the age of 87.

The little southern bank is still in operation, and after-hours cleaning crews occasionally still hear voices coming from the second floor. There hasn't been an attempted holdup or burglary since 1962. Is this building really haunted? A retired, convicted, bank robber seems to think so. And, for the bank, whatever is keeping the robber element at bay is working. It's hard enough to rob a bank with guards, sensors, cameras, and the like—why tangle with ghosts, too?

With its growing population and more banks or bank branches than ever before, America has seen the number of bank robberies reach an all-time high in recent years. This is not to say, however, that the *quality* of bank robbing has increased. To the contrary, the art form has been diluted as more amateurs dabble in the business, the most inept being those who rob banks out of desperation to support their drug habits. The venerated newscaster Paul Harvey has made it a point to regularly mention bumbling bank robbers on his radio show broadcast from Chicago. These remarks take place, on average, several times a month, and keep the general public abreast of bank robbing news. (I have not included any of his subjects in this work because there are more than enough to go around.) Far from glorifying the culprits, Harvey puts a little bit of spotlight on the simpletons who would be far better off if they had never been struck by the misguided notion that they could rob a bank.

Now, having looked at typical examples of today's losers in the bank robbery business, we'll turn to what the future holds for the profession. Where will new technology, societal trends, and economic prosperity lead the common criminal in coming years? Sadly, from the looks of things, not all that much is going to change.

Chapter 6

A New Breed

"We must change to master change."
—Lyndon B. Johnson

Far too many people think that bank robberies follow a predictable pattern; this is not the case. For example, there have been many bandits who have used guns, but also some who have used knives, bows and arrows, crossbows, bombs, plastic toys, swords, hand grenades, clubs, baseball bats, and electronic stun guns. In other words, if it looks like a weapon it's probably been used in a bank robbery. In fact, the most often used weapon is a finger. Stuck inside a jacket pocket, a finger can give an accurate impression of a lethal weapon. Of course, just as various are the getaway vehicles: cars, trucks, motorcycles, bicycles, roller skates, boats, planes, helicopters, and skate boards.

The incredible variety of methods used to rob banks suggests that an equally diverse pool of people are committing these crimes. In the past, surges in the number of bank robberies could be fairly traced to dire social conditions: the aftermath of war, economic depression and recession, and, in a unique case, Prohibition. Yet, in the 1990s America enjoyed an unprecedented stretch of prosperity while bank robberies reached an all-time high. Why did this happen?

Federal as well as local authorities have come up with some possible explanations for the recent rash of robberies. These include the proliferation of state-sanctioned casinos throughout the nation and the recent explosion in on-line stock trading. Aside from the professional bank robbers, whose numbers are constant, the authorities are aware that most of today's robberies are committed by novices. The snatch-and-grab kind of holdup has always been associated with the individual who has had recent or recurring money problems. This person has "hit bottom," and can see no other way to attain the money he or she needs short of a bank job. Many of the communities that promote riverboat gambling or other types of betting estimate that their citizens could be losing as much as a million dollars a day. That money has to come from somewhere, and when a person finds himself broke, he may turn to robbing banks to make up the difference.

On-line stock trading, now a multibillion-dollar-a-year hobby for many Americans, has become the new-age shill game. People can, and do, lose millions of dollars at the click of a computer mouse. Gambling and trading stock will always produce far more losers than winners, and the sad fact behind the statistics is that most of the losers are not wealthy to begin with. In most cases American gamblers cannot afford to lose their life savings because there is no other nest egg waiting for them. An ill-considered attempt to get rich is more likely to plunge an individual into the cruel despond of debt. And desperate men and women will do desperate things; they may even rob banks if conditions get bad enough. When these people are added to the usual crew of down-and-out drug users who need more funds to support their habit than they are capable of earning, it is easy to see why the crime of bank robbery retains its popularity.

This is not to say that if someone loses a large sum of money on a riverboat or in a stock deal he is going to rob a bank. But a significant percentage of people accustomed to high risk have given bank robbery a try. Unfortunately, the odds on a successful snatch-and-grab bank heist are about the same as winning a poker game with a full house, and for the neophyte stock trader those odds could be even greater. On the amateur level, stock traders, gamblers, and bank robbers share two common traits: a determination to obtain large amounts of money with the smallest possible effort; and the courage (or stupidity) to wager their life on a chance.

On the professional level, gamblers or stock dealers are akin to the expert bank robber in the sense that they study their occupation intensely and are well aware of risks. It is more often the beginner—who loses his nest egg or paycheck—who resorts to extreme measures to recoup his losses.

Still, the parallel increase in bank robbing and national prosperity is not due solely to gamblers, of whatever ilk. The phenomenon can
also be attributed to the fact that good economic times have simply
raised the stakes too high for many average citizens attempting to lead
a "normal" life. Gone are the days when a second-hand car, a modest
house, and a chainlink fence would suffice to establish a young family
as middle class. In the 1990s, bombarded by news of freshly minted
millionaires on every side, many people came under pressure to "keep
up with the Joneses," buying SUVs, computers, swimming pools, and
all the other prerequisite status symbols of the new prosperity.
Naturally, Americans, as revealed by credit card statistics, have gone
deeper in debt than ever. The truth is, some folks are better suited for
a modest lifestyle without feeling pressured to sport a Mercedes in the
driveway or a six-foot television in the den. For a growing number of
desperate individuals who simply weren't prepared for a decade when
they were supposed to be rich, the solution has come through a phrase
that anyone can utter: "This is a stick-up."

With the term "new breed" of bank robbers, however, I do not
mean to describe more amateurs driven for whatever reason to make
the biggest mistake of their lives. Instead, we'll take a look at a few
notable exceptions to today's recent rash of amateurs. This chapter
will examine some of the newer methods and characters popping up
daily in the bank robbing business, some more successful than others.
In the bank caper business, it's not only the amount of the haul that
sets robbers apart, but how they go about getting it. The ingenuity of
the human mind reveals itself in surprising ways, especially when it
comes to getting rich. Like most of the other robbers in this book, the
people in this chapter have made it their life's work to figure out just
how that is done. Some fail where others succeed, and some have
found success in ways that no one else had thought to try.

A SUCCESSFUL HEIST OR NOT?

With the advent of computers, bank robbery has taken on a new twist.
Two 20-year-old hackers pulled off a very successful bank robbery
some time in 1990. The target (denied by the bank in question) was

the Citibank of New York. Through a series of oversights by this corporation these two young men were able to access the Citibank computer. With a number of complicated maneuvers they managed to move funds from New York to a Swiss bank account. To do this they had to circumvent the Federal Reserve ID numbers. They then had to move the money through the intricate structure of the bank's electronic system. This heist took the men one week to accomplish and they supposedly moved $66,000 each to their accounts in Switzerland.

The two men have never been named and the scuttlebutt within the computer hacker community doesn't give this incident all that much credibility either. Regardless of this, there is an open FBI file concerning this robbery. Whether or not they get credit for their crime, such robbery by computer is entirely possible, as we will see with this next short story about the "burglary" described by many as the biggest bank heist of all time by computer.

ROBBERY BY COMPUTER

Before I get into particulars about this case I need to lay a little groundwork. Electronic transfers of funds from one bank to another began around 1918 in the United States. This method of moving money was devised by the Federal Reserve System. The heart of the procedure was a device called the Culpepper Switch, buried in the side of a mountain in Culpepper, Virginia. At this time it was a combination of telegraph (Morse Code) and standard telephone service, where available. This switch was a security device that enabled banks to encode their business transactions, keeping the transfers confidential from prying eyes and ears. The system handled this kind of business until the late 1950s.

The first illegal electronic transfer of funds from a bank to a crook took place in 1922. It involved taking money out of the loop between a member bank of the Federal Reserve System and a Federal Reserve Depository. This occurred on the East Coast and the amount of money diverted was thought to be about $80,000. The robber, much to the bank's chagrin, was never discovered.

By the late 1960s, the banking industry had ascertained that computers were going to be the wave of the future. Crude computers had been in use, but had more problems than they were worth. After most bugs were worked out, the Federal Reserve incorporated them into its daily transactions. The Federal Reserve went online with computers in 1970, utilizing them in wire transfers. In effect, they replaced the old telephone and telegraph systems which had been in use since shortly after the turn of the century. Funds which had been transferred in the past from member banks to the Federal Reserve were now transmitted via computer. Federal ID numbers were added as a safeguard. The idea was relatively simple: if you didn't have all the numbers in a specific order, then you could not access this program.

As described above, a couple of hackers did access this program in 1990. In the years since this 1990 robbery the banking system has upgraded its software and hardware in an effort to prevent this from happening again. Most of this modernization came in the form of an electronic hub to handle the traffic. In short, no one bank has the final say-so on any given transfer. The transfer is, in effect, routed though this hub and then dispersed to member banks. The hub arrangement is the modern version of the Culpepper Switch. The security is built into this program in such a way that no hacker can get around it— hopefully.

The theory is that when a request is made for a transfer of funds from one bank to another, it goes through the people who oversee the hub. They need clearance from both banks to complete the transfer, and this is accomplished with instructions given by the computer and known only to the person on the sending end of the hub. The receiving end enters their code, again by computer, to the hub. The electronic hub then takes this information without any human intervention and matches the request with the receiver. If all the codes are correct, the transfer is completed. This is an oversimplified explanation of what goes on, but hopefully it gives some basic background information. As late as 1995 there were still small banks not hooked up to this new system, but most of the nation's larger banks and all those overseas are online with this arrangement.

The man who may have pulled off the biggest single bank robbery in history—in 1996—has never been caught. Law-enforcement agencies are aware of who he is, but not much else. To make matters worse, there is a question as to whether this robbery ever occurred.

The bank isn't talking (so I won't name it) and computer buffs around the world question whether there was enough technical knowledge available to pull it off. This is the most common story of how the events transpired, so perhaps it would be best to leave any judgment up to the reader.

The interest on bank accounts, for the most part, is computed on a rounded-off number. The odd fraction, depending on whether the number is rounded-off high or low, is placed into the bank's own account. In a very minuscule way the bank earns a fraction of a cent, or points, on each computation of this sort. One would think that this small amount of money on the interest wouldn't amount to much, but it does. And the biggest bank robbery in history was with a major bank with worldwide branches, totalling assets in the trillions of dollars using this interest.

Our robber was an employee of the bank, and it would be possible to consider this robbery an embezzlement, but later I will explain why this is not the case. Our thief set up several dummy accounts using the bank's computer. His access to the bank's system was his only tool. Using numerous assorted approaches to the deposits, he funneled the interest which had been rounded-off high into his own bogus accounts. These accounts were installed in the bank's own system, but nobody bothered to check them out. The accounts merely showed up as a business account that seemed to have a lot of money. There were no deposit slips, memorandums or any other identifying paperwork which could tip off random checks by other bank employees or even the computer's own system of checks and balances.

The thief set up the scheme in such a way that the computer system itself made the deposits off the interest of other large accounts. By clipping a point or two off each dollar in interest, the money mounted up. These points found their way, with computer help, automatically into the bogus accounts of the bandit. When the totals deposited had reached an acceptable level, he transferred the entire account, by wire, to an overseas numbered account in his name. When our thief moved the money out of one bank to another he, in effect, robbed the first bank.

To do this our robber had to get around the ID numbers used by both ends of the transaction. The bank where he worked dealt in overseas transfers all the time, so moving funds from the United States to

Switzerland was not uncommon. His position in this bank allowed him to oversee the transfer. In that he was also a customer of the Swiss bank he was knowledgeable of its procedure. After the money had been deposited in the second bank, the thief dissolved the dummy accounts, essentially leaving no trace of the transactions.

The interest, in theory, was so small that not even the computer system itself picked up on the fraction of a point which had been diverted. The transfer of the funds was not discovered either. So he got a few thousand dollars, right? Even the lowest estimates of this robbery, which took about six months to pull off, give the numbers in excess of $50 million. However, no bank would willingly admit that an employee got away with better than $50 million of its depositor's money, so it has never been confirmed. Other computer experts say it didn't happen, the FBI says it didn't happen, the bank says it didn't happen, but there is a suspect. A suspect normally suggests that a crime was committed, so of course there has to be some merit to the story. The fact that nobody can prove it happened is the only fly in the ointment.

The technique that this man used for the heist has now been changed so that it can never take place again—which, of course, is something our robber could care less about. Looking back on many of the earlier stories, this guy was no different from most robbers we have looked at throughout this book. He knew where the money was and he had a plan of how to get it. He entered the banking system— just as surely as the guy with a cutting torch—and took the loot. He may have been different from the armed robber, in that he didn't use force to get his money, but he is a bank robber just the same. Computer systems that banks use for transfer and computations of their money have built-in alarms. He defeated them just as decidedly as a burglar would get around a physical alarm system in a bank building. He needed to get in and out of the system just as efficiently as any burglar needs to come and go from a robbed vault. He needed a fence for the hot funds, and the Swiss were amenable enough to conceal this money, like millions of other dollars, within their numbered accounts. When all of its parts are broken down, it becomes pretty clear that this really was one of the more brilliant bank robberies every committed.

Most depositors, be they individuals or businesses, don't know what happens to that little bit of interest that's rounded-off. Most people would be unaware that this money finds its way into the coffers of the bank and in fact makes the bankers just a little richer every day. This bit of "loose change" can add up to a whole lot of money though, and it only took the mind of an employee to figure out how to take that away from the only other people who knew how the system worked.

Aside from the incident in 1990 and the larger one in 1996, computer-facilitated bank robberies are all but nonexistent. One of the few things bankers got right early on was how to stop embezzlement by means of computers. It is true, however, that a few talented hackers have managed to gain access to banks' databases. But what the banks didn't spend on other security measures they spent on systems that are all but impervious to outside forces. This is not to say that hackers don't attempt to circumvent these systems, because they do—every day.

The actual fear of the man on the street is that some computer "geek" is going to take all of his money out of the bank. In reality this has not happened nor is it likely to. The fear of professional law-enforcement is that this same geek will someday figure out how to do it, but that fear has been somewhat lessened by banks' continued efforts to update software and to hire the best people to create fool-proof systems of defense. Firewall systems automatically deploy when a hacker is discovered in the system, and many are changed weekly—if not daily—in order to maintain the integrity of those firewalls. Although most people feel that computers in the right hands can do almost anything, this is just not so when it comes to stealing from a bank. There are simply too many professionals working against the would-be technological thief.

The New York bank that was robbed (or not) in 1996 was the result of an inside job. Therefore the common assumption would be that some other guy sitting in front of a monitor in the back of the bank could do the same thing. Pulling off another heist in the same manner would be almost impossible today. It could be compared to jumping off a 20-story building—you only get to do it once! Apparently, this technical loophole was closed in early 1997, and there have been no documented computer-assisted bank heists reported since. This is not to say, however, that some time in the not too distant future it couldn't be accomplished by a hacker. The chances are extremely low, but in the world of bank robbing any small chance is a reason to try the impossible.

THE VULNERABLE ATM's

A new kind of banking practice evolved within the last 25 years as a direct offshoot of computers. In the early 1970s a very bright Englishman devised an automatic machine to dispense cash during times when the banks were closed. By using a special card, banking patrons could remove cash from their savings or checking accounts without human assistance. The card notified the bank, electronically, that this person had this amount in his or her account and was entitled to it. The appropriate amount of cash would then come out of a little slot in the machine and the transaction was deducted from the patron's bank account.

It was only logical that this new form of banking could be added to the list of options for bank robbers. These ATM gadgets, loaded with cash and weighing upwards of a thousand pounds, became new targets for enterprising thieves. Men dressed as construction workers, using chains, dollies, and brute force, have managed to steal these machines. After they are taken they are then loaded onto a truck, transported to a secure place, and cracked open. They have been taken right out of the sides of banks, shopping malls, or just about anywhere else the bank owner has placed them. It's one of those bank heists in which guts plays an important role; in fact, this kind of robbery is committed, for the most part, right in front of onlookers and the occasional law-enforcement representative. In short, many of these robberies are successful even with lots of witnesses watching every small event take place in front of them.

People who attempt this kind of heist are just a little different from the strong-armed holdup bandit. Although they may be armed, their activity is not what would be considered an armed robbery. It would fall into a burglary classification, with a little twist. Most of these robberies are committed during nighttime hours and are not a quick or quiet kind of heist. Just given the size of the machine, it takes some courage to go after one. Crooks not only have to remove it from the building, but then they have to hoist it into a vehicle in order to haul it off. Television cameras are located in these machines, so the burglar needs to be aware that he could have a picture of himself taken for further reference by the authorities. If that camera is defeated, there may well be other cameras located in the area to record anyone who should tamper with the machine.

It's impossible for me to give an average amount of money that would be inside an ATM. Some banks prefer to limit the cash in their machines to no more than $25,000, which may be enough of a deterrent to keep thieves from going after one. There just isn't enough payback for an ambitious thief to chance a prison sentence. Regardless, hundreds of ATMs are stolen every year and discovered in vacant lots around the country. Just as an example, consider this true account of one such heist.

On a bright, sunny day in April 1998, two people walked into a Kansas City, Missouri, convenience store. The woman was obviously a security person of some sort. She had the uniform, badge, and demeanor of a "rent-a-cop." With clipboard in hand she approached the manager of the establishment, presenting a work order for the ATM in the corner of the store, which was nothing unusual. Her assistant pushed his two-wheeled dolly to the machine and waited for instructions. Once the work order was signed by the manager he went to work. Twenty minutes later the two were finished. The male assistant rolled the ATM to a waiting truck while the lady kibitzed with the store's staff. It was a simple transaction as far as the store was concerned. Besides, the whole thing was videotaped with the store's security camera; it really was nothing unusual.

Later that day, the manager of the store called the bank that owned the ATM to find out when the repaired machine would be returned because she had several requests from customers who used the machine. Well, you can imagine how surprised the manager was when a bank representative, the Police Major Crimes Unit, and a couple of FBI agents turned up in the little neighborhood establishment. There had been no work order from the bank to repair that machine. By that night the videotape was broadcast on all local stations in the hopes that someone might be able to identify the repairman and the security officer. A bank robbery? You bet, and one of the slickest heists ever seen on regional television.

How could this have worked so well? The two people had a solid plan. They had a plausible reason to remove the machine, as far as the manager was concerned. They even had paperwork to enforce their necessity for doing what they were doing. In no way did they give the store's staff, or any of the 10 customers present, any basis to be suspicious of their assignment. Once again the time-tested method of looking like you belonge, or hiding in plain sight, facilitated a flawless robbery. The machine has never been found—and neither have the robbers.

ATMs have also provided a means for criminals to pull off robberies on bank premises, if not to rob the banks themselves. A few years back a New York publisher and his wife-to-be decided to go to the movies, but first needed to get some cash from a nearby ATM. The door was stuck and they couldn't get in. At least a dozen people were visible through the glass walls of the enclosed ATM room and the couple was infuriated that no one bothered to help with the door. With only minutes to go before their movie, they started banging on the glass, yelling "Let us in!" Finally a gentleman opened the door and it was only then that the couple realized a holdup was in progress. Two gunmen were leading each of the ten other people up to the machines where they were forced to withdraw $500 (the maximum) from their accounts. It was a rare case where victims had indignantly demanded to join a robbery. A few weeks later the couple read in the *New York Times* about the demise of a salt-and-pepper team that fit the description of their robbers. Caught in midtown while perpetrating a similar caper, one had been killed and the other wounded by police.

PATTY HEARST & THE SLA

There have been many examples of groups of men and women who band together to perform robberies, but there is another segment of the bank robbing population that operates a little differently from that type. These are so-called militia groups or cults.

In the late sixties and early seventies America saw many bank robberies. Paramilitary survivalists had discovered they could supplement their war-chests by robbing banks. Some of these groups came out of their mountains and took on the establishment on a regular basis. There are countless examples of home-grown militia groups who robbed banks up and down the West Coast as well as in other Western states, but for the most part theirs were poorly organized and less than stellar undertakings. In the past few years, a number of banks have fallen to this element, but the numbers have decreased since the FBI made its presence known in this area of enforcement. In the overall scheme of things, these confederations have all but ceased their bank-robbing endeavors.

This was not true during the mid-1970s. The world's attention became focused on such cult groups when images of Patty Hearst participating in a bank robbery began to pop up on the television screen. Many people will never forget the closed circuit television pictures of this hippy victim holding a gun during the heist. The daughter of California publishing billionaire Randolph Hearst, Patty had supposedly been kidnapped and held hostage by a radical leftist organization that called itself the Symbionese Liberation Army (SLA). Those who witnessed the bank robbery firsthand, however stated, "She absolutely was an active participant!"

Later, Patty would claim she had been brainwashed and had no real part in the robbery. Dubbed Tanya by the SLA, her movements were followed by the entire nation for several months through the media. There has always been some question as to whether she had been released by the SLA or captured by the FBI. A noted attorney, F. Lee Bailey, handled her bank robbery defense, though she was convicted just the same. Hearst received a seven-year prison sentence, of which she served only 28 months. No doubt a lack of substantial evidence, and her father's money, played a part in this shortened sentence.

Her supposed captors all met untimely ends at the hands of law-enforcement personnel. William and Emily Harris, who were part of the team who abducted her in the first place, were arrested and tried; they received 10 years apiece for the kidnapping. After her release Patty married one of her bodyguards and settled into a somewhat mundane lifestyle. Patty Hearst will hardly be remembered as a bank robber, but her exploits with the militia group do place her among the most unlikely of bank robbers.

WILLIAM SCOTT "HOLLYWOOD" SCURLOCK

The old mentality of rushing into a bank with guns drawn and shouting violent threats to anyone within earshot is still frighteningly prevalent. The following story about Scott Scurlock combines the desperation of many of the losers in bank robbing with a certain innate leadership ability that set him apart from most amateurs.

Occasionally there emerges a robber who becomes so adept at the profession, simply through attempting so many heists and learning from his mistakes, that he gets catapulted into the rare ranks of the gifted professional; Scurlock was one such individual. In his younger days, Scurlock was a risk-taker and a daredevil. Along with a few childhood friends, there was nothing he and they would not do for a little excitement and danger. As a natural-born leader Scurlock led his little band of followers on countless treks into the unknown areas of crime and drugs. These relationships with school chums would carry him past high school and college, and would even last into adulthood. Charming, with drop-dead good looks, Scott Scurlock demanded and received respect from his friends. The understanding was that Scurlock could cope with every situation life had to offer. Two of his closest followers, Steve Meyers and Mark Biggins, would emulate their trailblazer so much that they were both led into one of the most dangerous occupations in the annals of crime—bank robbing.

Scurlock loved the high life. He thought nothing of spending money and usually had very little trouble finding someone to give him a supply. His inherent charisma enabled him to obtain the money, women, and pleasures that eluded most of his friends. When a different drug culture emerged in the late 1980s and early 1990s, Scott was captivated by the amount of money he could make. Using skills obtained in college, it was but a short jump for him to start producing one of the components of Crystal Meth. His true criminal career had begun.

Scurlock located outside the community of Olympia, Washington, and supplied drug dealers all over the country with his product; and, not surprisingly, the cash rolled in. He settled on some land and proceeded to build a home for himself when his business was really thriving. With his friends he managed to build an elaborate tree house in the woods adjacent to the property, a structure that would become one of the largest edifices of its type in the nation and was even written up in *The Seattle Times*. In 1978, Scurlock had the money to travel first class and to obtain all of the goodies a man in his late twenties would need. And, of course, he still had his loyal friends.

Things began to change, however, in the mid-1990s. One of Scurlock's dealers was murdered and this frightened the otherwise calm dealer into curtailing his manufacturing. The money slowly dwindled and he became harder to get along with, as he took to drinking and using pot to ease the pain and frustrations of his life. When he was desperate for funds he turned to his friends for help—as he had always done. His comrades, only slightly aware of his business dealings in the world of illegal narcotics, agreed to help get their leader back on his feet.

With absolutely no experience robbing a bank, Scurlock, Mark Biggins, and a woman named Traci attempted the impossible. On June 17, 1992, Biggins and Scurlock entered the Seafirst Bank on Madison Avenue in Seattle. Traci remained outside a few blocks away in the getaway car. Minutes after it had begun, Scurlock and his accomplice emerged from the bank with $19,971—but there had been mistakes. The mistakes were not in terms of Scurlock's plan or how he was dressed, since the disguise he wore made identification impossible, and he was not caught during the robbery. His mistakes were more akin to the common errors amateurs make when they first attempt a robbery: he only took money from the tellers' cages and was unsure of how to control the people inside the building. He and Biggins had also planned to steal a car from one of the bank patrons, but Biggins forgot to get the man's keys, so some time was lost. In spite of these minor errors, the robbery was successful.

The loot was divided among the three back at the tree-house compound in Olympia. Biggins was almost sick with fear and disgust over what he had done, whereas Traci and Scott were ecstatic with the pure excitement of the act. Months passed by and the money slowly ran out. Biggins had moved to another part of the country but remained in touch with Scurlock, as did Traci. Scurlock waited 10 months before he began planning another bank job. Unwilling to ask for help this time, he decided to undertake this next robbery by himself.

During the gap between his first robbery and his second he improved on his disguise. This included theatrical makeup utilizing rubber components of a nose, chin, and facial flaps; also, a reddish-blond wig gave the impression of either a badly burned individual or an old man. These disguises would remain part of his modus operandi throughout his career, as would the high-top sneakers he always wore.

Scurlock, not content with the take from the first armed robbery, decided to hit the same bank again. He did this on August 20, 1992, and relieved the establishment of $8,125 from the tellers—still a small amount for a bank robbery. But the most important aspect of the heist was that he controlled the crowd better. Three weeks later, Scurlock robbed the U.S. Bank, West Seattle, of a little over $9,600. Internal bank cameras now noticed that he always carried a large semi-automatic pistol, later identified as a .40 caliber Glock. But as usual, these pictures and the witnesses could not make a clear identification of the heavily disguised robber. Because his luck was holding out, Scurlock went after the third bank just eight days later. The University Savings Bank in Laurelhurst, netted him $5,740. Naturally, it did not take him long to realize that he was putting a lot at risk for a paltry amount of money. Thus, he began looking for the bigger score.

Now nicknamed the "Take Charge Robber" by local and federal authorities, Scurlock and his modus operandi were becoming well known in Seattle's rash of bank robberies. Before this, Seattle had the fourth highest number of bank robberies in the nation. Now this new bandit was playing hell with those statistics, and law-enforcement officials knew he had to be taken off the streets.

On October 5, 1992, the Great Western Bank lost $27,400 to this robber in weird disguise. The only difference between this holdup and the others was how it was accomplished. The unknown robber had finally discovered where the real money was kept—the vault. In the five months since he burst onto the bank-robbing scene in Seattle, Scurlock had stolen about $50,000; with his newfound knowledge about the vault, that figure would escalate considerably. Although his exploits were still considered amateurish, even cops knew that he was learning quickly and would soon be more dangerous.

Another robbery with a similar modus operandi took place on

December 18, at the Seafirst Bank on Black Lake Boulevard in Olympia. This holdup had all the earmarks of the "Take Charge Robber" but was a little different. Had the robber moved to another town, changing his style a little? The authorities did not believe so, and attributed the December crime to a copycat bandit. Scurlock would discover that the heist was actually pulled off by his first accomplice and friend Mark Biggins. He was furious with Biggins for holding up a bank so close to his home in Olympia, and ended up not speaking to the man for months afterward.

Law-enforcement officers, realizing that they were losing ground on this robber, formed a task force in early 1993. It included people from the Washington State Police, Seattle Police, ATF (Alcohol, Tobacco and Firearms), HUD (Housing and Urban Development), DEA (Drug Enforcement Administration), FBI, and the Secret Service, with officers from local county sheriff's offices also helping out. The mission was to catch the robber in the act, at any cost.

As usual for Scott Scurlock, the money eventually ran out and he began looking for someone who could act as his eyes and ears while he took care of business in the bank. With some serious convincing, he managed to get his old friend Steve Meyers into the business with him. They hit the Seafirst Bank, Hawthorne Hills, on November 24, 1993, for $98,500. On January 12, 1994, they robbed the U.S. Bank, Wedgewood, in Olympia for $15,800. A month later, on February 17, 1994, Scurlock and Meyers robbed the Seafirst Bank, Hawthorne Hills, again—for $114,000 this time.

While the authorities were getting increasingly aggravated over the string of robberies, a new moniker was coined for the elusive bandit: "Hollywood." Scurlock's disguises would change from time to time but he was still an unknown to surveillance cameras and witnesses alike. Officers working on the cases began noticing that the only constant was the high-top sneakers, made by Converse. A ball cap, or a floppy hat, sometimes rounded out the unidentifiable bandit with the uncanny luck. Once this new "handle" was mentioned in the newspapers Scurlock became elated. At last, he had achieved notoriety for his efforts in the bank-robbing business! His exhilaration was so monumental that he even took time to drive past his just-robbed target to watch the police running around looking for him. He was a faceless celebrity, famous and without identity all at the same time.

It could have been his own perceived prominence that got in the way of good sense during a holdup in Portland. Scurlock and Meyers barely escaped capture when everything went wrong and they had to make a run for it without any money. Undaunted, the pair held up the First Interstate Bank, Queen Ann Hill, Seattle branch on July 13, 1994, and escaped with $111,800. In December of the same year, they went back to Portland and relieved the U.S. Bank, Woodstock, of $22,000. The money was small but they were not discouraged. They next took on Seattle's Wallingford District's First Interstate Bank but, again, there were problems. Police were notified before they even got into the building and they had to make a hasty exit. When an exploding dye packet of money went off they also tossed $11,924 on the ground during their escape.

During the robberies Meyers manned the radio and advised Scurlock about police radio messages. Scurlock was always the man in the bank. This same arrangement was in place when the two of them robbed the Seafirst Bank in the wealthy Seattle suburb of Madison Park; their total take was $252,460. The pair had been using at least two cars for their escape for quite some time. When Scurlock walked into any bank, he now took charge of the employees and customers before he got down to business. He would always ask for the vault manager to escort him inside. There he would fill nylon bags full of cash, ever vigilant in spotting dye packets or bait money. He seemed to know what he was doing every time he pulled a job, and it was about this time that the authorities began to believe that "Hollywood" could be one of their own. The bandit carried an automatic pistol just like a cop, knew how to control a crowd, and didn't seem to get flustered easily or run hastily from a job. Certainly the signs pointed to it being an inside setup, but this new paranoia proved wrong; Scurlock was simply a very good bank robber with a commanding personality.

While some cops were studying camera images, other officers were piecing together a profile of "Hollywood." His last holdup had netted the bandit over a half-million dollars so they knew he would lay low for a while. It was estimated, because of the precise timing of the robberies, that he would be looking for money by late January, 1996. His lifestyle, however extravagant it might be, seemed to require quite a bit of money to maintain. Also, the robber liked staging his heists on rainy days, and seemed to dedicate his efforts to a particular section of Seattle. All of this was added to the thumbnail sketches that the investigators were compiling. Of course, Scurlock was oblivious to all of these efforts.

Scurlock and Meyers were joined by Mark Biggins, Scott's first bank-robbing accomplice, for their next heist. On January 25, 1996, the three struck the First Interstate Branch Bank, Seattle, for over $141,000. This time, Biggins entered the bank with Scurlock to facilitate crowd control—which he bungled horribly. As they were leaving the bank, an employee got a license number of the getaway car, but it did not help the authorities all that much; the car was later found abandoned and wiped clean of fingerprints. To the police, the only significant aspect of this heist was that the predictions of the time of Scurlock's robbery attempt were pretty accurate. By then, however, Scott Scurlock had robbed 15 banks, and this was his only pattern helpful to police officers.

Four months later, on May 22, Scurlock and Meyers hit Seattle's First Interstate Bank for almost $115,000. Biggins was not a part of the heist, but this really did not matter to the police. By this time, they were desperate to catch "Hollywood"; he was by then the most sought-after bank robber in Washington state, Seattle in particular. A $50,000 reward was offered by the authorities for the arrest of this increasingly troublesome robber, along with his accomplices.

The heat was on and Scott Scurlock knew it. However, he was also aware of his luminary status in the community. After "Hollywood" had been invented by the newspapers, the "Robin Hood" aura around the crook began to form. It was said that some Washingtonians, usually in bars, would cheer when he struck another insured bank. The tall man with an announcer's voice had reached his celebrity nirvana. He had achieved the fame he always wanted, and had the money to enjoy it at the same time.

Now Scurlock informed his cohorts, Meyers and Biggins, that he intended to hit three banks on the same day. His targets would be the Roosevelt branch Seafirst Bank, the Green Lake Bank, Seafirst, and the Lake City Bank, Seafirst. This was to be their last job—the crowning achievement. After all, they had already stolen over a million and a half dollars during their brief careers, and Scurlock assumed that he could add another two or three million with the triple heists. However, by the end of the summer of 1996 he had changed his mind. They would only rob one very lucrative bank that would be full of money, based on the day they robbed it, and that would be sufficient. Or, so the plan went.

FBI agents and local police investigators knew it was crucial that they catch this robber. The time would inevitably come when Scurlock would lose some of his luck and would end up killing someone out of desperation; law-enforcement had to quickly prevent that from ever taking place. The Seattle-area banks were staked out in sectors around the clock, with a particular focus on those that he had hit in the past. Air units (helicopters) and ground units were coordinated with the stake-out teams. It was the most massive mobilization in Seattle's history to apprehend a single bank robber. All of the authorities engaged in this manhunt knew that the rainy season was in full swing and that this was "Hollywood's" favorite time of the year.

At 5:41 P.M. on the day before Thanksgiving, November 26, 1996, a silent alarm was sounded at the Seafirst Bank in the Lake City suburb of Seattle; the task force activated. The robbers were efficient and cool, and also very unaware that an alarm had been sounded even before they entered the building. After gathering up the money and exiting the bank, they headed toward their car. Shortly after the holdup, one of the task force members—Mike Magan—drove two other officers to the scene and picked up a description of a white van. A few miles away, he located the suspects' vehicle and pulled in behind it. Magan called for back-up right away, and when the van pulled onto a residential street, he had the full support of the huge Seattle task force in tow.

As two armed men exited the van, shots were fired by the officers. The men from the van did not return fire, but rather got back inside it and drove away. A short time later the van stopped again and this time the occupants fired at the officers. Once more, after a brief exchange, the van pulled away and stopped on a hill. Gunfire split the night as the police and the suspected bandits exchanged shots. The van then rolled down the hill and into a house, but not before the driver bailed out and scurried down an alley.

Mike Magan called for a cease-fire when the shooting from the men subsided. Two wounded suspects were removed from the vehicle and were placed on the ground. An arsenal of weaponry and enough ammunition to sustain a sizable firefight was discovered in the back of

the van. Police officers now fanned out in the general neighborhood
where the driver, Scurlock, had made a run for it, but he could not be
immediately found. The search continued for many hours with no success, and the police feared that he had escaped. They had not yet identified the suspects, so they had no idea whom they should really be
looking for.

Steve Meyers had been wounded twice, once in the left shoulder
and once in the right arm; neither wound would be fatal. Later he
would give the authorities Scott Scurlock's name and his place of residence in Olympia. Mark Biggins, however, had been hit in the right
thigh, arm, and through the back of his stomach; he was in critical
condition. While the doctors fought to save Biggins' life, investigators
were questioning Meyers about everything. Biggins would survive and
later tell his story to the authorities after going through surgery. He,
too, identified Scurlock and Meyers as his two accomplices in the robbery. Both men, however, left out a lot of their own backgrounds in
the bank-robbing business. It would be discovered that the money in
the van amounted to a little over one million dollars; it was the men's
biggest score yet, and the man who had masterminded it all was
nowhere to be found. "Hollywood" had disappeared.

On Thanksgiving Day, 1996, shortly after the search began, a man
was discovered hiding in a truck camper that had been placed on
sawhorses for storage in the backyard of a home. Seattle police and
FBI agents were called to the scene and arrived within minutes. The
house was only about five blocks from the shootout the day before, so
despite the police's fears "Hollywood" had not gotten far. The man in
the camper did not want to talk to anyone and the authorities were
not about to waste time convincing him. Dozens of shots were fired
into the camper, and the man inside fired back when pepper spray was
let loose within the shell—with little result. Next, two tear gas canis-
ters were fired, and again there was no response from inside the trail-
er. It was now feared by the officers that whoever was inside was dead.
After a reasonable wait, and with darkness falling, the commander of
the SWAT team forced the door open. It took only seconds for him to
find the body of Scott Scurlock huddled on the floor.

An official autopsy would reveal that Scurlock had died of a self-
inflicted wound from a Glock automatic that had been placed under
his chin. There were six other wounds on his body, but they were all

attributed to shots fired after he'd already killed himself. In the end, it was the same weapon he had used in all of his holdups that had ended his life.

For the officers involved, and the community in general, "Hollywood's" career in robbing banks was officially over. This gifted and intelligent man, who could have utilized his natural leadership skills to be successful in nearly anything he tried, instead chose a life of crime and paid the highest price. There is no question that Scott Scurlock had worked his way up from amateur status to become a fascinating professional in the world of bank robbery. His mistake was simple and not uncommon in this line of work: he was too predictable.

Meyers and Biggins were federally charged with one count of conspiracy to commit armed bank robbery, one count of armed bank robbery, and two counts of assault on a federal officer. Their conviction carried a maximum sentence of 60 years in prison, but after a plea bargain in February 1997 both were sentenced to 21 years for their crimes. Meyers went to the federal penitentiary in Sheridan, Oregon, and Biggins was placed in the federal facility at Terminal Island, California. At the turn of the century these men were still incarcerated, although there is a plan underway to reduce their time served to only 12 years. There is also some question as to whether Meyers and Scurlock held up a Wells Fargo armored car shortly before the now-fatal last bank job, though this is still under investigation.

We will now look at one final pair of bank robbers, who also operated out of Seattle. They had far better results in terms of money than "Hollywood" and his culprits, but in the end a life of crime did not turn out to be what they had expected.

THE TRENCH COAT ROBBERS

Ray L. Bowman and William A. Kirkpatrick, two men in their mid-fifties, were known collectively as "The Trench Coat Robbers." These men were arrested for a $4.5 million Washington state robbery, now considered the largest bank robbery in American history. And this was merely the culmination of a very lucrative 15-year career in the business of robbing banks.

There is no question that these two men were good at what they did, but their final mistake was classic stupidity. Their last robbery, which took place in February 1997 in a suburb of Tacoma, Washington, was a textbook heist. Not unlike their other robberies, the two men walked into the Seafirst Bank in their traditional disguises of trench coats and masks. They forced three women into the vault and filled bags with cash for over 25 minutes before leaving.

The two got away from the robbery without any problems, but the FBI and local authorities had them as suspects from the very beginning. The problems arose when Kirkpatrick purchased a Minnesota log home in 1998 with $183,000 in *cash* and thus aroused the suspicion of a local IRS agent. Kirkpatrick, sensing that everything was falling apart, made a mad dash across the country, emptying safe deposit boxes. As he was racing through Nebraska he was stopped for speeding, and the trooper discovered $1.8 million in the trunk of his car. Investigators later recovered another $1 million in cash from his home and local bank safe deposit boxes in Parkville, Missouri.

Bowman had likewise been gathering up funds from assorted bank safety deposit boxes. However, in his haste, he overlooked a couple of stashes that were recovered later. In spite of this, the police managed to retrieve a little over $1 million in cash from his home in December 1998. Kirkpatrick's girlfriend, Myra J. Penney, had no intention of going to prison for helping a couple of bank robbers get away with their crime, so she cooperated with authorities. The two robbers had been in touch with each other and Myra knew it. She passed this information on to the authorities, and soon the police put two and two together—they had their Trench Coat Robbers.

Both men were indicted in Seattle with conspiracy to commit bank robbery, armed bank robbery, using a weapon during a violent crime, and transporting stolen property across state lines. Some of the money was difficult to recover, however, due to the fact that these men had failed to pay the rent on their safety deposit boxes (which contained several million in cash).

Since they had never been arrested for the crime of bank robbery before, they were considered first-time offenders. Both men received in excess of 35-year sentences for their crimes. In spite of a lengthy career that netted the robbers many millions of dollars, they only made one serious mistake: they dealt in too much cash. Their convictions on these charges will, however, keep them safely behind bars for the remainder of their natural lives. They were not sloppy bank robbers, they just got complacent with their success.

BANK ROBBING SCAMS

The average person would no more attempt to steal money from a bank than he would attempt to jump off the Golden State Bridge in San Francisco. However, there are "legitimate" companies in the United States which sell supposedly foolproof information on how to rob any bank, all targeted at the amateur criminal. Without ever requesting to receive such product offers, brochures from such companies have been sent to me using U.S. postage bulk rate—one from Texas and another from California. Of course, the brochures were labeled with warnings such as, *"For informational purposes only"* or *"We do not promote nor condone any illegal acts of any sort!"* or even *"Not to be used to make money with."* Along with these comprehensive disclaimers is the "real" company directive: to inform honest people what some unscrupulous individuals are up to.

Some of the items that caught my attention were scams such as: "A.T.M. Fraud Made Easy," "A.T.M. Theft—Non-Technical Stuff," "Time-Delayed Self-Disintegrating Checks," "Plastic Bank Jobs," "Disappearing and Appearing Inks," "Hacking Telecheck & Telecredit," "Ultimate Checking Scam" and the ever-popular "How to Steal Anything." This last one instructs the reader on how to circumvent alarm systems, how to plan the caper, and how to dress.

For an example of how ridiculous these pamphlets are, take a closer look at the one called "Plastic Bank Jobs." The author of this $6 work claims that $100 million a year is stolen through electronic methods, be it modified credit cards or swipers. The latter, a machine the size of a pack of cigarettes, can transfer the information from a credit card magnetic strip for use at a later date. Also discussed are EMP (Electromagnetic Pulse) devices, which can be used to knock out other electronic machines, including computers. And, the writer states, if you do not know where to buy such objects, for just $10 he will tell you how to build one yourself. One must keep in mind that simply owning one of these objects is illegal. However, the pamphlet covers that too, since it also has a flyer on how to "hack" your way out of any predicament by computer.

Consider for a moment the following claims, found all over those mailed pamphlets: "Before this check hits the bank, it will vanish! Leaves no trace a check ever existed, paper and all! Very illegal to do. *For informational purposes only!*" Another publication explains bank scams using disappearing and appearing ink. The purpose of these two forms of theft is to void a check 30 minutes after writing it or to cause the original writing to disappear within 24 hours. Of course, one of these suppliers of illegal information also provides recipes for how to make thermite, pipe bombs, zip guns, silencers, counterfeit coins, exploding paint, a fully automatic gun using a 9-volt battery, a pocket flamethrower, and even a devise to change your fingerprints. In the event that a robber, using such sophisticated equipment as homemade exploding paint, has to make a run for it, there is also a pamphlet on how to jam all radios, including police bands, with a simple device that costs less than five dollars.

For most people, this information is just another reason to laugh at how far companies will go to earn money by fooling people. But for the dim of wit or simple of mind, some of this information could be dangerous. A desperate individual willing to spend money on such garbage might, conceivably, attempt some of the nonsense that the pamphlets make sound so easy. His or her chances of being successful, of course, are limited at best.

Some of the objects advertised by these people are modifications of legitimate tools used by professionals in the business, which the flyers vaguely allude to in their claim that the information is written by ex-detectives and accomplished thieves. Most assuredly, the only people getting rich through the publication of this "criminal expertise" are the publishers who convince ignorant, desperate people that a life of crime is as easy as plugging a 9-volt battery into a handgun. The result of such mindlessness is often ruined lives and simply more criminals being housed away in state penitentiaries.

NEW CENTURY, NEW METHODS

Any respectable researcher, after compiling years of information on a given profession, would have to wonder what kind of impact that profession will have in the future. For bank robbing, this is especially important. Given that history is only an account of what happened yesterday, one must assume that thieves will still ply their trade far into the future, just as they have done for thousands of years. The adaptability of the common brigand in the last hundred years has not only kept pace with technology, but has often surpassed it to surprise even the most advanced banking establishments. The general law of the universe, that "every action produces an equal and opposite reaction," has never applied to bank robbers. If the thief never exceeded the conventional then there simply never would have been bank robberies in the first place.

Bankers have used the most modern of methods to thwart the inevitable holdup or burglary with little success. One can, therefore, assume that this trend will continue unabated. Bankers will throw up their bulwarks, be they physical or electronic, and the clever thief will consistently defeat them. Taking into consideration that building materials and deterrents will improve as the years tick by, so will the outlaws' determination and need to excel beyond even the best defenses. When the new breed of brilliant minds take over in a world controlled by computers and the best-quality building materials ever seen, there will inevitably be a whole new kind of criminal to contend with, and more likely than not he will continue to win some of the battles.

The traditional armed robbery will someday give way to more congenial techniques of a less violent nature, at least in the more sophisticated banks. The advent of faster and more efficient computers will bring about a whole new modus operandi, one that banks will not be able to fight initially simply because no one has seen the ways to utilize such tools. Other traditional deterrents, such as reinforced steel, are already being replaced by other building substances like new alloys and carbon-fiber products that make banks even stronger in appearance. The days of the snatch-and-grab bandit, and even the "drill through the roof" burglar, are numbered. These days, the holdup man encounters bulletproof glass which cannot be destroyed or leapt over as in the days of Jesse James—if he can even get to that part of the bank. The closed-circuit television bank teller is already apparent in some banks, which eliminates the teller even being part of a robbery attempt in the first place. With today's advances in computer graphics technology, could the animated teller be far away? It would be reasonable to suggest an interactive banking encounter with a cartoon in the near future, similar to how many ATM machines work today.

Credit cards are becoming "smarter," as is the technology to protect the information they represent. Debit-banking transactions have already eliminated the need for most people to carry cash. The day will probably come when hard currency will be obsolete in most advanced societies. Direct deposits will be accomplished through computer transmissions and wire transfers, eliminating the need to even see a paycheck or to carry around cash at all. The average person might just carry around one card that contains his or her financial data and any purchasing or billing information needed for his or her finances—all with a protective code that would eliminate a robber's thieving abilities. Without cash to carry away in a bag slung over his shoulder, the burglar's role would become obsolete.

The bank as we know it today will someday be nothing more than a protective fortress of digital details. Information useless to anyone but the banker and the patron will be stored only in computers—beyond the reach of even the most clever of thieves. A person's monetary worth will no longer be represented by the thickness of his wallet, but will simply appear as a number in a vast digital system that the bank will only store for its customer as a center of finance. The hold-up man entering such an establishment will be almost laughably outdated—a relic of a time when flashing a gun in a bank meant free money.

Will these far-sighted predictions cast the bank robber and burglar into legend and lore any time soon? The answer is no, not right away. Such changes will probably occur in the next hundred years or so, depending on the progress of technology and the willingness of people to forsake that wonderful feeling of carrying around a wad of cash. The day of the plastic ID card is coming, but it will take several generations of computer-literate people to make it a reality that is acceptable and advantageous. Bankers and nations alike already know that their systems of commerce have to progress in order to survive the coming age, which will ultimately mean the elimination of hard currency for a simpler economic system.

No, bank robbers are not going to drift off into oblivion any time soon. If anything, the epidemic of robberies that began in 1831 will continue for quite a while longer, inhibited but never destroyed by increasingly better technology. The romantic aura of bank robbers past and present will continue to fascinate Americans and people worldwide with headlines of multimillion-dollar heists and holdups. Innocent people will continue to die at the hands of the killer bandits and the public will clamor for more prison time for the culprits. But bank robberies will continue. The spirits of Jesse James, "Bearcat" Starr, and Willie Sutton will continue to inspire imitators, most of whom will meet disaster, but a select few of whom will just as surely prosper.

Conclusion

"The darkest hour in any man's life is when he sits down to plan how to get money without earning it."
—Horace Greeley

Thieves have been around since the flickering sparks of primitive communal living. The bank robber is simply the logical evolution of that aboriginal thief, updated with the most recent advancements in his craft. In prisons today, the professional bank robber is considered royalty by many fellow inmates; he is a true expert in the art of illegality, a standard bearer of the underside of the culture. He has achieved a status in a profession which demands respect from lesser criminals, and is a role model for what they, too, could become.

Such status is somewhat ironic given the humble beginnings of the profession. The relatively simple plan Jesse James devised was to successively employ surprise, strength, and speed to make off with as much money as possible from a vulnerable target. Despite far more failures than successes in the century since, the essence of bank robbing has remained constant, the progression required for success both logical and predictable. You can bet that the bank president who loses $50 million today will be just as surprised as the banker who met Jesse James for the first time. What we have discovered with this book is that bank robbers are truly an adaptable lot. If the rules and obstacles change, so will the bank robbers.

There will always be bandits, armed or not, willing to take extreme risks for quick wealth. Most will be the snatch-and-grab kind of robber, but there will also be the heavy hitters. They will take the time, do their homework, and figure out how to defeat the alarms. They will get into the vault and will take the bank's money with them when they leave. The only thing that changes is the method used. It would be foolish for bankers to think they are going to finally beat these people who rob banks; it isn't going to happen. In the foreseeable future, technology will slow the robbers down, but it will not stop them.

When we look at these bank robbers we see a lot of similarities. For the most part, professionals are not concerned with jail time. The judicial system has become so overburdened with cases that most non-violent robbers know they will get out in a reasonable amount of time. The thief knows he will probably pull off more heists than he will ever get caught for, anyway. Sadly, over 150 years after the profession of bank robbery began, there is still no bank immune to holdups.

Every bank robber we have examined has had a common bond with every other robber: a desire to hit it big. This has applied equally to the superstars and the failures. True, some of our examples were of the kind most accurately termed "desperadoes," but for the most part the successful ones honestly enjoyed robbing banks; they enjoyed the thrill of planning and executing a heist. This was their life's calling and some became very good at it. Not unlike some doctors, lawyers, and businessmen you would see on the street every day, good bank robbers, too, take pride in their work.

As with any occupation there are certain risks associated with it. Occasionally a doctor will kill a patient, a lawyer will lose a case, and a businessman will make mistakes and perhaps go bankrupt. Likewise, it is true that the bank robber will miss an alarm, underestimate the thickness of the steel, or be killed by a posse. But there is always the possibility of a substantial conquest. The robbers' triumphs can be measured in hundreds of thousands, if not millions, of dollars.

A one-word definition for a bank robber would be "gambler"; he is willing to risk life and limb on his expertise. He is betting his skill and daring against a system dedicated to the safety of the institution's money. At the split second the robber draws that gun, saws the hole in the roof, or breaks the computer code, he rolls the dice of fate. The bet will always be the same: his skill, guts and determination against all of the bank's money.

Given the desperate nature of many bank robbers, their consequent erraticism, and the persistent sprinkling of real pros in the business, authorities have been unable to develop an exact science to prevent robberies from occurring. One thing all authorities can agree on is that criminality is too random to ever anticipate completely. Fridays and Saturdays seem to be the most common days of the week for a bank heist, but even this is not carved in stone. The second that banks assume they are only vulnerable on weekends, they will find themselves assailed on Mondays and Tuesdays. A bank robbery can, in fact, take place on any day of the week, at any time of the day or night, and by absolutely anyone with the brass or bad judgment to go through with it.

The major, professional burglaries are more rare and necessarily take place when the bank is closed. The decision of when to do the job is determined from reconnaissance missions by the burglar, who must measure the risk of security with the time it would take to get past all the systems. Even the robber sometimes doesn't know when the heist will be set in motion, so one can only imagine how nervous the banker must be at all times—he, like the criminal himself, has no idea how secure he is until the robbery is actually attempted.

Imagine for a moment that you are in a bank when it is being robbed. What should you do?

Law-enforcement personnel have been instructing bank employees for years on how to behave during a bank robbery. These rules are simple and apply to customers as well as to members of the banking staff. Most important, do what the bandit tells you to do—immediately. Make no movements toward the robber at all. Simply obey his orders without any extra motion to throw him off. Attempt, if possible, to make a mental note of how he is dressed, what kind of weapon is being used, how he looks physically (hair, nose, distinguishing mouth features), and which direction he takes when leaving the establishment. Under no circumstances should a person attempt to restrain the robber or run after him once he has left the building, unless he is a law-enforcement officer. If it is possible, and can be done safely, getting a license plate number and description of the getaway car is very useful to the police.

Other than these simple directives, any confrontation or involvement with the robber should be kept strictly to the law-enforcement officers. Keep in mind that any thoughtless move could cost you your life or the life of another innocent person. The victims of a bank robbery will, without a doubt, be under a huge amount of stress during the actual event. That anxiety, however, is comparable to what the robber is experiencing, and he likely has a gun to help release any of his unwanted stress. Many bank robbers, as we have seen, are also homicidal maniacs, and a fair number are suicidal besides. Above all else, never give the robber a reason to hurt anyone; the money is just not worth it. For the employee and the average citizen, most bank robberies are survivable without injury. It is usually the simple and unexpected miscalculation that causes an otherwise "routine" criminal act to end in disaster.

The more ridiculous stories in this book generally had one aspect in common: They involved an amateur with visions of grandeur who decided on a whim to run into a bank, flash his gun around, and demand some cash. The unpredictability of this event, and the potential for violence, is what makes the holdup perpetrator so hard to prepare for or even profile. Statistics reveal that branch banks are targeted more often than main banks when a holdup is attempted, a fact attributed to less security and clientele to deal with at such places. The main bank could have two or more armed guards on duty at a time, while many branch banks don't even think it necessary to have one. Even the rankest amateur knows that this places the theoretical odds in his favor.

Well-organized, professional armed robbers are the only kind of people who would intentionally opt to take on a main banking establishment. They have the experience to handle the guards and the multiple security systems, and are most likely known by authorities either by their modus operandi or from prior arrests. Once the police or FBI know who the robbers are, it's all basically a game of chance for when the authorities will catch up to them. Eventually someone will make a mistake, and it is up to the police to make sure that they are there when this happens.

For all the somewhat brilliant schemes detailed in this book, there are thousands more so mundane that it would be impossible to even count them all. Bank robbery in America has become so uncreative, in fact, that the FBI no longer even investigates such crimes unless there is substantial publicity surrounding the robbery. The average robbery does not involve murders or anything that the authorities haven't seen a hundred times before, so there is a pattern to investigating them that even the smallest town sheriff can handle. This also gives the public a barometer of sorts, in terms of how large a particular robbery was after it happens. If the FBI is involved in an investigation of a bank robbery, you can be assured that the thief was a talented professional who knew exactly what he was doing.

Violence in bank robberies will tend to bring FBI interest as well, along with more media involvement than with regular robberies. The most famous names in this book are those associated more with violence than skill: Jesse James, John Dillinger, Bonnie and Clyde, Jimmy "The Gent" Burke, and a few others. These individuals regularly incorporated wanton violence in their crimes without any consideration for human life. Among professional, or career, bank robbers, however, vicious and unprovoked loss of life is almost nonexistent. The professionals who have killed for apparently no reason at all are often called "Killer" or "Mad Dog" robbers; it is impossible to predict their violent actions. A robbery with a death or injury involved is always given a lot more attention, and since the days of J. Edgar Hoover, law-enforcement has made it a point to pursue such criminals with considerably less mercy.

The amateur robber is more apt than any professional to shoot a bystander. Foolhardy amateurs in any profession make mistakes and get flustered when they lose control of a situation. Couple that fact with a gun and a room full of nervous people, and the situation becomes volatile. Some of these killings can be traced directly to television violence or glamorized crime in films. Far too many of these punks only see what a gun does to a television character, and never stop to think what a high-powered weapon can actually do to real human flesh.

There are hundreds, if not thousands, of bank robberies remaining on the books of the FBI and local authorities. Unless by some miracle there is a break in any of these cases, they will most likely remain unsolved until the six-year time limit expires. Statistics reveal that 75 percent of the nation's bank robberies are solved within a short time—which means that a bank robber goes into a robbery attempt facing fairly steep odds. The remaining 25 percent of robberies are by professional robbers, who will not leave any clues behind for the police to follow. The days of the bandit outrunning the cops from the scene of a crime are over, as we saw with the man and woman who attempted to drag a bank employee away from the scene as a hostage. In the end, they had no place to go, because the authorities were quicker and got them surrounded. Today's true bank robber knows that he has to be skillful to pull off a job successfully; the days of relying solely on luck or on the paucity of law enforcement have passed.

Crime experts point to the growing trend of using credit cards and online transactions as a potential deterrent to bank robberies, but even this does not hold a promise of ending them completely. There will always be the need for cash in some respect, if only as a secondary option for the consumer. Banks will probably always be the only natural place for money to be held, even if on a temporary basis. Bank robbers can feel assured that their profession will not disappear in the near future for a lack of opportunities.

The law of averages indicates that a typical citizen will most likely never be in a bank when it is held up. Nor, fortunately, will most people ever see the aftermath of a bloody shoot-out. Violent events leave people traumatized for a long time after the event. Sadly, movies often tend to portray robberies in an exciting light, as if the daring criminal is an object of admiration and intrigue. Such fictional accounts of what movie producers view as the typical robbery are almost always unrealistic and sorely lacking in any of the real elements that are present in robberies—the fear, the tension, the tangible sense of violent threat. The consequences for robbers are severe, leading to either long prison sentences or to years of bad dreams for any innocents that are involved. Those who base their understanding of bank robberies on depictions that come from Hollywood should question their grasp of the subject.

Ironically, the largest number of daily bank robberies takes place in Los Angeles, the city where most of the movies about bank jobs originate. This is not to say that other metropolitan areas do not receive their fair share. Robberies take place in densely populated areas far more often than in rural settings, so St. Louis, Detroit, New Orleans, and Chicago have their own sad roster of tales to tell. But the West Coast of the United States claims more robberies than any other area of the country. The combination of New York, New Jersey, and New England runs a close second to California.

Large cities such as Los Angeles and New York drastically drive bank robbery statistics upward, so the sense of a national epidemic may not be as pronounced as it seems. However, one cannot ignore the threat that still looms over each financial institution in the country. The ominous truth is that banks will add more security, authorities will develop newer ways to catch the bad guys, buildings will become more impenetrable—and the robbers will still try to figure out how to beat 'em all. On average, a bank is either robbed or burglarized somewhere in the United States every 45 minutes.

Appendix A
Crimes in Time

1782: The first federally chartered American bank is established.

1831: First recorded bank burglary, netting $245,000.

1834: First major U.S. safe manufacturer, called Mosler Safe Co.

1850: Pinkerton's Agency security service is established.

1852: Wells Fargo is established.

1859: Brinks Armored Car Company is established.

1863: First armed bank robbery, netting $5,000.

1865–1884: George Leslie nets a remarkable $12 million.

1866: First train robbery by the Reno Brothers.

1866: First organized daylight armed bank robbery by Jesse and Frank James, netting $17,000 on Valentine's Day.

1876: James Gang and the Younger Brothers attempt first robbery of two banks at one time.

1882: Jesse James is murdered by Bob Ford, former member of his gang.

1911: First car used in a robbery, in Paris by Jules Bonnot.

1918: World War I ends, causing a recession and string of bank robberies.

1920: Henry "Bearcat" Starr uses first automobile in an American bank robbery.

1921: Starr killed by a banker during failed robbery attempt.

1921: First time aircraft used to hunt bank robbers.

1922: First electronic transfer of funds from a bank by a crook takes place, netting $80,000.

1924: J. Edgar Hoover becomes head of the Bureau of Investigation in Washington, DC.

1928: Infamous Thompson "tommy" gun introduced.

1929: Stock market crashes, causing massive employment and sudden outbreak of bank robberies.

1931: Harvey Bailey nets $1 to $2 million in a single armed heist.

1931–1934: "Pretty Boy" Floyd nets $1.5 million.

1932: First reported bank robbery by Bonnie and Clyde.

1932: First appearance of radio-controlled police cars, in New York City.

1933: Roosevelt creates the Federal Deposit Insurance Corporation, increasing federal interest in bank robbing.

1933: Union Station Massacre in Kansas City, Missouri.

1934: Hoover's agency is reorganized and retitled the Federal Bureau of Investigation (FBI).

1935: Bonnie and Clyde killed by lawmen, their car shot up with hundreds of bullets.

1950: First Brink's Armored Car Co. heist, netting $2.7 million.

1957: First surveillance camera used in the St. Clair Savings and Loan of Cleveland, OH.

1962: First time satellite used to capture a bank robber.

1965: Second Brink's heist, netting $430,000. Also the first documented use of a cannon during a robbery.

1966: Helicopters introduced to law enforcement for the first time.

1967: First time bank president and family are held as hostages.

1970: First computer used in wire transfers from banks.

1971: John Little is caught for the final time, ending his crime spree.

1972: Amil Dinsio nets $30 million, becomes nation's most successful bank robber.

1974: Patty Hearst abducted by the Symbionese Liberation Army.

1977: Last of the Davis County robberies occur, the suspects never to be found.

1978: Largest heist in U.S. history: Lufthansa heist nets $8 million in cash and jewels.

1980: Largest single bank burglary in U.S. history: $20 million.

1981: Largest armed robbery in U.S. history: $3.3 million.

1990: First computer-assisted bank robbery.

1996: First bank robber to be caught using the Internet, from the Ten Most Wanted list.

1996–1997: New York bank possibly robbed by computer of $50 million.

1997: Wells Fargo armored car heist by Philip Johnson, netting $22 million.

1997: Trench Coat Robbers commit largest single two-man armed bank robbery in U.S. history, netting $4.5 million.

1998: Largest criminal shoot-out in U.S. history takes place during a bank robbery in Hollywood, California.

Appendix B
Bank Robbing Films

It may come as a bit of a surprise that many bank robbers give credit for their holdups to an unusual source. Many of these miscreants, when asked, "Why did you do it?" answer, "I saw it in a movie!" If one views some movies on the subject, this isn't as ludicrous as it might seem. Slick scriptwriters dream up complex and intriguing plots for bank robberies, and inevitably someone tries to see if they will work in the real world. Hundreds of would-be famous bank robbers spend their time walking around prison cells because of what they perceived as a foolproof plan. This isn't something new, either. Bank robbers have been portrayed for decades as cunning and smart. This outlaw is capable and, at a moment's notice, can change his plan for the ultimate success of the goal. The bank robber in the movies is cool and calculating, unusually suave with the ladies, and totally fearless in the face of danger. However, for the petty crook who has decided to expand his expertise into the world of robbing banks, these stories are mostly fiction and tend to get them in trouble more often than not.

Over the years Jesse James, Butch Cassidy, Bonnie and Clyde, the Newton Boys, and countless others have been portrayed in films depicting their genius. The plots are airtight, the bandit does his thing, outsmarting the law at every turn. What the would-be robber doesn't see in the film is the part of the actual story that was manipulated by the scriptwriter. The neophyte bank robber doesn't know about the days, months, and years when the "star" has to hide out just to stay alive. He will never understand that the real character had to keep looking over his shoulder forever. He won't know about the lack of trust that develops within the psyche of the crook for everyone and everything around him. All the viewer generally sees is the thrilling material the producers and writers wish to show in their presentation.

In the old days it was the dime novel that touted the exploits of our nation's bank robbers. With the advancement of technology came radio program serials that depicted the America outlaw hero. News broadcasts and newspapers took up the gauntlet to extol the feats of bank robbers.

From the onset of motion pictures, including the silent era, robbers were a hot topic. The first commercially successful movie about robbers was *The Great Train Robbery*, made in 1903. After that monumental movie, it didn't take the most brilliant film producer to discover that crime paid well. All through the twenties, thirties, forties, and fifties, crime dramas found their way into this country's theaters. How many "high profile" bank robbers of the twenties and thirties saw or heard accounts of derring-do? And did these stories contribute to their careers in banditry?

Then, with the advent and proliferation of television, the bank robbers came into the home. In recent years the television documentary has highlighted obscure facts about our most well-known bank robbers. The glamour of robbing banks for a living is alive and well in America, and around the world, too. It would only stand to reason that someone will attempt to emulate what he or she sees on television and in the movies. The jails are full of men and women who saw something in a movie that gave them the inspiration to try the same thing. In some cases the amateur was arrested, just like his movie icon, doing exactly the same dumb thing. For the most part, "professional" bank robbers don't need to watch movies in order to get ideas. It's often only the beginner who is looking for just the right script for his shot at the big bucks who will try even the craziest scheme seen in a movie.

I will include a short list of films dealing with some of the major characters or themes discussed in this book—to give the reader an idea of how Hollywood has displayed these criminals. These movies are, for the most part, grossly inaccurate when describing the true life of any bank robber. Some are more entertaining than others, but if one is looking for strictly factual accounts of the stories described, then movies will not be the best place to look. In terms of entertainment value, some films naturally succeed far better than others. That judgment, however, will be left up to the reader.

Jesse and Frank James

There have been at least 17 films about this pair of outlaws. In most, they were the main characters, but in others they only attained a cameo mention in a bigger story—often only to "legitimize" the Western feel of the movie. In few of these films, however, was the true disposition of Jesse James brought to light in a reasonably honest way. Movies have often forgotten, or misconstrued, the fact that James was a cold-blooded killer; when imbibing painkilling drugs, he was simply ruthless.

For pure entertainment value, I will list some movies the two James brothers played a role in—even if that characterization was hopelessly far from the truth. The 1939 film *Days of Jesse James* starring Roy Rogers is considered a classic Western by many critics, though the romanticized portrait of the outlaw would force this author to advise viewing the film with a critical eye for accuracy. A film similar to the Rogers flick is *Jesse James*, starring Henry Fonda. Again, this 1939 film makes a hero out of a killer, presenting a man who could be revered despite his many vicious crimes. Another movie that bears mentioning is *Jesse James Rides Again*, with Clayton Moore, more famous as television's Lone Ranger, playing the lead role. This 1947 picture primarily covers the Northfield, Minnesota, bank job.

The best of the movies on the James Gang, as well as the entire subject of the Old West, however, was 1981's *The Long Riders*. Starring the Keach brothers, Carradine brothers, and Quaid brothers, the film adds a bit more nobility to its characters than warranted, but otherwise provides a surprisingly realistic glimpse into the period.

Butch Cassidy and The Sundance Kid

These two killers/thieves have been portrayed in just about as many films as Jesse and Frank James, usually with the same premise: two close buddies head out West to have some fun and get in trouble along the way. The professional nature of their crime, and their utter brutality at certain moments, is usually ignored so that their friendship can be focused on. This rarely makes for good history, but some of the films have been entertaining and I'll list a few of them here.

Paul Newman and Robert Redford portrayed this pair of mischievous bank robbers in a 1970 movie called *Butch Cassidy & The Sundance Kid*. Surprisingly, this film accurately described some of their exploits. It held true to the accepted belief that Cassidy never killed anyone while Sundance liked to shoot his guns a little more often. The film did romanticize their lives to some extent; however, mostly this was used to portray them as only a couple of friends out to have fun, while entertaining the audience at the same time. Overall, this was not the most accurate Western ever made, but it was not the worst either.

Simitar Video has released two films about these outlaws lives, with varying results. *The Real Story of Butch Cassidy & The Sundance Kid* (1993) is the earlier of the two, and does a fairly good job of representing the outlaws. *Outlaws: Billy the Kid & Butch Cassidy and the Sundance Kid* (1999) describes their lives in relation to other outlaws of the period. This second film is a Western documentary-type piece and is probably the better film released by this company. Butch and Sundance were never the best bank robbers, but their story can be interesting and any of these films will be a good supplement to their story, if only to give the reader a more visual sense of the period.

The Dalton Gang

The Dalton Gang, infamous for its 1892 Coffeyville, Kansas, raid has been portrayed in a few films dealing mostly with this one famous event. While none of those movies are remarkable as either historical or entertainment films, a good background for this group can be found in the documentary *The Dalton Gang*, a 1999 release from Winstar Home Entertainment. This history of the gang is part of their "Gunfighters of the West" series and does a commendable job of covering the gang and its place in the shoot-'em-up history of the Old West.

Bill Doolin

The man who survived the Coffeyville massacre has been the subject of a couple of films over the years, usually in association with the Dalton Gang. In *The Doolins of Oklahoma*, a 1949 film starring Randolph Scott and released by Columbia Pictures, Bill Doolin is portrayed as the typical outlaw Westerner—a title he could have fit fairly well. *The Last Ride of the Dalton Gang* also includes Bill Doolin in his role at Coffeyville and afterwards; this was a television movie made in 1979, and starred Bo Hopkins as Doolin and Dan Collier as Frank Dalton. These two movies have the distinctive Western feel of the time period, and are legitimate movies as far as decent acting and script are concerned. The bank robberies are exaggerated to add dramatic effect, so I would only caution the reader to view either of these films with a suspicious eye for accuracy.

Bonnie and Clyde

The star-crossed lovers premise of Bonnie and Clyde has captured audiences for years now, and studios are well aware of their star power as criminals. The earliest, and most famous, of the films made about these two killers was *Bonnie & Clyde*, a 1967 film starring Warren Beatty and Faye Dunaway. This movie had a distinctly romantic feel that fit the press' view of the killers but hardly stands up to the reality of the crimes they committed. A more accurate portrayal of their characters appears in Oliver Stone's film *Natural Born Killers* (1994), starring Woody Harrelson. The maniac nature of these people, and their utter abandon of thoughtfulness when committing their vicious crimes, truly reflect Bonnie and Clyde.

One of the more ridiculous of the many films made about these criminals has to be *Teenage Bonnie and Klepto Clyde*. This comedic movie places the two as soul-searching teens whose innocent adventures land them in trouble. More than anything, this movie simply shows how the media has loved to glamorize and exploit their actions, to the point of making a joke out of two cold-blooded murderers. Sadly, the true-life story of Bonnie and Clyde is hardly as romantic and amusing as many of the films made about them would like to suggest.

Charles "Pretty Boy" Floyd

This man has been included in many films over the years, usually as an accomplice to a crime or as a big-name character lingering in the background. Perhaps the most notable examination of his life in any film is the A&E Biography released about him, simply called *Charles "Pretty Boy" Floyd* (1998). While it is true that this is not a movie in the strictest sense, it does give a more visual film representation of the man and his relation to the society of his era, and for this reason I think it is a notable work. His other depictions, either in movies with no historical basis whatsoever or in "re-creations" of his crimes, have simply been too romanticized to be considered reliable. Martin Sheen portrayed Floyd in a television movie in 1975 called *The Kansas City Massacre,* one of the worst movies ever done concerning that incident at Union Station.

The Newton Boys

The film concerning the Newton Boys is somewhat typical of the bank-robbing films that have been made over the years. The 1998 film, starring Matthew McConaughey, is called *The Newton Boys* and covers a string of bank robberies. The Boys are portrayed as non-violent, comical robbers who handle their crimes in a lighthearted way. While not particularly accurate about the fear involved in bank robberies, the film is a typical Hollywood representation of such crimes and could be studied on that basis alone, without paying too much attention to the historical inaccuracies.

Willie "The Actor" Sutton

The mastermind behind his own freedom and the great self-promoter Willie Sutton had a television movie made about his life in the 1960s called *The Willie Sutton Story.* The movie was fairly accurate in most respects, even if it was not a commercial success. For additional material on Sutton's life that is more reliable than any film yet been made, I would suggest reading his book, *Where the Money Is.* This is a relatively honest approach to his life of crime and should give more insight as to who this man was and what he meant to bank robbing.

Brink's Armored Car Company Heists

The first Brink's robbery is re-created in *Brink's Job*, a 1980 film starring Peter Falk. The movie is more comedy than historical analysis, but it does give the viewer a good sense of the time period when these heists were performed and of what was required of the average thief to get around security back then. The second Brink's heist is the subject of 1974's *Thunderbolt and Lightfoot*, starring Clint Eastwood. This is primarily a comedic movie that is entertaining in a lot of ways, with the high life of the thieves (after the robbery) accentuated to the fullest. It is not particularly accurate about the actual planning it took to perform this heist, but is a good movie nonetheless.

Patty Hearst

A 1989 television movie was made about the Patty Hearst abduction and bank robbery, taking the victim's point of view to tell the story. Called simply *Patty Hearst*, the movie starred Natasha Richardson and painted a sympathetic portrait of the young woman after she was "kidnapped" by the Symbionese Liberation Army. The bank robbery is not the focus of the film, but it does add to her infamy, and it is interesting how the filmmakers demonstrated Patty's brainwashed view of the event and the Stockholm Syndrome.

Miscellaneous Bank Robbing Films of Interest

Kansas City Confidential (1952): This action film does not concern a bank robbery entirely, but does use the premise as background for a larger string of crimes. It includes an interesting robbery sequence and stars John Payne as the principal thief.

The Great St. Louis Bank Robbery (1959): Steve McQueen stars in this re-creation of an actual St. Louis bank heist. One of the more notable features of the film is that the St. Louis police officers who were involved in apprehending the suspects appear in the film as themselves, lending more credibility to this film than to many others of the genre.

Dog Day Afternoon (1975): This movie starring Dustin Hoffman and Al Pacino presented a generally accurate picture of the frustration of a failed bank robbery. Like *Reservoir Dogs*, the character studies reveal the lack of trust among thieves—a topic particularly relevant to many of the gang robberies that appear in this book.

Black Sister's Revenge (1976): Jerri Hayes stars in this bank-robbing film that focuses on a woman thief who turns to a life of crime in order to free her boyfriend from jail. There are few bank-robbing movies that star women in prominent roles, disregarding Bonnie Parker of course, so this film could be an interesting study piece for how such robbers are perceived.

Dillinger (1990): Warren Oates plays the famed gunman in this sensationalized view of John Dillinger's life. The gun battles in this film are extraordinary and his bank-robbing days are covered, so the movie may be of interest to fans of the genre. The film is available from Goodtimes Home Video.

Goodfellas (1991): This film, starring Robert DeNiro, Joe Pesci, and Ray Liotta, was loosely based on the December 1978 Lufthansa heist, though the heart of the picture is day-to-day life in the Mob. In a *New York Post* poll of police officers this movie was found to be a favorite for its accurate portrayal of Mafioso as petty thugs.

Reservoir Dogs (1992): While not strictly about bank robbing, this film starring Harvey Keitel explores the relationship among thieves as trust breaks down amid failure. The prevalence of backstabbing among thieves has facilitated many law-enforcement captures over the years, including the Boston "Cops" robbery.

Killing Zoe (1994): This is a decidedly strange movie in the tradition of *Natural Born Killers*. It examines the psychological condition of bank robbers who kill during the heist, and uses film techniques to create a paranoid-like atmosphere that must reflect the psychosis of some of the robbers who attempt drug-induced robberies, such as Betty Oldham. *Killing Zoe* is strange, but it does cover dementia in robberies, which is certainly a cause of far too many recent attempts.

Dillinger and Capone (1995): I include this film simply to show readers how Hollywood twists facts to create entertainment with crime. John Dillinger is teamed up with Al Capone in a bank heist that never could have happened, leading to eventual problems between the two thieves. The movie is, of course, total fiction, but it does fit the genre and illustrates how far Hollywood will go in using name recognition for a movie.

Heat (1995): I confess that after viewing the spectacular gun battle in this movie I declared it hopelessly unrealistic. Not a week later every news station in the country was carrying live footage of the North Hollywood heist (pages 87–89) which made the roaring cinematic street battle between Robert DeNiro's gang and Al Pacino's LAPD look tame by comparison. Thus humbled, I have no further comment other than that the byplay between Val Kilmer and Ashley Judd, culminating in the latter's slight flick of a wrist, is a highlight.

Many other movies have been made about bank robbing throughout the years, such as those depicting the Ma Barker Gang, "Machine Gun" Kelly, "Baby Face" Nelson, and Jimmy Valentine—all bank robbers of varying talents. Hundreds of films pertain to bank robberies alone, without the big names to capture the audiences. It would be virtually impossible to document them all or even pick a Top Ten list. Sadly, most of these films are based on fictitious events and have no bearing on what takes place in the real criminal world of bank robbers. Some characters have been presented as the romantic rebel, waging his or her own kind of mischief on society, while others take a more grizzly bent. All of these films have that one central component of film-making that does not ever allow an accurate picture of the real bank robber: the Hollywood touch of glamour.

The bank-robbing lifestyle is difficult and stressful, involving years of hiding out all because of perhaps five minutes of intense action. Films will continue to try to strike a balance between romanticism and facts, but until precisely the right combination is reached, many of these robbers' stories will remain clouded in as much mystery as they have been in documented reality.

Index